A French Genocide

a french GENOCIDE

THE VENDÉE

REYNALD SECHER

Translated by George Holoch

UNIVERSITY OF NOTRE DAME PRESS

Notre Dame, Indiana

© Reynald Secher, 1986

Translated by George Holoch from *Le génocide franco-française: La Vendée-Vengé*,
published by Presses Universitaires de France, Paris, 1986.

The publisher is grateful to
THE FRENCH MINISTRY OF CULTURE — CENTRE NATIONAL DU LIVRE
for support of the costs of translation

Library of Congress Cataloging-in-Publication Data
Secher, Reynald.
[Génocide franco-français. English]
A French genocide : the Vendée / Reynald Secher ; translated by George Holoch.
p.   cm.
Includes bibliographical references and index.
ISBN 0-268-02865-6 (cloth)
1. France—History—Wars of the Vendée, 1793–1832—Atrocities.
2. Church and state—France—Vendée—History—18th century.
3. Vendée (France)—History.   4. France—History—Revolution, 1789–1799—
Influence.   5. Vendée (France)—Church history—18th century.   I. Title.
DC218.S43313   2003
2003047333

CONTENTS

Part Three   The Period of Instability

Part Four   Consequences

TABLES

FIGURES

MAPS

THE HISTORY OF THE WARS OF THE VENDÉE HAS ATTRACTED MANY writers, and the subject might seem to be exhausted. However, they have not revealed the reasons for the movement nor its short- and medium-term consequences.

Undertaking a new investigation including all the events and all the insurgent territories would merely have produced yet another compilation. This is why, for a thesis for the *troisième cycle,* I chose a community in the north of the military Vendée, La Chapelle-Bassemère, at the junction of Anjou, the Vendée, and Brittany, and on the banks of the Loire.[1] This area provides an excellent vantage point, a place where ideas, ideologies, and ways of life came into direct and vigorous conflict. Reactions were of varying degrees of violence, and they deeply affected the local population. However, I could not restrict myself to this narrow canvas and necessarily had to consider the Vendée as a whole.

Historians have generally tended to study the movement from the Revolutionary and Jacobin point of view. As for historiography on the Vendean side, it is not very convincing, made up as it is essentially of personal, partial, and impassioned testimony.

It is commonly thought that most documents related to the military Vendée have disappeared, but the reality is entirely different. A substantial quantity of data was deliberately preserved by one or the other of the belligerents. For example, the mayor of Challans, in flight, had his archives transported in a wheelbarrow.[2] Some were stored in official or private structures; ignored or geographically inaccessible, they were therefore preserved. Others were collected and lovingly preserved by individuals, such as the abbé Pierre-Marie Robin (1748–1805), the refractory curé of La Chapelle-Bassemère who saved a portion of his parish registers.[3]

But a distinction must be made between official and private documentation. The former, unevenly catalogued, is scattered in public collections—the fort of Vincennes, national, departmental, and communal archives—and it contains unsuspected riches. As for the latter, deposited in bishops' palaces, local churches, headquarters of religious orders, and in some private houses, it is little known and therefore little used, but it sometimes provides great surprises.

Oral tradition survives but is of varying interest depending on times, informants, and places; it remained relatively vivid until the 1960s, as in all of provincial France. Now it has almost disappeared; only the elderly still have some original portions of it, and it is therefore urgent to take advantage of them.[4]

The two world wars obviously transformed the traditional Vendée. In the first, the men mobilized went through the actual experience of war, and in the second, captivity affected thousands of young men for a number of years. These prisoners acquired experience on model farms in Czechoslovakia, Germany, and Austria that gave them an image of a different rural life, which they experienced as more evolved, more modern. During this time, the women, left to work on the land, challenged even further the traditional division of labor. After 1945 communities that had become self-critical, dissolved into generalized doubt. The proliferation of means of transport and the spread of consumer society provided their death blow.

This sketchy description partially explains the difficulties encountered by researchers in reconstituting the life of the military Vendée through its habits and conflicts as well as through local political events and economic vicissitudes. Although it is obvious that I encountered the same obstacles, I must recognize that I benefited from certain advantages, of three kinds. The first was access to a significant stock of family documents and to a relatively intact old oral source. The second was my knowledge of the Vendée, my birthplace, in which my family has deep roots. Finally, many people provided close cooperation.

I thank the professors on my jury, Jean-Pierre Bardet, Louis Mer, Jean Tulard, Yves Durand; André Corvisier for his advice; Pierre Chaunu for his writings and his encouragement; and I express particular gratitude to Professor Jean Meyer, who supervised my work in a friendly, attentive, and active way, and to his wife, for her gracious hospitality.

A French Genocide

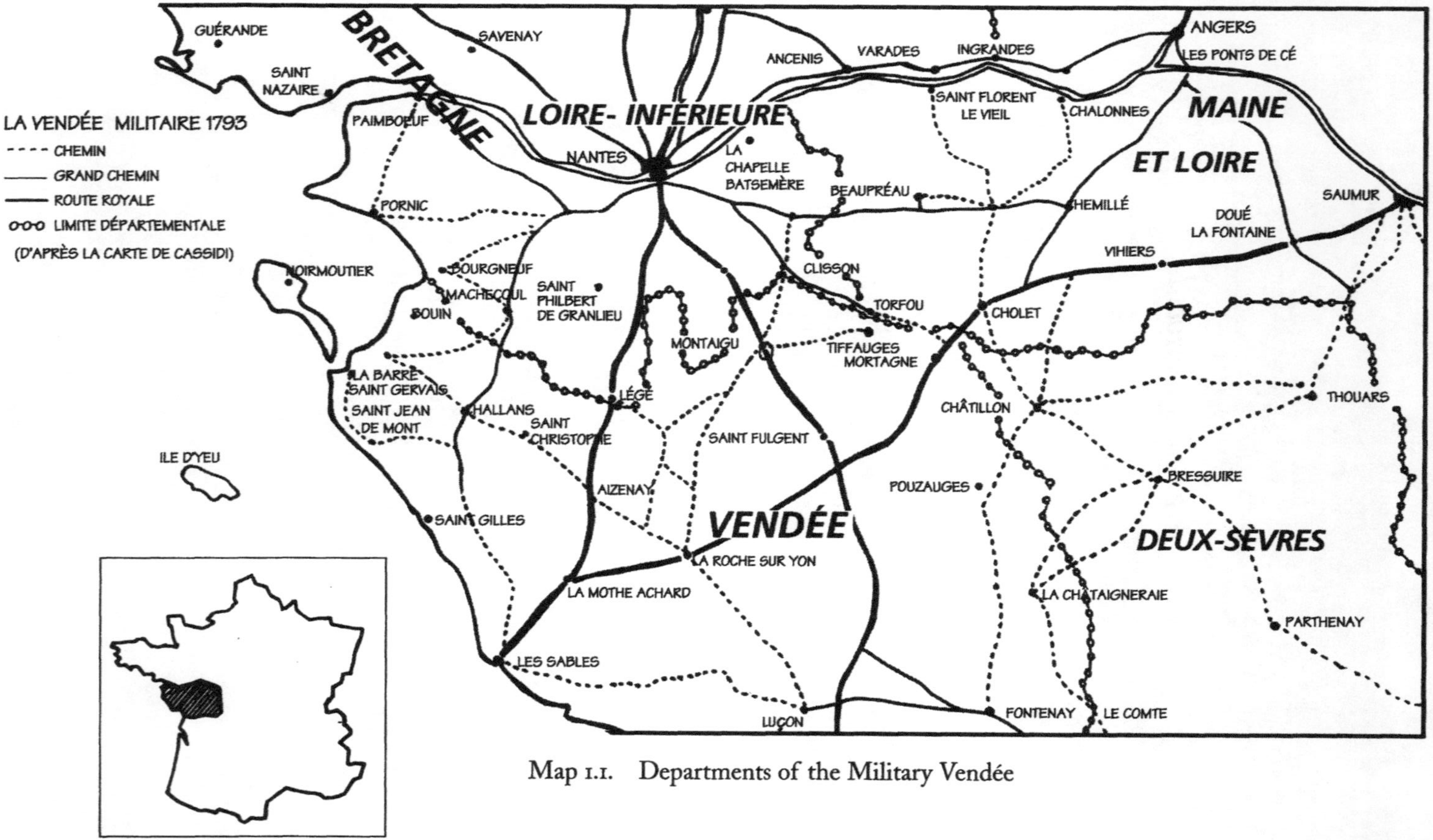

Map 1.1. Departments of the Military Vendée

LA VENDÉE MILITAIRE 1793
- - - - CHEMIN
———— GRAND CHEMIN
———— ROUTE ROYALE
○○○ LIMITE DÉPARTEMENTALE
(D'APRÈS LA CARTE DE CASSIDI)

Introduction

While all provinces became departments, the Vendée is the only department that became a province. With a vigorous gesture, it upset the official geography, breaking the narrow limits that had been imposed on it. It moved to the banks of the Loire, it took a piece of the Deux-Sèvres that it liked, and seized a part of Anjou, all at top speed, in a few days and for good. For the whole world it had become a sister of Poland and Ireland.

This painful birth took place to the sound of the parish tocsins and the rolling of drums, the singing of hymns in the north and *La Marseillaise* in the south. Thus, from its birth it had the reputation of being warlike and heroic. Warlike and heroic it certainly was, but with such simplicity that, though armed, it remained a peasant society.[1]

THE TERRITORY OF THE MILITARY VENDÉE COVERED ROUGHLY TEN thousand square kilometers. It was bordered on the north by the Loire, from Saint-Nazaire to Ponts-de-Cé; on the east by a fairly straight line from Ponts-de-Cé to Parthenay; on the south by a more wavy line connecting Parthenay to Saint-Gilles-Croix-de-Vie on the Atlantic coast. The seven hundred parishes that rebelled apparently had no distinguishing characteristics: they did not belong to the same provinces (Anjou, Brittany, Poitou) or to the same departments (Loire-Inférieure, Maine-et-Loire, Vendée, Deux-Sèvres), did not have a common history or the same economic resources, and were opposed on certain points. Moreover, the reference to a common identity came not from them but from Paris, following the defeat of General de Marcé at Pont-Charron on March 19, 1793. By choosing the word Vendée, the politicians hoped to impose a rather reductive form on the movement. By extrapolation, they quite naturally extended the characterization to any region of France hostile to the regime and to all centers of refractory priests. And yet, according to Doré-Graslin, all these parishes answered present to the tocsin, even if their hearts were not in it.[2]

Why the Vendée and not the rest of France, certain historians wonder. The question is badly framed. In fact, at the time of the Vendean uprising, a number of departments were in turmoil: in the west and the southwest (Caen and Bordeaux set up independent governments), in the southeast (Toulon surrendered to the English, Lyon became an armed camp). Indeed, in the course of the spring and summer of 1793, the central government maintained control in only thirty departments at most. The Revolution had disappointed; worse, it had created fear.

Then how can we explain the fact that the insurrection was not general? We can suggest two reasons: the lack of a concerted plan among the rebels, and the extensive and energetic activity of the extreme minority in power. The Bolshevik Revolution seized power in similar circumstances.

The Montagnards had a leader, Robespierre, a will, and means. On October 10, 1793, the Convention decreed that the provisional government of France would be revolutionary until peace had been attained. Robespierre defined the meaning of this without ambiguity:

> The aim of the constitutional government is to preserve the Republic; the aim of the revolutionary government is to establish it . . . It is thus subject to less uniform and less rigorous laws, because the circumstances in which it finds itself are stormy and shifting, and especially because it is forced constantly and rapidly to put forth new resources to confront new and pressing dangers . . . The revolutionary government owes to good citizens all the protection of the nation, it owes the enemies of the people only death.

The democratic constitution of the year I, subjected to popular approval, ratified by 1,800,000 votes and solemnly promulgated on August 10, 1793, was then piously stored in an "ark" of cedar wood and placed in the Convention chamber.

The revolutionary ideological system armed itself with adequate structures and means to carry its fight to the end: the Committee of Public Safety, created by Danton in April 1793, which took on the important role it is known for in the following July; the Committee of General Security, charged with surveillance of suspects and control of the police and revolutionary justice; the Revolutionary Tribunal, whose magistrates and even presiding judges were appointed by the Convention. As a consequence, the system was transformed into a purely political instrument, made up on the one hand of national agents, chosen by the same organ and set up in every municipality and district, and on the other of representatives sent on missions, invested with dictatorial powers to carry out the revolutionary laws.

The Terror was imposed in the name of justice, equality, and efficiency: "We must govern with steel those who cannot be governed with justice," proclaimed Saint-Just. Whoever refused to submit became an outlaw and was thereby condemned to death.

The Vendean reaction was thus rooted in this insurrectional context. It was effective because the Vendeans, with their backs to the wall, were determined, organized, and naturally protected by the wooded landscape.

The entire West was involved, to the great terror of local patriots. The improvised containment of the cancer by the military prevented a general uprising. This in itself was the first great Republican victory, totally ignored except by its contemporaries. From that moment on, the Vendée was doomed.

PART ONE

Before the War

ONE

Hope

PETITIONS, TRIALS, AND *CAHIERS DE DOLÉANCES* WERE UNANIMOUS: the West, like the rest of France, was suffering from the centralizing evolution of the Church and the monarchy which had been particularly pronounced since Louis XIV. More than the distant king, the administration was the principal target. It was openly criticized for fostering the growth of new irregularities and new privileges, for perpetuating the old ones, and in a supreme paradox, for lacking rationality. More seriously, it was accused of conducting a systematic policy of repression and of penalizing any form of local and personal initiative.

THE PERCEPTION OF THE ADMINISTRATION BY THE POPULATION

The administrative structure, indispensable for the new State's centralizing purposes, was seen as "a devourer of money, of work, of men" without compensation. This voracious appetite was chiefly evident in taxation, the corvée, and the militia.

Taxation

Two kinds of taxation affected the Vendeans. The first variety was common to the kingdom as a whole, the second more confined to certain professions and geographical locations.

Taxation had generally grown heavier in the course of the eighteenth century for two principal reasons. The first was the creation of "novelties":

a tenth (1710), a twentieth (1749), another twentieth (1756), and a third twentieth (1783). The second reason was that at the same time, in absolute terms, the rate of each tax was constantly on the increase. In raw figures, locally, the progression was slow between 1725 and 1775; it accelerated between 1775 and 1789. It seems that the total taxation doubled over sixty years.

The administration itself was sometimes surprised by the magnitude of certain taxes. For example, the financial administration of Brittany was surprised by the sum paid for garrison expenses by the parish assembly of La Chapelle-Bassemère, which it found high.[1]

This flagrant increase was badly received by the population, all the more because every year from the pulpit it was promised moderation or even decrease. Protests came principally from those who were most heavily taxed, who saw their taxes increase more quickly because of the decline in the number of taxpayers.[2] The causes invoked—reasons of state, the American War of Independence—were locally neither understood nor accepted.

The special taxes were extremely varied and are therefore difficult to catalogue. For example, places located on the Loire were affected by fisheries duties instituted in 1716, a tax on vineyards, and even a charge for maintenance of the bridges of Nantes.

The Corvée

Challenges to the corvée were also widespread. Here, too, communities were affected in two ways, by a royal corvée and by another that was called "personal."

The royal corvée, established by Orry (1689–1747) in 1738, was exploited to the maximum by financial administrations because it made possible the launching of a major program of economic development. One of the most spectacular aspects of this program was the construction of the road network. Theoretically, this corvée should have required at most two weeks a year from each community; each day should have lasted from seven to five o'clock in the summer, and from eight to four o'clock in the winter. In reality, the day was often very long and extremely costly, the source of many complaints. A letter from the parish assembly of La Chapelle-Bassemère, sent to the Parlement of Brittany on January 14, 1781, is explicit on the subject:

> Imagine the inhabitants obliged to go on the corvée; you see them coming out of their houses that have often been flooded, hurrying into

boats too fragile to carry them, their animals, and the tools needed for the corvée, travel at the mercy of the winds over a space of water greater than a league, at the risk of sinking at any moment.

If they escape from danger and reach the opposite bank without mishap, from there to their workplace, there is at least another league; they have to get there by roads that are often impassable, over rutted paths, for corvées are almost always more frequent and more necessary in times of bad weather because of the rain that ruins the major roads.

When they finally reach their workplace, what time remains to them for work? Much of the day has already passed; they soon have to start thinking of the return, which will present again the same dangers and obstacles. This is how the petitioners have to use several days to complete a corvée that would take only one if they were on the spot. This is how, against their will, they lose to the corvées precious time that they would give to cultivating their fields.[3]

This corvée in kind provoked easily understandable discontent, all the more because some parishioners had themselves excused from it.[4] Finally, it required important preparatory work.[5]

From the beginning of the reign of Louis XVI, its reorganization was requested on many occasions:

> We are deeply convinced that the inhabitants would gain a lot by paying to have the work done that they owe on the part of the road attributed to them. We also think that their example could usefully be followed by other parishes and that interesting information would be derived from this experience to decrease the burdens of the corvée and to perfect the administration of the major roads.[6]

The corvée's abolition in 1786 satisfied the demands. However, the new tax established in compensation was so heavy that the inhabitants complained to the provincial administration.

Personal corvées might be seigneurial or parishional, or both. They were so varied that it is difficult to determine both their quantity and their exact content. They might be used to build dikes, to dig ditches or wells, or to clear roads. To these demands was added another, concerning the militia.

The Militia

As Carré very judiciously notes in an article entitled "Des milices de la monarchie à l'insurrection de 1793," the Bretons, like the inhabitants of Anjou and Poitou, were deeply concerned by the militia.[7] Contrary to an assertion by Michelet, there were very few refusals and troubles associated with recruitment. While the rate of desertion in Brittany was on the order of 4.5 percent, compared with a 2 percent average for the kingdom, in Poitou it was 1.8 percent, the lowest rate. This is not the place to rewrite the history of the militia under the Old Regime, but one of the most widespread commonplaces on the origin of the wars of the West consists in saying that the populations had no experience of conscription or that it had not been burdensome.

Two stages may be distinguished. In the seventeenth and early eighteenth centuries, there were urban or bourgeois militias, as well as a coast guard militia made up of the inhabitants of maritime regions, excluding seamen themselves. After the defeat of Corbie in 1636, Louis XIII and Richelieu began to put into operation a veritable general mobilization; when the danger had passed, they gave it up. In 1688, out of necessity, Louvois created the Provincial Militias, drafted in time of war: in 1711, Brittany had to supply 2,150 men.

However, it was not until 1726 that these militias became permanent. During the three major wars of Louis XV, the number of militiamen reached approximately 350,000, not including naval enlistees and others. For example, in 1762 their number in the royal regiments reached approximately 91,000.

Contrary to another widely accepted idea, the coast guard militias of Poitou, Anjou, and Brittany were, on occasion, sent to fight outside the national territory. For example, in 1746 militiamen from Poitou and Anjou were sent to Canada. In 1759 many Bretons died in the naval battle of the Cardinaux. In 1779, 12,000 of the coast guard at once were sent as assistant artillerymen. Similarly, during the American war, the militia was called upon. Bretons and Vendeans were used to fighting not only in their region but also abroad.

After the reform of 1765, Brittany owed seven battalions of "Land Militia," reduced to six through the intervention of deputies at court, charged by the Estates with defending the interests of the province.

When the order to levy militiamen arrived, explains a chronicler, the parish authorities in charge drew up a list of bachelors aged eighteen to forty. Each man on the list received notice of the day and place where the drawing was to be held.

Most of the time the place indicated was the town hall of Nantes for southern Brittany and the principal towns of subregions for the other provinces. The drawing was sometimes done on parish territory. The officers of the king appeared first with a police escort. The young men who claimed exemptions stated them on arrival. When the interviews were over, the drawing of tickets was carried out. There were as many tickets as there were men on the list eligible for service . . . the others being blank. Both kinds were mixed in a hat which had to be held at the level of the heads of those who were doing the drawing, and each one came up according to his place on the list. Everyone who drew a blank ticket was free to resume work in the fields, while the others made a point of thieving and carousing until the day they had to report for duty.[8]

The parish assembly was responsible for equipping each militiaman: "a hat, a jacket, brown serge pants, a pair of shoes and leggings, two shirts, a canvas knapsack, and a hair band."

The uniforms themselves were supplied by the king. For the purchase and maintenance of this equipment, there was a supplementary tax on parishes in addition to the capitation. In the late eighteenth century, the total expense for each man drafted varied between one and two hundred livres. "When they arrived in town, the militiamen received pay on which they had to live; besides their pay they were given only lodging 'with a place by the fire and a candle from the landlord.' Exercises lasted only a few weeks, and then they returned home."[9]

For as long as he was in service, the militiaman was prohibited from leaving the territory of the parish. Every time he was called up, he had to be ready to go to the assembly point. Failure to do so incurred a punishment that was usually ten more years of enlistment. The judgment was read during the sermon at high mass. Service lasted for four years in 1765 and for six beginning in 1775.

All bachelors between eighteen and forty were eligible for militia service. In certain serious circumstances, married men or widowers without children were also called up, first those below twenty and then, if necessary, above that age.

Men who worked on the land were very discontented with this situation, and this unhappiness was frequently expressed in the *cahiers de doléances*. It was everywhere expressly requested "that the militia, that takes the laborer from the bosom of his family and depopulates the countryside, be abolished."[10] Vineyards suffered even more because they required "for their maintenance many hands and a large number of growers."

More than against recruitment itself, the populace complained particularly, as it would a hundred years later, that the militia "reduced the taste for agriculture! Indeed, a large number of these militiamen, the exact percentage of whom is uncertain, refuse to return to agriculture. Either they enlist in the 'national' army, or they go to work in town, where they stay for the rest of their life."[11]

However, this argument is not enough to explain the general outcry of the populace against the militia, which directly affected only a limited number of inhabitants. The decisive element was the major psychological problem created by the anxiety that lasted until the age of forty about the fate of those eligible, bachelors or married men without children. Pétard states it explicitly in his work on Saint-Julien-de-Concelles:

> Militia service was considered by our peasants as the heaviest burden placed on them. They found it very painful to escape from a year of service and then to be on the next list and so on until they were married. Bachelors especially continually complained about a law that kept them in suspense until the age of forty.[12]

As much as possible, the parish assembly reduced the burden of the militia by purchasing volunteers to replace recruits; for five recruits, it would buy one volunteer. The sums spent were divided among all the names listed for the year's drawing. In 1741 in Saint-Julien-de-Concelles, five volunteers were paid "in all 595 livres" in addition to 97 livres for equipment. In 1751 Louis Aubert acknowledged "having received from the parish assembly the sum of one hundred forty livres for militia service." Samson, from the village of La Boissière-du-Doré, received as much as 400 livres in 1779 "to serve in the name of the parish."

Moreover, the administration, which was thought of as doing nothing but restricting, arresting, and systematically rejecting any novel ideas, was disparaged by force of circumstance. There was nothing new about this situation. On the other hand, the administrators systematized certain aspects of it. Thus, the functions of general taxes, requests for levying local taxes, the management of parish assemblies, the planting of vines, and so on, were subjected to a detailed critique carried out by subordinate officials and then transmitted through the administrative hierarchy. It became more and more difficult to cheat, for example to establish an unequal distribution of tax burdens, to divert parish assembly funds, or to fail to maintain Church property. Beginning in 1732, for instance, removing or replanting of vines had to be declared to the administration or a fine would be levied. And the administration remained oppressive; it threatened to send garrisons at the expense of the populace in cases of rebelliousness. This blackmail sometimes became a reality, as in 1783 in Saint-Julien-de-Concelles. In the month of December, all the roads near the Loire were washed away, the countryside was ravaged, and the crops destroyed.[13] As a result, the parish assembly refused to send laborers to the other side of the river for the royal corvées. Soldiers were immediately sent to the territory and the populace had to give in to armed force; it was given two weeks to comply. The news spread through the countryside; the people were upset and afraid and complained that "times are hard."[14]

Whatever their demands, communities had the impression that no one was listening, or worse, that they were being systematically opposed. For example, they were not allowed to raise a local tax to pay for a deficit, to tax the curé and some nobles for their lands subject to flooding; despite their protests against the burden of the corvées on the major roads, the work required was increased. Taxes proliferated: in 1787, in Brittany, after consideration by the Estates on January 19, vineyards with mixed species were subjected "to duties of the hundredth denier, of registration, and two deniers per livre." The parish assemblies later deliberated on what they considered a violation of their customary rights and forcefully protested by petitions. It was a futile gesture; the decision of the Estates was maintained. The inhabitants affected would not fail to refer to this when the *cahiers de doléances* were prepared.

The populace compared their new situation with the "old days," which were seen as a kind of golden age that was regretted, idealized, not forgotten, and that had been violated. There was thus obvious local resistance only awaiting an opportunity to come to the surface.

In this context, the nobility was often led to perform a significant role. The nobles interceded with the authorities to limit abuses or to make them aware of the inherent difficulties of certain decisions. As a general rule, the nobles made it their duty to provide firm and effective leadership for the population, directly or through the intermediary of their representatives, such as notaries. They were able to decide on the construction of dikes, the digging of wells, the clearing of ditches, and the like. If necessary, they did not hesitate to remind the clergy of their primary obligations, and they were sometimes prodigal with their time and their money.

The local seigneurial system was characterized by its extreme flexibility. It was all the more easily accepted because its advantages seemed greater than its drawbacks, which consisted essentially of taxes, most of which were symbolic.[15] Some historians have spoken of oppressive duties, citing the *quintaine* as an example. In fact, this interpretation is mistaken for two reasons. The first is because this game was an occasion for diversion in which nearly everyone was eager to participate. In the second place, those who refused to attend or to break lances could pay to be excused. In addition, a certain number of seigneurial fees, like the hundredth denier and the *lods et ventes,* had become royal taxes.

The great majority of the inhabitants had little to complain about in this system, and besides, they could rather easily evade its restrictions. For example, a large number of peasants hunted. This situation explains, among other things, the considerable number of rifles in the country under the Revolution and the peasants' skill in shooting. This situation was probably truer of the north than of the south. Other similar infractions may be mentioned. For example, on September 19, 1780, the Marshal Duke of Fitz-James presented a petition to the king and his council: "He constantly observes that the duties for the Loire are not paid. In the month of April 1780, for example, the customs employees on duty saw two individuals," one, Jacques Boiffraud, pulling a boat loaded with goods, and the other, Pierre Bouillé pushing it upstream on the Loire. "They had no pass, and the employees seized the boat, the sailors, and the goods. Boiffraud escaped . . ." They were jointly sentenced to a fine of 60 livres.[16]

These facts explain at least partially the extreme poverty of Vendean nobles, except for a few who lived luxuriously at court. The inhabitants, as a result, spoke little or not at all of abolishing the "feudal" system. As a matter of form, they asked for "a softening,"[17] and perhaps above all a rationalization, particularly of the system of justice.

The situation was seen differently where the Church was concerned.

The Perception of the Church

Grievances were addressed principally against the regular clergy, the chaplains, and the parish assemblies (*fabriques*). The regular clergy were criticized for their opulence, their avarice, the harassment for which they were responsible, and their very way of life. The chaplains were accused of drawing the revenue from their livings without respecting their obligations, such as that of residence. They even sometimes paid wages for another priest to replace them. This situation was considered irrational, because these livings had been established by and for the benefit of the parishioners. Because the services required were no longer performed, it seemed logical that the money be restored to the community in the form of a tax.

The Council of Trent, royal edicts, and decrees of the Parlement had ordered the establishment of the parish assembly and regulated the administration of its holdings.[18] This organization had been set out in very general terms that did not interfere with local customs nor, later on, with numerous particular regulations.

At the outset, the *fabrique* was made up exclusively of members of the clergy charged with drawing up a list of the poor. It later became an assembly of laymen elected by the parishioners to oversee the community's possessions. Locally, its origin went back to the early seventeenth century. Before then, parishes had no political body. Meetings must have been similar to those of Saint-Julien-de-Concelles described by Pétard:

> At the end of the parish mass, the inhabitants present met in full assembly and deliberated all together on their common interests. Decisions were made by majority vote. Churchwardens or treasurers appointed by these assemblies copied down the decisions on loose sheets of paper and later carried them out in the name "of the majority of the inhabitants." These large gatherings had more than one drawback. Discussions were interminable, the results questionable, the recalcitrant opposed one assembly to another and had a second come to conclusions that contradicted those of the first. It became necessary to entrust the discussion of common interests to smaller and better-defined assemblies.[19]

The Parlements, aware of the difficulties created by the situation, corrected them with a series of decrees between 1644 and 1718. This institutional organ, the *fabrique*, consisted of two elements: the assembly of deliberators, having a merely consultative role of proposition and recording; and the office of *fabriqueurs*, a genuine executive organ accounting for the effectiveness of the institution.

The Parish Assembly

The assembly consisted of members, by right or elected, and it had little power. The members by right were the curé or his representative, that is, the rector, and the fiscal procurator or the notary. The first two represented spiritual authority, and the others temporal authority.

The elected members, whose numbers varied depending on the size of the parish, were co-opted. To be eligible, one had to be male, of age, Catholic, a former *fabriqueur*, on the list read and approved by the assembly, and above all solvent: *fabriqueurs* were personally responsible for any possible mishandling of funds. Theoretically, any parishioner might be chosen. In practice, the final condition turned the institution over to the well-to-do strata of the population, chiefly peasants, and to a lesser extent coopers, artisans, and bourgeois. An impecunious parishioner might occasionally be appointed, as in 1735 in Barbechat,[20] but then a relative had to provide a financial guarantee.

Custom was very precise with respect to the internal structure of assemblies. The procedure was minutely regulated in order to avoid any problems. The assembly had to meet in plenary session at least once a year, as required by decrees of the Parlement, presided over by a bureau assisted by a clerk and possibly commissioners.

The bureau directed the debates. At its head were the rector and the syndic of the nobles. As such, they, along with a *fabriqueur*, each held a key to a chest with three locks.[21] They presented to the assembly new laws and demands from the nobles and heard claims that they passed on to the proper authorities. They were assisted by a clerk appointed every two years by the assembly. He took down the minutes in a register whose pages had been stamped, numbered, and dated by the chief judge of the provincial court. He was forbidden to write deliberations on loose sheets of paper "likely to disappear," as was the custom for popular assemblies.

"The choice of clerks," writes Pétard,[22] "was not difficult for the assembly, for several would present themselves when the office became vacant, because of the payment received, from thirty to fifty livres during the eighteenth century."[23]

In order to settle particular problems such as a trial, or to supervise public works, special commissions might be set up. They were appointed by the assembly and automatically dissolved when their work was done.[24]

Custom provided for a minimum of four "ordinary" meetings each year. There might also be other "extraordinary" meetings, whose numbers were limited and varied. The presence of all members of the assembly at each meeting was obligatory; it was carefully recorded at the beginning of the minutes "failing which the deliberations are carried out at the risk of the fortune of the said former *fabriqueurs*." In addition, a member who had not justified his absence was theoretically fined ten livres for the first and twenty for the second. After a third absence, he was excluded and replaced.

When the date of the meeting had been decided, the curé announced it a week beforehand, during the sermon at every service. For their part, the *fabriqueurs* informed every member with a note composed in the following terms:

> By virtue of the notice of public convocation certified by the honorable rector, the *fabriqueurs* in charge of the parish inform the former *fabriqueurs* that they are to assemble next Sunday in order to consider and deliberate upon the matters that will be presented, failing which the said *fabriqueurs* leave everything at the risk of the fortune of the said former *fabriqueurs* and require that the inhabitants appoint two other *fabriqueurs* in their place, protesting that, should the said inhabitants fail to aid in this request, they declare that they leave everything at the risk of their fortune.[25]

A week later, the meeting took place after high mass, under the *chapiteau*[26] in summer, in the nave in winter, as the decrees of the Parlements required, for example this one from Brittany dated May 7, 1691:

> The Court has ordered and orders that in the future all deliberations of the parishes of the province will be held in the parish sacristy or in a decent place that shall be chosen for this purpose by the parishioners; prohibits them from holding any meeting elsewhere, nor in

cabarets, and prohibits notaries from reporting any such meetings on pain of nullity and fifty livres fine.[27]

According to custom, the assembly was called by ringing the bell fifteen times. Everyone freely expressed an opinion, beginning with the youngest. Discussions might be animated and last a long time.[28] They concluded with a vote first by the members of the assembly, then by the fiscal procurator, the notary, and finally the rector. Each participant placed his paper in the "box." After being mixed, the voting papers were unfolded and read aloud by the rector in the presence "of the officers who might also read them." The agenda was adopted by a single vote, requiring a relative majority.

In practice, the specific powers of the assembly were limited, with their essential purpose to determine the actions of the *fabriqueurs* in office. In the spiritual realm, the assembly held essentially a power of appointment and budgetary control; it appointed the *fabriqueurs,* the woodsmen, the *égailleurs,* and the sacristan. The latter was given the duty to

> prepare the church every Saturday and festival eve throughout the year, to keep the lamp burning day and night, to clean cobwebs from the church, to sound the bells for a quarter hour to summon people to high masses, to take care of the cemetery, to maintain the walls, and to dig graves three and one half feet deep.[29]

In addition to the income from these various activities, the sacristan took up a collection in the parish each year and received fixed honoraria for ringing the bells for baptisms, weddings, and funerals.

The audit of the budget took place at the end of December each year during a plenary meeting. In addition to the assembly members, all the former *fabriqueurs* "who have given their accounts and paid their balances" were present. The purpose was to "discharge" the former active members and to "charge" new ones. The *fabriqueurs* had to present themselves with an account book and read it out in public. They faithfully set forth, in a very detailed way, the balance sheet of their management and what they were passing on to their successors. According to custom, the reading began in this way:

> Account both of debits and credits that the *fabriqueurs* in charge during the course of this year represent before you, the honorable rector and former *fabriqueurs* of the parish, which account they represent, fol-

lowing the declaration of His Majesty, to be examined in the spiritual and temporal realms, in the manner in which it should and as follows. This discharge of account the said *fabriqueurs* in charge intend to place into the hands of honorable persons . . . *fabriqueurs* in charge appointed for the next year by the assembly of this parish, following the capitulary act of . . . The said new *fabriqueurs* present declare, each one individually, that they will well and faithfully conduct themselves in the following manner.

Then, the *fabriqueurs* described orally what they had carefully written down, concerning their receipts in the spiritual domain. This enumeration consisted of a detailed inventory of all the ritual objects contained in the sacristy and all sums received. The meeting concluded with a "joyous discharge" meal. The rector, members of the assembly, and *fabriqueurs* sat at the same table.

The assembly also had to accept or reject pious donations and establish concessions of tombs in churches, until that was prohibited by the Parlements in 1755.

Finally, the parish assembly held a certain power of initiative, which consisted of maintaining and decorating the church and regulating the price of "chairs, benches, and stools." In reality, its authority was confined to the nave, the choir being under the authority of the *décimateurs*. Ordinarily, in order to simplify operations, chairs were rented out by the year.

In the temporal realm, the essential task of the parish assembly was limited to recording the lists drawn up by the *fabriqueurs* and to drawing up the list of young men subject to militia duty, and thus subject to the corvée and to taxation. On occasion, at the request of the *fabriqueurs*, it might decide to levy exceptional taxes. In this case, it sent an express written request to the king who had to agree to it.

In practice, the range of action of the parish assembly was very limited, and this was all the more true because there was frequently disagreement among members. Real power, in fact, belonged to the *fabriqueurs* who, locally, made up a genuine executive organ.

The Fabriqueurs

There were rarely more than five of them, depending on the size of the parish. Two lists of notables were drawn up each year by the *fabriqueurs* in charge. They were submitted for the deliberation of the parish assembly. To remove a name from this list was to do a reputedly serious injury to the man concerned. Abbé Pétard cites an example from the parish of Saint-Julien-de-Concelles.[30] In the month of December 1718 Michel Robin, "finding himself omitted and believing himself overlooked and claiming to have been included in previous lists," had no hesitation in bringing the two *fabriqueurs* in charge, Bezeau and Laurent, before the provincial court in Nantes. He reproached them with having changed the list without informing the parish assembly, which was contrary to the decrees of the Parlement. Indeed, the court nullified the election of the new *fabriqueurs,* which it considered marred by illegality. The assembly was thus obliged to hold another meeting to approve the list, which would be read and made public by the curé in his sermon. Every person named was informed by a note. A week after the proclamation, the assembly proceeded to the election. Following tradition, it took place toward the middle of September in the great nave of the parish church after high mass. The vote was by secret ballot.

Those elected received a note written by the *fabriqueurs* in charge, made public in the rector's sermon, and composed as follows: "The *fabriqueur* in charge informs . . . of . . . that by the chapter of last Sunday he has been appointed *fabriqueur* for next year. He advises him therefore to be ready to begin his duties following custom."[31]

Fabriqueurs were elected for one year, but their mandate was renewable. In addition to their traditional principal functions (making inventories of goods, making collections, establishing agendas, drawing up rolls, holding police powers), they might occasionally take up other problems (building dikes, filling in ditches, and the like), and propose the base for new taxes to be debated.[32]

Despite appearances, the power of the *fabriqueurs* was real and very important. In fact, there was no means of controlling them even in budgetary matters; only the balance of accounts had to be respected and the allocation of expenditures known. Moreover, if problems arose during meetings, the *fabriqueurs* did not summon the parish assembly, or they avoided "errors" by the choice of questions to be debated. On no account could their actions be challenged. They held a kind of immunity that made them indifferent to any action by the parish assembly and more precisely by the rector. In case of opposition or serious problems, it was always possible for them (they pointed it out every time) to go to court, to resign their office, or to debate their management in front of the population. The only effective counterweight for the parish assembly was to reject their accounts, on the condition that expenses were not justified.

Those elected were essentially connected notables making up a numerically small group. They thus benefited from a favorable complicity on the part of the population, which expected material advantages from them, particularly relief from taxation or understated declarations of cattle ownership. The *fabriqueurs* undertaxed themselves, and their friends profited from this, as the administrator's envoy Groleau noted in 1777 at the establishment of the capitation list in La Chapelle-Bassemère, the basis for all taxation and for corvées:

> Through the examination that we have made, we have noticed several omissions and have noted that the deliberators who worked on its establishment discharged themselves from one *toise* of road, and their friends from one half *toise,* to the detriment of the whole number of those obligated, as can be seen by the marks next to the names of those reduced.
>
> So the said deliberators are to be condemned, not only for the inaccuracy they have included in this list, but also for having abused their office by discharging themselves and their protégés, although the syndic of the same parish made observations to them about this reprehensible point.[33]

This undertaxation automatically created overtaxation for the rest of the population. In the case of a challenge, there were allegations of the antiquity of the lists or other arguments, and promises to establish new ones.

Along with the parish assembly and the *fabriqueurs,* there were other people working for the *fabrique*. These were chiefly the woodsmen, responsible for the management of trees dedicated to various saints; and the *égailleurs* and the collectors, appointed every year in January by the assembly and charged with the distribution and collection of the different taxes. Theoretically, they were financially responsible for mistakes made by the *fabriqueurs*.

The word *"fabrique"* implied the body of administrators charged with governing it, but also the possessions and revenues, the value and number of which varied according to the size of the parish.

The institution, which functioned well early on, aged very badly. Those responsible for the crisis were the members of the assembly who fail to answer in sufficient numbers the call of the bell and do not provide warning of their absence three days in advance. Intrigues and disputed feelings take shape, and they are pretexts for several to withdraw, without deliberating, and finally these different reasons have led to neglect of the interests of the church and those of the assembly.[34]

The deliberative body respected its obligations less and less. It thus left the executive authority without control, with all the abuses that situation involved, particularly in matters of managing the budget. As a consequence of this negligence, many problems arose between the *fabriqueurs* and the rector. Their causes lay in the perpetual budget deficit, principally due to two factors: tax payments advanced by the *fabriqueurs* not reimbursed by the parishioners; and diversion of funds, either by individuals or by the group as a whole. It is even possible to suspect in some instances the tacit agreement, or even the complicity, of the parish assembly.[35]

Rectors were often forced to file complaints in provincial courts or even before the Parlements. This management explains in part the dilapidated state of most religious buildings on the eve of the Revolution, a situation sometimes aggravated by the rivalry between two parish assemblies.

The community as a whole was thus aware of the aging of this institution. It would see it disappear with no regret in 1789, to be replaced by the commune and its municipal council, symbol of the secularization of the community.

The reproach had less application to the secular clergy charged with the cure of souls, whose liberal sentiments cannot be questioned. The *cahiers de doléances* of Brittany, Anjou, and Poitou accentuate the same tendencies: guarantee of individual freedom, distribution of taxation among the three orders, increase of the number of schools in the countryside, access of citizens to all employments, rationalization of the system, and the like. The clergy was thus fundamentally in agreement with the population.

The First Revolutionary Accomplishments

THE VENDEANS WERE THUS NEARLY UNANIMOUS IN WISHING FOR change; they therefore gave a very favorable, indeed an enthusiastic welcome to the fundamental principles of the Revolution of 1789. The *cahiers de doléances* were prepared and municipal governments elected with feelings of elation, and there was no regret for the disappearance of the old parish institutions.

There were high hopes because, in addition to the problems created by the administration, the economic situation was far from flourishing. Abbé Le Mercier, rector of La Chapelle-Bassemère, describes it in his parish register:

> The winter of 1783 was remarkable for the overflowing of the Loire, which was so great that in living memory, its like had not been seen since the year 1711. The water began to rise on March 4, Mardi Gras, and by Sunday almost the whole valley was inundated and the houses abandoned. All the roads were swept away, causing considerable damage to the parish.
>
> These sad events were followed by an extraordinary summer. For about four months, the sky was covered with a thick fog which barely permitted a glimpse of the sun. Morning and evening it was red, the color of blood; at noon it was pale, and yet the heat continued to increase so much so that it was hotter than it had ever been. All the journals talked about this fog, and all the scientists investigated it . . .

The winter of 1784 can be compared to that of 1709. We can say that it was cold from the beginning of the month of September 1783 until the end of April 1784. But it was bitterly cold for two and a half months. During this time, such a great quantity of snow fell that the octogenarians were sure that they had never seen as much and for such a long time. It is true that it did not snow throughout the cold period, but there was snow on the ground for at least six weeks. There also was such a large amount of freezing rain that in the spots where the wind had not left any snow it was impossible to stand, and when the sun shone the trees glittered more brightly than the finest diamonds.

The winter of 1785, while not one of the harshest, was one of the longest. Leaves did not come out on the vines until the month of May, and they flowered before the end of the month. The grape harvest was one of the most bountiful. And the wine was excellent.

The spring of 1787 and three-quarters of the summer were extraordinarily dry, so that no hay was gathered, fodder was sold at an excessive price, and meat became very tough in 1787. The year was rich in wheat, there was a rather large quantity of wine, but inferior in quality to that of the preceding years.

In 1788 there was no wheat and much flax; there was neither winter nor summer. The grape harvest was so abundant that in living memory there had not been such a large quantity of wine since 1742, but the wine was of mediocre quality.

The year 1788 is forever memorable because of the cold at the end, that is, during the months of November and December. Ice began to appear in the river by September 26 and by the thirtieth, the whole river was frozen. December 17, 18, and 19 were notable for a biting cold.

But the most terrible days were the mornings of December 30 and 31, when the temperature fell to eighteen and a half degrees below freezing, which had never been seen in Paris.

Winter was long, since there was constant freezing from September 24 through January 13, 1789. The ice did not begin to disappear until the 21st. It caused the greatest ravages along the upper Loire. It carried off bridges and roads and inundated more than five hundred houses. Fortunately, the ground was very dry when the cold came on. During the whole cold season, it was covered with snow and ice so that it was extremely difficult to walk. All the cabbages and other vegetables died, but the snow preserved the grains that are now very fine.[1]

Following these crises, which affected not only peasants and wine grow-ers, the distress that the Estates General intended to remedy was expressed by a desire for rationalization and simplification. These were the major themes of the *cahiers de doléances*.

THE *CAHIERS DE DOLÉANCES*

In accordance with the regulation of January 24, 1789, the *cahiers* were put together in the course of the first three months of the year. Participating in their composition were men "twenty-five and older, included on the tax rolls and domiciled in a particular parish."

Generally speaking, throughout this large quantity of documents, a substantial number of which were copies, two principal sentiments were ex-pressed. The first was an attachment to the monarchy, which may have been genuine or a mere formality. This was not confined to the countryside, since Nantes erected a statue to the king.

The second characteristic of these *cahiers* was to call contemporary so-ciety into question, particularly its lack of coherence. Principles were not always directly attacked, but they were everywhere criticized. There were demands for the disappearance of abuses that had grown out of particular circumstances. Lacking that, there were proposals for modifications or backup positions if the demands might appear too bold. It is clear that the principle of legitimacy represented by custom and tradition had been re-placed by that of reason.

As a general rule, the first subjects broached had to do with purely local problems: Loire flooding, ecclesiastical benefices, distribution of taxes, and collection of tithes, except for those for the rectors; this latter complaint was a direct attack on the curés holding parish livings, on abbés, canons, and other clergy, and on nobles who had sometimes seized them. These griev-ances were indeed justified; a large number of rectors in charge lived poorly. Holders of benefices did not even respect the very minimal obligations due to the community, such as maintaining the choir of the parish church in "good condition."

The second set of subjects dealt with more general demands, such as justice, communes, and church collections. However, they were always sub-ordinated to local interests and even narrowly conceived in the framework of the parish. This individualism and independence of mind, which are explained by history, topography, and the wealth of the soil, are essential for an understanding of the later reaction. Relief from taxation and militia service produced great and lasting hope, tied to the hope for the equality of all in the face of social burdens.

Some *cahiers de doléances* were different in character. This was true for Barbechat, located in the future canton of Le Loroux-Bottereau. Only those who could sign their names were recorded. These were thirteen peasants, four blacksmiths, two *septiers*, two millers, and a clogmaker. Sixty-eight articles were drawn up with the aim of presenting a constitution and carrying out various reforms. It seems improbable that this was the work of the inhabitants, which makes it of minor interest.[2]

Following this confusion of ideas, new administrative structures were put in place, namely, the municipal governments.

THE ESTABLISHMENT OF MUNICIPAL GOVERNMENTS

The idea was unanimously accepted because it confirmed the Revolution in a tangible way. In accordance with the law of December 22, 1789, parishioners paying a minimal contribution equivalent to three days' work, having taken the civic oath, and being at least twenty-five years old, voted for the municipal council, the size of which varied with the size of the commune. "These elections are carried out in the accustomed manner, at the end of the parish mass and to the sound of the bell."[3]

It is difficult to get a general picture of the origin of these councillors. The analysis carried out for La Chapelle-Bassemère, although of limited application, provides interesting details.[4] Those elected—that is, the president, eight officers, and sixteen notables—were essentially inhabitants of the village and of large hamlets, who were the only ones able to fulfill the conditions required by the law:[5] nine coopers, two men with private incomes, two tailors, a hatmaker, a baker, a blacksmith, a wigmaker, a notary, and only seven peasants. Fifteen members out of twenty-four were artisans or merchants, thus holding a large majority. The average age was forty-eight, which was relatively old.

A majority of councillors and peasants were in support of the new ideas. They saw themselves reflected in the measures taken in Paris, which were apparently in their favor. They were thus given, with no supervision, considerable power, which they had been waiting for for half a century.[6] Simultaneously with these elections, the old parish structure disappeared.

THE DISAPPEARANCE OF THE PARISH ASSEMBLY

The assembly died from its inability to resolve all the problems directly or indirectly confronting the community. Various basic causes explain this rapid change.

The first came from the members themselves. At the end of the Old Regime, the institution was in part spinning its wheels, for lack of representatives. In addition, some inhabitants were using the structure to undermine ecclesiastical power. As soon as the first Parisian insurrectional movements were announced, most *fabriqueurs* resigned. The clergy, surprised by the sudden spread of this attitude, were powerless to deal with it.

The second cause had to do with the community itself, hostile to an institution that recalled the Old Regime with its hierarchy, its privileges, and its abuses. With the disappearance of this structure, bourgeois, artisans, and prosperous peasants hoped to acquire property, particularly "unoccupied" or common land, and other land as well.

The final attack came from the National Assembly. Indeed, by the passage of two laws, the nationalization of church property on November 2, 1789, and the sale of that property in July 1790, the parish assembly lost any reason for existence.

This idea was well received in the military Vendée as a whole. Concretely, the first properties sold were the chaplaincies and lands of the regular clergy, provoking no reservations in the population. These lands were acquired by representatives of the whole society, including future army generals such as Stofflet and Jaudonnet de Laugrenière, who bought a parish church and a priory.

Depending on the size and use of lots, purchasers came from different backgrounds. Acquirers of large tracts were generally from outside the commune, especially in the south. In the north, the situation was fundamentally different: lots were small and prices relatively low. In La Chapelle-Bassemère, the total of the first sales reached 87,221 livres. The purchasers were only local residents. They were divided as follows: artisans, 65 percent; professionals, 13 percent *rentiers*, 3 percent; peasants 10 percent; undetermined, 10 percent.

Eighty percent of the value of land sold went to inhabitants of the village, the only ones with "good hard" currency, because they were merchants or artisans.

The old structure died all the more easily because no one protested, including the parish clergy and the clerical Catholics. Most of the former were favorable to the new institutions that had been proclaimed, and possible challengers had neither the time nor the means to oppose them. As for the latter, who were not very numerous, they were obviously afraid to speak out because of the revolutionary atmosphere.

Besides, any reaction was impossible. The new administrative structure that had been put in place unquestionably corresponded to the wishes of the majority of the population.

THREE

The End of the Honeymoon

HUNGRY FOR REFORM, THE PEOPLE HOPED TO HAVE THEIR CRITICISMS heard at the national level through the intermediary of the new representatives. The strongest criticisms were obviously tied to certain hopes, more or less conscious, arising from the moment or going far back in time. In fact, not only were demands not listened to, but even worse, the abuses of the administration and the gendarmerie and the mistakes of the government aggravated the situation.

THE REFUSAL TO LISTEN TO THE POPULACE

Endowed with new power but inexperienced in its exercise, the municipal governments tended to rely on superior bodies: districts, departments, government, National Assembly. The hierarchical authorities, traditional as well as revolutionary, were more than willing to respond favorably to this appeal.

The municipal governments were thus concerned to impress the authorities and to anticipate recommended measures. In a few months, an impressive range of problems was thereby created. Some were particular to a few communes, others were of a general order.

In any event, one of municipal governments' first tasks was the establishment of boundaries on the land. This initiative could not fail to provoke an uproar. Indeed, a large number of hamlets, villages, and *fillettes*, for various entirely legitimate reasons, demanded independence from the old parishes, the *matrices*.[1] As an example, let us consider the case of La Chapelle-Bassemère and Barbechat.

The first crisis went back to the seventeenth century with the desire of chaplains to unify parishes. The inhabitants of Barbechat resisted, particularly beginning in the 1780s. To defend their rights, they relied essentially on two means, petitions and trials, without success. Of the various solutions proposed, such as the creation of a permanent post of vicar, none was adopted. The two communities were thus in favor of the Revolution; each one hoped that it would lead to recognition of its own rights.

To break the deadlock, the inhabitants of Barbechat decided to take unilateral action. Despairing of obtaining their "autonomy," on February 22, 1790, they elected a mayor and municipal officers whose first concern was the proclamation of a new independent commune.[2] La Chapelle-Bassemère complained very bitterly to the departmental directory. On August 2, 1790, the procurator-syndic of Nantes sided with La Chapelle-Bassemère.[3] The municipality of Barbechat was ordered to cease all activity. The reaction was immediate; the inhabitants of Barbechat directly addressed the National Assembly. The petition sent on September 1, 1790, recites the facts and openly expresses desires and grievances in relation to La Chapelle;[4] the terms of the instruction of December 14, 1789, concerning the formation of new municipalities applied to Barbechat. The village had a church with a pulpit, confessionals, banners, baptismal fonts, and a cemetery, and the community contained more than five hundred communicants — that is, seven to eight hundred inhabitants. The creation of an independent commune "is the wish and in the interest of the public." According to the councillors, "It is the only way to bring about peace and concord." The response of the National Assembly was final; it confirmed the decision of the directory of Nantes.

This example is far from unique. We might mention Saint-Julien-de-Concelles,[5] Le Loroux-Bottereau,[6] and La Benâte,[7] among others. Worse, some old parishes found themselves included within new communes, and we should not forget sensitivities connected to belonging to a bishopric. The "cantons" most favorable to the Revolution felt betrayed, all the more because the abolition of privileges meant the loss of their ancient rights, while the powers of the municipalities were increased.

This deterioration of good relations was also caused by the increase in taxes; in certain communes they doubled between 1789 and 1792. Added to this were obvious abuses of distribution, as the inhabitants of La Motte-Achard pointed out.[8] There was nothing new about this, but there had been hope that the Revolution would remedy the situation. Various "voluntary" subscriptions to assist the families of national guardsmen suffering the effects of poverty[9] or to finance the occupation of troops[10] aggravated the situation all the more because any refusal brought on a surtax.[11] To these measures was added the patriotic contribution established by the decree of October 6, 1790, affecting all individuals paying taxes of four hundred livres or more.[12]

The mayors in charge of establishing tax rolls, justifiably or not, were accused of following their own interests and not respecting their primary obligation to serve as an intermediary between the populace and the government.

THE EXPRESSION OF THE NATIONAL WILL

The municipal governments gave the impression that they were prostituting themselves to the government authorities. They served them scrupulously, forgetting all consultation of their constituents. The December 1789 decree of the National Assembly, moreover, was in full agreement with this practice. Article 55 specified that municipal bodies "will be entirely subordinate to the departmental and district administrations for everything having to do with the functions they will have to perform by delegation from the general administration."[13]

The decree of October 21, 1789, concerning martial law against crowds had already been a major step. Indeed, municipal officers of places in which there was a risk of disturbance were obliged to deploy police forces. In case of negligence, "they were held responsible."[14]

The decree of February 26, 1790, strengthened their police power considerably; it was extended to proper collection of taxes (article III). In the case of insurmountable problems, municipalities were expected to come to one another's assistance (article IV). In the case of incidents, the commune was answerable (with recourse against individuals responsible) before the local tribunals, on a complaint by the district directory.

A letter of December 4, 1792, sent to the department by the municipal government of Savenay, is revealing in the desire it expresses to strengthen the bonds among all the "bodies of the administration": "This union is especially valuable at a time when a mass of corrupt and widespread insurrections are widely spreading poison and contamination in every direction."[15]

The law, source of the general will, for which the municipal governments held the "precious trust," became the only rule to be respected: "It serves as a rallying point for the most distant parts of the empire. It truly puts into practice the unity and indivisibility of the Republic. It brings together all the administrations in the same spirit and a single justice." Consequently, the law has to be faithfully executed; that is "the most solid, the incomparable advantage of republican government."

From then on, the inhabitants observed, with a certain fear, they now had to submit to forces from outside, not necessarily favorable to the community. This was the death of a certain form of autonomy to which Vendeans individually were so strongly attached. We might say that by the end of 1791, and even before, in a large number of communes, the municipal governments no longer represented the popular will. It is obvious that resistance took root at the most humble levels.

The Realization of the Unpopularity of the Administrations and the Means Adopted to Remedy the Situation

Some organs of government rapidly became aware of the unpopularity of the administration. During a debate on February 19, 1791, the directory of the department of Maine-et-Loire attempted to understand the reasons for this development. It set forth various arguments, particularly the fact that "this administration tries to keep itself from public view; it fears examination, inspires mistrust, and creates a bad opinion of its operations."[16]

It was asked to display its conduct in the open and to put all those under its administration in a position to understand its work. To do this, two methods were adopted. The first was to give every citizen the full right to consult the registers, the second to print all operations in order to make them public. "Unfortunately," concluded the report, "while the first method is already in operation, in fact, only the inhabitants of Angers have made use of it."

As for the second, which "would much better have fulfilled its purposes," they could not "turn" to it for lack of financial means. A third solution was then proposed: to print in the form of weekly periodicals the minutes of plenary sessions, debates, and decisions, and correspondence with the National Assembly, the districts, and the municipalities. "Young men would thus be able to familiarize themselves with the great principles of the new constitution, and to follow its development and application."

The report concluded that any infraction would no longer be excusable and would thus be subject to punishment.

In fact, although the department was publishing bulletins every week by the month of March 1791, they were seldom read. Neither citizens nor even the local administrations knew the documents. The result, according to the general council, was a total disorganization caused by "wicked subalterns." Law and justice were constantly violated, and the honor of the nation outraged by "the atrocious and abject bureaucracy that has infected it." The solution would be "a purge and the recall of the faithful servants whose zeal and talents had been ignored and proscribed, and who demand the honor and glory of effectively serving the nation."[17]

When the situation became too tense, troops were sent; for example, 150 men were sent to Guérande in December 1790 "in order to keep order among people with bad intentions."[18] To avoid any problems, the populace was disarmed, as in Saint-Lumine-de-Coutais in December 1791, seeing that they "are insubordinate toward the higher administration."[19]

The recognition of failure was obvious, even within the upper levels of the administration. From then on the mistrust of the local populace was understandable, all the more because the central government was to make more and more mistakes.

FOUR

The Mistakes of the Central Government and the Excesses of the Administration

ANGER WAS RUMBLING IN THE COMMUNES OF THE VENDÉE, BUT THE National Assembly paid no attention. Even worse, it took a series of measures that crystallized discontent. The administrative hierarchy stiffened and exaggerated them, either from ineptitude and misreading of the laws or on its own initiative.

THE MISTAKES OF THE GOVERNMENT

The definitive break of the populace with the government authorities was consummated by the proclamation of the Civil Constitution of the Clergy.

The Civil Constitution of the Clergy: July 12, 1790

By this law, the National Assembly decided on the abolition of religious vows and confirmed the nationalization of Church property. The State, having assumed responsibility for support of the clergy, could reorganize it as it would any other public service. "It was," wrote Lallié, "a flame of discord cast in the midst of a nation attempting to re-establish itself."[1]

For Mourret:

It was a mistake, a deliberate and not an accidental mistake, which was to oblige the clergy, in order to remain faithful to the Church and to its priestly vows, to refuse to obey the State. The aim of the Assembly was clear: it wanted to establish a national Church in France, and at the same time it settled all the relations the Church was to have in the future, with the Pope, with the State, and with the people.[2]

Most members of the National Assembly[3] and of the Convention were rationalists and for that reason anticlerical. The mixture of Gallican (from the Parlements) and Protestant "philosophy" of the new masters was catastrophic, all the more because it was joined to a total misunderstanding of fundamental French psychological realities.

Article IV of Section I of the Civil Constitution prohibited any church or parish in France, as well as any French citizen, from recognizing under any circumstances the authority of a bishop appointed by a foreign power. The allusion was obvious; earlier, Camus had said in the National Assembly, "[W]hat is the Pope? A bishop like the others . . ." He went on, "It is time that the Church of France was delivered from servitude."

Article XIX was more explicit. The Assembly decided that any elected bishop would no longer have to address the pope to receive canonical appointment. It would now be enough to inform him out of politeness, in witness of the unity of the faith and of communion with him.[4]

Each department became a diocese, with administrative rigidity predominating. Fifty-two bishoprics were thereby wiped off the map. Parishes were similarly rearranged and chapters abolished.

Like the curé, the bishop was now elected by a plurality of votes of all active citizens, including Jews, Protestants, and unbelievers. The bishop would subsequently request canonical appointment from his metropolitan. The leader of his diocese, he nevertheless depended on a council made up of vicars-general who had voting powers equal to his own.

In addition, the elected bishop took a solemn oath to supervise the faithful in his charge and to support, with all his power, the constitution decreed by the National Assembly and accepted by the king. "At bottom," according to Jarnoux, "the Civil Constitution of the Clergy was unacceptable because it denied the exclusive spiritual power of the Church, a power received from God Himself."[5] It was a direct attack on the faith.

In late September 1790 the Civil Constitution of the Clergy was posted in departmental capitals. The event, writes Gabory, was like a thunderclap.[6]

The patriots greeted it with joy. In Nantes, Coustard de Massy, president of the department, mounted the pulpit in the cathedral to praise Louis XVI.

Priests had thus become nothing but civil servants. Salaries allocated varied as a function of the size of parishes and the extent of duties involved. In November 1792, however, the Christian Brothers teaching order was excluded on the pretext "that it was surprising that men who held principles opposed to the Revolution wished to assume responsibility for public education."[7]

Although some members of the clergy willingly accepted the new situation, a substantial number rejected it. Consequently, on October 25 the directory of Loire-Inférieure sent to the nine districts of the department a circular containing directives designed to repress "the stubbornness of these churchmen."[8] On October 4 it had already ordered all curés and vicars under its authority to deliver from the pulpit a decree requiring the sale of Church property.

Reactions proliferated. On November 10, 1790, 103 priests of the Nantes diocese signed a protest addressed to the Assembly. Its author, the curé of Saint-Lumine-de-Coutais, a former deputy to the Estates General named Chevalier, wished to demonstrate that the Civil Constitution destroyed the hierarchy of the Church, made France a nation in revolt against the papacy, and subjected religious authority to civil authority. In the preamble, he emphasized that he was not protesting against the loss of property: "Taught by a poor God, we ourselves have learned to make sacrifices." Nor did he wish to provoke a rebellion of the people against legal authority: "We consider this authority to be a real power for you the legislators, and it is toward you as well that we direct our hopes."[9] The signatories had their pay reduced or abolished.

As for the bishops, the reaction of many of them was unambiguous. In March 1790, 134 of them condemned the Civil Constitution. By the end of April 1790 the bishop of Nantes had left his diocese "with the heartfelt hope that calm and good sense would return to the country."[10]

The State had already intervened in the domain of the Church. For example, it had ordered that incense be burned in churches only to honor the Divinity. This restriction was received and posted in Nantes on June 19; the traditional use of incense, following the Roman ritual, as a sign of respect for the priest, his ministers, the faithful, and the bodies of the dead, was forbidden.

The directory of the district of Paimbœuf zealously applied this decree and on August 23, 1790, decided to have it publicized by priests in their parishes. An interesting reaction was that of Abbé Robin, who had been rector of Le Pellerin since May 28, 1782. He deliberately failed to publicize it on the grounds that it was an attack on the rights of the Church.[11] Incidentally, his arguments give evidence of solid training in philosophy and theology.

On September 8 the municipal government took note of the arguments of the curé, who nevertheless asserted his obedience to the law while at the same time making very pertinent remarks about the timeliness of making the decree public. If he did not accept it, "this was also because it would only have increased the terror of the people, who fear that religion is the target, and it would have been futile because never had the said rector or his vicars received or demanded incense at holy mass since he had been rector." In other words, the decree was obeyed de facto, but was unacceptable de jure. He also observed that

> being obliged to publish the decrees on pain of being deprived of the status of active citizen, he had made a solemn oath to publish and to recognize the decrees of the Assembly insofar as they contained nothing that might bring harm to religion. The directory of Paimbœuf could not find fault for his not publishing a prohibition of doing something that the directory does not do, that has to do only with him, and which can only be prohibited by the authority of the assembled Church; otherwise, this would be an attack on its rights which the Estates General declared, in a solemn decree, having no intention of reducing in the slightest way. In addition, like any other citizen, he had the right to freedom, leaving to the municipal officers the duty of publishing the decree at the end of mass.[12]

Nevertheless, the municipal government thought it appropriate to make a major case of the matter. On September 10 Mainguy, the commune's prosecutor, sent a report on the rector's sermons to the directory. After making his refusal public, Abbé Robin explained that he was ready to undergo martyrdom to defend the integrity of the Christian religion. "I hasten," said Mainguy,

> to give you some fragments of the remarks and incendiary speeches that were made, after high mass last Wednesday, by *sieur* Robin, the curé of the parish . . .

The said Robin, after making an apology for his own person in the most flattering and extended manner, set forth statements that are, according to many people, against the orthodoxy of the Gallican Church.

"Speak, gentlemen, speak, must we give up the Church of Jesus Christ to serve as a temple for idols? While I did indeed subscribe to the federation agreement of July 14, I did so not out of mere servility. The priest at the altar is Jesus Christ Himself and incense is due to him. If I am brought to justice, put in prison, locked in chains, if I am struck and killed like Saint Paul, I will die for the religion of Jesus Christ. As a Christian, I will never leave the Christian religion. As a minister at the altar and a pastor, I will defend this holy religion and the flock that has been given me."

Later, the municipal government wanted to be protected by superior authorities. It requested instructions from the director of the department, claiming that it did not know what measures to take in the situation:

I would be obliged to you, sir, if you were to outline the action I and the municipal body should take. We have on our side only our probity and our attachment to the Constitution and are ignorant of the formalities that should be observed in such a case. The gentlemen of the directory of the department are in a position to verify the leniency and the moderation of the conduct of the municipality and of my own through the documents that I sent with my last communication.[13]

This report is interesting in its admission that "the people are grumbling against the municipality which they accuse of secretly being the source of these orders, that do not come from the National Assembly," and that they are already prepared to follow their rector without hesitation. "The women and girls are lamenting the loss of their religion," confesses Mainguy, and "are expecting that their curé will be put in prison and perhaps put to death because he is defending that holy religion and he anticipates the prohibition of baptism." This document implicitly reveals the fear of an insurrection.

On September 18 the abbé sent another letter to the directory in which he explained his position in detail. He repeated and expanded his earlier arguments.[14] Not knowing how to counteract the influence of the curé, who was claiming to use his freedom as a citizen to follow his conscience, the municipality seems to have carried out a whole series of harassments against him. They lasted for three months, from September through November 1790, but confirmed a pre-existing anticlerical attitude. Many examples demonstrate this: the curé's taxable income was increased from 398 to 998 livres; his servant, aged sixty-seven, was taxed despite the exemption decreed by the National Assembly for any servant over the age of sixty; the number of parishioners was underestimated in order to reduce his pay, and so on. Abbé Robin tried to justify himself and sent several official letters with this aim, with no results.

On November 9, 1790, in the face of threats, the rector fled Le Pellerin and took refuge with his family, "which worriedly opposed his return." From there, on November 17, he sent a letter to prosecutor Mainguy; he would return to Le Pellerin only if the municipal government ordered it and at the same time guaranteed his freedom. He complained of the harassment to which he had been subjected and explained his departure:

> I hasten to reveal to you the true reasons for my leaving so that my absence will not be the occasion for imputing new crimes to me, when you have the opportunity to confer with the municipal authorities about the means to remedy it.
>
> I left Le Pellerin on November 9, alone and unaccompanied throughout my journey; it was about two o'clock, and I spent the night at Saint-Aignan. I left the next day at eight to consult about what steps I should take, and I returned to spend the night at Saint-Aignan, where I arrived at five the next day. I left at eight to return to my family, where I am now . . . This, Sir, is my true itinerary which will prove to you that I have not covered my steps with the dark of night, as I have always behaved among you. Any other delay and circumstance would on the contrary be an outrage to truth, and here are the real justifications for my departure. For some time, Sir, justice and peace, inseparable accompaniments to true happiness, had been denied me, and I merely groaned in secret. Then I suddenly learned in confidence and from three different people in succession, that a secret hatred had openly been declared against me which aimed at nothing less than taking my life and burning my house. Who would not have trembled at such news. I confess that despite all the reluctance I had had until now in believing in the reality of the threats with which I was constantly assailed, I was unable to prevent myself from believing in the plausibility I found in them, in recalling

that three months earlier honest people had said that they had been threatened with being attacked at home if they did not stop seeing me, and being unable to conceal from myself that I had previously been threatened with prison, and constantly hearing from the public the insults and the threats made here and there in societies against priests, and particularly against me, that all come from the same source. But I myself heard, on my way to see a seriously ill parishioner on the seventh of this month, from your mouths made to speak only of peace, a torrent of sarcasm prohibited by the National Assembly. Finally, could I fail to believe in threats from various sides knowing that at bedtime at home, at nine o'clock, I saw and was not mistaken, I saw men running on my paths with torches in hand. At ten-thirty, I had the foolhardy courage to go and see: I found my door open, and everyone had gone home.

Consider, Sir, whether such an event, which was not a visit, was not capable of confirming for me the truth of the threats that had been made against me. Despite that, I maintained the most scrupulous silence about everything that prudence had required me to do, and I would have presented to your assembly everything that fell under its authority. But suddenly, three different people informed me that my door had been broken down, as well as the doors of a few other people whose crime was to grant me entry to their houses, and that the time of execution was near. The days Friday and Sunday were mentioned. I was asked to keep it secret. I swore secrecy and will keep it at the risk of my life, but I thought I should leave, determined to resume my post only if you order it, that is, the municipal authorities.

1. Good protection against whoever threatens my life, since it is your duty to see to public and individual safety.
2. You must remedy the injustices about which I have rightly complained: 1. for the patriotic donation; 2. for my capitation; 3. for the counting of parishioners . . .

Those, Sir, are the true sources of my troubles and the only cause of my departure.[15]

This affair, one example among many others, justified the alarm of the population at the blunders of the various administrations. Even before the question of the constitutional oath was posed, and much earlier than historians have thought, the problem of the independence of priests from the government arose locally.

The Constitutional Oath: November 27, 1790

On November 27, 1790, the Assembly decided that all ecclesiastical officials had to take an oath to the new Constitution of the Church or else be removed from office and deprived of their salary. "Finally," wrote the administrators of the directory of Nantes, "the day of the Lord has arrived and the heavenly Zion will shine with a brighter and purer light."[16]

However, the oath was paradoxical. One of the grounds for attack against Catholicism was the existence of monastic vows, and this produced the prohibition and abolition of religious orders. But the same men took as the basis for everything the secular oaths that were only a caricature of their clerical counterparts.

Each priest then had to deal with a question of conscience. Should he submit and remain in charge, or on the contrary refuse and be excluded from his employment and pursued by the authorities? The National Assembly had given the example. Only two of the forty-four bishops present had accepted. A special deputy expressed surprise, protesting that

> religion is not in danger: the dogma is preserved in all its purity, the ritual is restored to a state of dignity and decency unknown for too many years, the habits of the ministers at the altar become more austere. We must return to the primitive institutions of the Church, imitate the virtue of the apostles and the divine savior of the world . . .[17]

In January 1791 the bishop of Nantes, responding to the wishes of the local clergy, asked priests to refuse the Civil Constitution, not to take the oath, and to remain in their parishes.[18] On March 10, 1791, Pope Pius VI sanctioned and legalized this refusal in the eyes of the populace.[19] He repeated the condemnation the following April 13. The brief was of extreme severity. The Civil Constitution was declared "heretical and schismatic" and aimed only at the annihilation of religion. Catholics were already aware of the situation, but from then on they knew that there were no more illusions and no possible compromises.[20] The flight of the king on June 11 proved it to them.

By January 1791 the departments had recognized the failure of the law. To make this explicit, various proclamations were posted, including one in Nantes on January 15.[21] It spoke primarily of confidence, patriotic zeal, truth, conscience, and religion, the two latter notions being hierarchically subordinate to the law:

The law requires, finally, that priests swear to support with all their power the Constitution decreed by the National Assembly and accepted by the king. What does this mean? That religion being in the State, its ministers must be subject to the laws? Either it is to govern the empire or it must give way to the government; priests live under political law, it is engraved on their cradle; they are born its subjects and the priesthood is for them only an adoptive condition.

There followed a long diatribe on the notions of good and evil connected to law and conscience.

Conscience itself is only the moral sentiment of good and evil . . . If this sentiment must reject the constitution of the kingdom, if this constitution is heterodox, the evil has already been done, because almost the entire Nation has sworn to accept and support it. Thus consciousness of the good now belongs to only a handful of individuals . . . privileged and clairvoyant beings, the only ones to whom the truth has manifested itself; dare to say it! All the rest are therefore guilty and in error. He is guilty in your opinion, he is in error, the monarch beloved of the French, the restorer of freedom and its most worthy bulwark, who accepted this constitution! Also guilty and in error are our august legislators who created this constitution, restored the rights of man, and avenged their country against the shackles of despotism! They too are guilty and in error, those brave citizens and soldiers who have all together used their weapons and devoted their lives to the support of this constitution; guilty and in error are all the men called to the administration. Let them tremble! The same oath binds them, they have all offended heaven and committed the same outrage against religion! Is it possible that this is what they want to prove and convince us of, the thirty bishops and a few priests who, following their example, have conspired against the Nation, its liberty, and its laws . . .

Those priests were already treated as fanatics who wanted to create the horrors of a civil war. The populace was implored not to listen to them and to turn their eyes toward the others, "the virtuous," who were competing for the honor of taking the oath.

The pope's brief was ridiculed. The Society of Friends of the Constitution of Niort "thinks that it is worthy only of contempt . . ."[22] One speaker proposed in an amendment "that it be covered with a sanbenito of black cloth, steeped in lavender oil, on which will be drawn the effigies of Royou, Mallet du Pan, Durozoy, and Suleau, and that escorted by these miserable champions, it be consigned to the flames in the courtyard of liberty . . ." He then proposed that its ashes be preserved "in a ram's horn to be administered as an emetic to the former prelates, abbés, canons, curés, vicars, chaplains and Beguines suffering from aristocratic congestion."

Contrary to what had been hoped, this kind of proclamation did not restore calm. On January 25, in a letter to the minister of the interior, the department of Loire-Inférieure admitted its failure:

> Until now, we had hoped to be able to maintain tranquillity, but we see that the oath to be taken by priests, and the refusal of a large number of them to do so, has stirred up the populace of the countryside. We have not yet experienced any excesses, but gatherings have been noticed which might become dangerous if we did not have a police force able to hold them in check.[23]

The departments had reason to be worried. Among the 1,058 priests and monks in the diocese of Nantes in 1791, only 159 took the oath, about 60 of them monks, and a certain number were later to retract. In Vendée, they were 207 out of 768, and in insurgent Anjou, 44 out of 332.[24]

This refractory clergy was summoned to the departmental capitals in the course of January 1791, on the fourth to Nantes. In this case, too, there was massive refusal; the rebels were considered to have resigned. The decree of November 29 prescribed that "no one may preach in any church without first having established his taking of the oath."

Events came to a head among the bishops. The constitutional bishops were elected: Servant for Luçon; Jallet, the curé of Chérigné, for Niort; and Mercy for Nantes. What authority could these prelates not recognized by the pope hold? They almost immediately resigned and were replaced by Rodrigue, the curé of Fougeré, a prior, immediately succeeded by Mestadier, consecrated in Bordeaux, and Minée, the son of a master surgeon who had been ordained a priest in 1770 and was a Parisian by adoption.

Minée was supposed to be consecrated in Nantes on April 10 by Gobel, the constitutional archbishop of Paris, and this caused an uproar. The priests composed a letter, and printed ten thousand copies, which were distributed throughout the diocese:

Your election is void and your consecration illicit. When you see coming to welcome you the municipal authorities in uniform, the administrative bodies, the national guard, when you hear the bells of your cathedral ring and the cannon roar, you will simply believe that you are wished for by the town and the whole diocese. But your illusion will end perhaps with the sound of the bells, the roar of the cannons, and the compliments, because the majority of the clergy of town and country will look upon you as a usurper . . . and that will be so no matter what is done to receive you well.[25]

Jarnoux recounts the arrival of the prelate in Nantes on Friday, April 15:

As soon as his carriage was in view on the road from Paris, toward the crescent, cannons and bells saluted his arrival. The municipal authorities and elected officials were all present to welcome him. Anticipating some possible disturbances in the crowd, the authorities had had it proclaimed a few hours earlier that they would accept no troubles. "We believe that we should warn the nice old ladies and determined bigots that forty to fifty young men, quite strong and vigorous, often armed with rods, blessed or not, will spread out through all the quarters of the town on the day of the arrival of the new bishop and on the day of his installation, to put to the whip whoever would have the impudence to indulge in unpleasant outbursts suggested by their idiotic hypocrisy."

On foot, the bishop advanced between two ranks of soldiers and national guards to reach the cathedral. There he gave thanks to the Eternal, while the organ played a well-known tune: "There is no better place than the bosom of the family." At the bishop's palace, he received the compliments of all the administrators of the department and the members of the tribunal. But the clergy was absent. This absence troubled him and he asked to have his official installation put off until May 1.[26]

On the day of his actual installation, Minée composed his first pastoral letter. According to him, nothing had changed for the present in the administration of the sacraments, nor for that matter in the teaching of the Gospel. He concluded by warning his flock against refractory priests who "hide the heart of a tiger under a sheep's coat." Similar reactions were shown in neighboring bishoprics.

A few days after the elections, the legitimate bishops reacted by writing to the members of their dioceses. Monsignor de La Laurencie warned that Minée should be considered a usurper.[27] On December 9, 1790, the legitimate bishop had been denounced before the National Assembly by a special deputy as a defender of the old order.

The bishop of Angers addressed a personal letter to his priests to congratulate them on their firmness:

> I had always expected that you would reject this civic oath and that no human consideration would be able to make you betray your conscience . . . Courage; continue to visit with zeal. We have a greater master to serve than the National Assembly, and it is He who forbids us most absolutely to take the oath that is demanded.[28]

These bishops were unanimous (it is impossible not to note the modern character of the position): the civil authority is an absolute sovereign, independent in everything that is under its authority, and the clergy must accept that. Moreover, this reaction troubled the government; it recognized that the majority of churchmen scrupulously observed the rules of submission to the civil authorities.[29] On the other hand, in a pastoral of November 23, 1790, the bishop of Luçon explained, "with respect to everything that concerns spiritual matters it can be accountable only to God, and sees only Him above it."[30] This was a divine and hence sacred hierarchy that could not be called into question:

> Jesus Christ gave the most explicit commandment to render unto Caesar that which was Caesar's and Himself gave the example in loyally following the precept, by performing a miracle to pay the tribute. Therefore be subject to the civil authority in everything within its competence not only from fear of punishment but also out of a duty of conscience. Give to each what is his due; tribute to whom you owe tribute, taxes to whom you owe taxes! Fear to whom you owe fear, and so on. However, that authority has limits beyond which it cannot go; there are sacred objects over which it may not hold power; and all the measures it would undertake to the prejudice of the spiritual Authority should be regarded only as errors into which it has fallen, and not as laws that it could have prescribed.

Spiritual authority is sacred, and any attack on it is a sin. The Church in the State therefore owes it to itself to be independent.[31] The new laws are anticanonical and call into question the divine order, hence they are impure, and it is unthinkable for the Church to submit itself to them. Any compromise "which might have brought about a better order of things and restored peace" became from then on impossible.[32]

The clergy, well-trained in the eighteenth century, could only fall into line behind the legitimate bishops and show it openly. As a result, few priests followed the legal prelates "regarded as usurpers, mercenaries, and intruders."[33]

Instructions from exiled bishops followed, particularly in order to "set forth rules of conduct for all cases that might be encountered," for it seemed impossible to foresee all the circumstances in which "these virtuous pastors" would find themselves.[34] These instructions, given in the form of catechisms, repeated the fundamental principles of canon law. They set forth only general rules so that the clergy as a whole would follow a uniform path "both wise and courageous." It was a matter of having them fulfill "the whole range of duties that circumstances allow." Confronted with this parallel organization of the Church, the local authorities were troubled and were to harden their position.

The Hardening of Local Authorities

The Growth of Conflict

Indeed, the populace very soon openly manifested its distrust of the municipal authorities and the administration. Everything became grounds for dispute, giving rise to countless conflicts. Difficulties arose in Beaufort as early as August 1790 over the leasing of benches in the church. Armed men demanded that they be replaced by chairs: "If their petition had been accepted, the council would remove them and would make them into a '*charibande*' (*sic*)." When the municipal government refused to consider their petition, according to the informant, they became "threatening" and spoke differently: "We've been led like sheep, we're going to become lions." The national guard put an end to the incident by an "organized dispersal."[35]

On September 10, 1790, the population of Sorges was desperate because of the high cost of wheat and bread, because of massive exports.[36] The same thing was true in Paimbœuf.[37]

There were more serious disturbances at Ponts-de-Cé on September 12, 1790.[38] The brotherhood of sailors dedicated to Saint Nicholas, which had been in existence for thirty years, expressed the desire to go into the church, led by its flag, to celebrate mass. Frightened by their vehemence, Mayor Hommedi made a report to the district. The next day at six in the morning, Foucher, a representative of the department, came to town. He was surprised to encounter several women armed with sticks and to hear the tocsin, and he was obliged to hide. The church was occupied and "a group of agitators" tried to stir the populace to revolt, but it refused. The mayor resigned, and the army had to restore order. After a long discussion, the mayor's brother-in-law was chosen to succeed him.

In Tillier and Viellevigne in January 1791 forty people threatened to set fire to the town hall. In the canton of Maulévrier, the tocsin was rung in seven or eight parishes; the country people were convinced that someone was about to seize the cannons belonging to Monsieur de Maulévrier. The inhabitants had seized them on July 22, 1789. "The people," explained the informant, "looked on this artillery as a significant conquest."[39] In this instance as well, municipal officers and "former judges" were accused of being the source of the problem.

The examples were many. Everywhere there was talk of treason and deceit. Sometimes there were threats to drive out the authorities. The municipal officers of Beaufort were even called bourgeois "who should be hit with rifle butts like dogs."[40] Anger was provoked by orders to burn silk and golden braids[41] and church ornaments, to remove copper or iron tombstones, and to confiscate bells.[42]

The Reaction of the Authorities

The patriots were worried by this latent insurrection. The refractory priests were universally accused of fomenting it, as in an anonymous letter sent to the department of Maine-et-Loire on May 26, 1791. They were accused of dividing parishes into two opposing parties, "constantly stirred up against one another, and this will end in explosions whose consequences will be extremely dangerous."[43] The accusation was repeated in many parishes in all the departments in crisis.[44] As a result, the priests designated were frequently harassed, with arbitrary tax increases, disruptions of masses, and the like.

The patriots were unanimous in favoring increased repression. Various petitions along these lines were addressed to the National Assembly, including one from the "Friends of the Constitution of Nantes," dated May 9, 1791.[45] It requested that a general law be promptly passed to remove the refractory curés. According to the petitioners, this was the only way to prevent bloodshed and at the same time assure the preservation of public order.

As Chamard judiciously points out, the Jacobins of Nantes were far from the relatively moderate spirit then prevalent in the National Assembly.[46] For example, the procurator-syndic Letourneux, while agreeing with the timeliness of the measure, had to admit that it was contrary to the current intentions of the National Assembly.[47] The department had a different opinion and on May 15 confirmed the petition of the Friends of the Constitution by a draconian and illegal decree that was fully executed throughout the department:

> The curés and other public servants who have not taken the prescribed oath may consider themselves warned, by the publication of this decree, that their own safety and the safety of the citizens in general urgently requires their removal and replacement by other civil servants acknowledged by the law, that if they were not to withdraw they would expose themselves to responsibility for the unfortunate events to which their actions, their speech, or even their mere presence might give rise. That as a consequence . . . one or two days before the day set for their replacement, they will be expected to submit to the said order, to vacate the premises and to leave their parish, and we declare that in every case, at the time of replacement, if they provoke any riot or sedition, the public order and the general interest would require that they be seized as hostages for public tranquillity and the restoration of order.[48]

Three days later, the department ordered that all chapels be closed and refractory priests forbidden "to celebrate the Holy Mysteries in them unless they have a specific mission from the constitutional bishop, countersigned by the constitutional curé."[49] Every municipality also had to keep close watch on nonjuring priests and if necessary begin legal proceedings against them. The department would then order the allegedly guilty priests to go to the departmental capital to remain under the supervision of the administrative authorities.

The situation in some communes was even worse. Even before the departmental decree in May, the district of Clisson planned major reprisals against the nonjuring clergy whom it accused of antirevolutionary propaganda following the celebration of Easter.[50]

Despite contrary orders from the legitimate bishops, a large number of these priests decided to abandon their parishes. Shortly thereafter, they received orders to go to the departmental capitals and to report to the department at noon precisely to respond to a roll call.[51] Some priests refused to obey and stayed in their parishes. The municipal authorities, who felt the situation escaping from them, sometimes encouraged the priests not to leave their posts, as the rector of La Chapelle-Bassemère explained to Letourneux, the procurator-syndic of the department:

> I was preparing to obey the decree, and therefore last Sunday after my sermon I asked the mayor and the municipal officers to transport me to the parsonage after vespers to take an inventory of the registers they had placed in my charge and to give me a good and proper discharge; my vicars wished for the same thing. But after vespers, Monsieur Rivière des Héry, the mayor, did me the honor to come to beg me to continue my duties with my vicars in order not to leave the parish without help. I felt obliged to acquiesce to his request and his reasons, and I convinced myself that this accommodation would not be considered a crime although it might cause a delay. The act will indicate my good will. That is the grace I hope for from you.[52]

On July 4, 1791, the department of Maine-et-Loire even required that nonjuring priests not leave their parishes if they were not replaced.[53]

The daily roll call was the source of deep disappointment for the authorities. In a session of March 6, 1792, one of the departmental delegates from Nantes complained about it:

> You can no longer hide from yourselves that although in the early days a significant number of priests came to be counted, the same thing is no longer true today. The number present decreases every day. For example, this morning, of one hundred thirty on the list, ninety-four were absent. There is only one remedy, we must consider holding them all in a single place.[54]

This appears to have been the first time that this idea was suggested. On March 12 the directory issued a decree along these lines.[55] It provided:

1. That in each district a list of names would be prepared of all the nonjuring clergy, active or retired, in the parishes.
2. That every nonjuring priest who had not indicated his presence in the department capital would be sought out and taken by force to the town of Nantes.
3. That a house would be designated to receive these priests, namely, the Saint-Clément house.
4. That their subsistence would be provided by witholding their salaries and pensions.
— and that a guard would be set up by the municipality to guard the house;
— and that the bishop and his council were invited to provide for the spiritual needs of the parishes thereby deprived of priests.

Similar measures were adopted in the neighboring departments. These principles, contrary to the Declaration of the Rights of Man and Citizen, were illegal, since it involved the imprisonment of citizens who had not been judged by a judicial process. It is therefore easy to understand the lack of zeal of the commissioners charged with the execution of these orders.

In order to accelerate the course of events, citizens spread the rumor in Nantes that a riot provoked by refractory priests had broken out in Saint-Joachim. The reaction was immediate. On June 4 a certain number of citizens of Nantes signed a petition addressed to the municipal government. Because of these disorders and the seditious gatherings in Plessis-Tison, they demanded that the department decree the detention of all priests in the town in Saint-Clément and the seminary.

On June 26 the procurator-syndic found a legal pretext in a decree of the Assembly authorizing the deportation of nonjuring priests merely on the basis of a denunciation by twenty-five citizens.[56] For him it was a matter of ensuring public tranquillity as well as the safety of "all those men of the Church." The priests were notified of the order on the following day at the roll call; a force of twelve to fifteen hundred national guardsmen rounded them up. Officially, after that date, no nonjuring priest was in office; the internally divided populace was apparently left to its own devices.

FIVE

The Role of the Refractory Clergy in the Resistance

THE DEPARTURE OF THE REFRACTORY CLERGY LEFT MOST PARISHES without a priest. Protest uprisings were infrequent, but dismay was nearly universal, as in La Chapelle-Achard. On April 27, 1792, Mayor Augard openly expressed his distress:

> When our curé was ready to leave, we all went to the parsonage to collect the registers of baptisms and weddings, and deposited them in a closet in the sacristy for which we have a key. Now, gentlemen, we need to know what course of conduct to adopt in this matter. When there is a funeral to be held in our parish, which does happen, what priest shall we ask for; as for baptisms, and who will record them?[1]

Farewells to priests were sometimes moving, as in Saint-Hilaire-de-Mortagne. Before leaving, the curé, Mathieu Paunaud, summoned his parishioners for the last time, and after making pious recommendations, said to them:

> Wherever Providence may lead me, I will pray for you; my heart and my spirit will be with you. Every Sunday if I am able, I will offer the holy sacrifice to God for all the inhabitants of this parish. And if, as I unfortunately fear, you are prevented from hearing mass from a good priest, I urge you to meet as often as you can, every Sunday, in the church, at the time when I have always been accustomed to say it with

you. At that hour, that is, around ten o'clock, I will go up to the holy altar and will celebrate for you. You will join your prayer to mine, and I have no doubt that the good Lord will take account of the intention you will have to follow the precepts . . . Do not go to mass held by any intruder.[2]

To widespread astonishment, the church remained open, and every Sunday the bell publicly summoned the faithful. Troubled, the revolutionary authorities sent gendarmes to put seals on the doors of the building. They used the opportunity to tear down a few crosses. They were greatly surprised the next day, a Sunday, to hear the bells ring out at ten o'clock. They quickly armed themselves and came running. The crowd of parishioners was spread out in the cemetery and kneeling on the tombstones, in a deep meditative silence. A dialogue took place between an old man and the sergeant:

> "What the devil are you doing here?"
> "When our curé left, he promised us that every Sunday at this very hour he would say mass for us wherever he might be . . ."
> "Superstitious imbeciles! They believe they hear mass from the place where it is said."
> "Prayer travels more than a hundred leagues, since it ascends from earth to heaven."
> "And do you believe you are in a church here, you savages?"
> "We are in a holy place, over the bones of our fathers."

The gendarmes attempted to force the people to disperse but, fearing violent reactions, they chose to back off. That very evening they sent a report to the revolutionary committee. Nothing came of the affair for lack of enough soldiers.

To the great distress of the people, there were no more baptisms. Funerals were celebrated without ceremony, in the presence of the sacristan or the gravedigger near the tomb. They were registered by the mayor or his adjutant, on the civil register, with the notation "for want of a priest in this parish."[3]

However, this uncertain situation did not last. Some individuals decided to use the edict of November 1787, which allowed non-Catholics to register the various ritual acts.[4] Moreover, the absence of priests did not last long, with the constitutional clergy quickly taking up its posts.

The Arrival of the Constitutional Clergy, Nicknamed *Truton* by the People

There were various situations, depending on the commune; people accepted these "intruder" (*truton*) priests with enthusiasm or indifference, or drove them out. The mayor might also on occasion "neglect" to introduce them, invoking various pretexts: absence of a mandate, lack of lodging, and so on. For example, Mayor Craipia of L'Orbrie refused to give citizen Cailleteau the keys to his church;[5] the same thing occurred in Saint-Lumine-de-Coutais.[6] The mayors and the new priests then called on armed force, of varying size, depending on the situation. Requisition in the name of the king explains the perplexity and confusion of those who saw Louis XVI apparently in agreement with the proceedings.

As a general rule, reports indicate that installations went fairly well. In the presence of the mayor, municipal officers, notables, and the people, there was the customary reading of credentials, followed, in accordance with the law, by the taking of possession and the presentation of the salary allocated as a function of the importance of the office.[7]

The first baptismal certificates were sometimes preceded by curious notes; this was true in La Chapelle-Bassemère, where the curé Caperon wrote, "Here begins the reign of the Republic."[8] The remark is rather strange because the deposition of the monarch was not proclaimed until August 10, 1792, four months later. We should probably understand the word "republic" in the sense of "public interest." According to the curé, revolutionary principles were finally going to bring enlightenment to the old customs of Christianity.

According to parish registers, it seems that the people hesitated to come to the intruders. In the eight months from March to December 1792, in La Chapelle-Bassemère, only one wedding was celebrated.[9] During the same period in preceding years, there had been about twenty.

For the administration of baptism, recourse to force of arms was necessary. However, many newborn children were baptized by nonjuring clergy. Michel, the curé of La Motte-Achard denounced this "very serious" abuse, and at the same time expressed indifference; he merely asked "that those gentlemen would have the kindness to send him the record of each baptism so he might inscribe it in the register" in his charge.[10] He regretted a refusal of cooperation that resulted in children dying without Christian burial. He exhorted the justice of the peace to write to those priests to have them send the indispensable documents.

Some less tolerant curés called on the army, like the curé of Saint-Lambert-du-Lattay.[11] In his unpublished memoirs, Abbé Conin reports that on August 20, 1792, the captain of the guard of Angers, named Payer, who had arrived in the commune the day before, on a complaint by the intruder, Dubourg, sent four national guards to families that had newborns. They brought eighteen of them to the church to have them rebaptized. Payer himself wished to be godfather to a girl named Godineau, with Perrette Androuin as godmother. To the question from the intruder priest, "What does this child ask?" the woman answered, "Nothing." The captain was furious and had her taken immediately to his headquarters in the hotel de l'Ecu. There her hair was cut, the kerchief she was wearing on her shoulders was removed, and, following the humor of the time, she was made to mount a donkey backward. She was then led through the streets of the town. Similar abuses cropped up in many places.

As for funerals, corpses were abandoned at the doors of churches and chapels.[12] In the absence of pallbearers, who were hard to find, national guardsmen, carrying crosses and banners, had to be used. Gasnault, the curé of La Séguinière, reports that these undertakers refused to enter the church: "they trot from the steps of the church to the cemetery and leave the cemetery at quick march," leaving him at the mercy of a "troop of mocking young men." In Saint-Lambert-du-Lattay, not only were the dead buried without notice, but the parishioners sneaked into the church to ring the bells for the ceremonies.

In their official reports, some intruders boasted of "good attendance"; it sometimes even seemed to them that they were well accepted by the people. Several documents from refractory curés assert the opposite. In Clisson, the *fabriqueurs* made fun of him: "The apostate curé is incapable of saying mass; a pig sty should be enough to house him."[13] Abbé Robin of La Chapelle-Bassemère declared that the people were hostile to the *truton* curé, and that only thirty of them went to his mass.[14] In Saint-Aubin-de-Luigné, the constitutional Abbé Besnard seized two broadsheets circulating among his parishioners. One was a coarse caricature depicting him with a rope around his neck, with the legend BESNARD IS HUNG, GOD WOULD HAVE PRAISED. The other was just as explicit:

> You know that Besnard is not the curé of Saint-Aubin-de-Luigné, only M. Boutini is the curé, and therefore Besnard is only an intruder, a robber and thief and schismatic and apostate, and we, the believers, would fall into error like him. A new song with a fine tune about Besnard:
> True Christians, groan that you see among you
> an unknown pastor who disavows us
> with no power or welcome from our true bishop
> who could give him any?
> an intruder like himself?

In Le Loroux-Bottereau, when the constitutional curé came to celebrate mass, he found the church so crowded that he had trouble making his way through the crowd that jostled him from all sides. When he went up to the altar, the church was empty.[15]

According to Abbé Vattel, these troubles increased significantly in early December 1791, to the point that he feared for his life.

> We are insulted every day even in the church. The new municipality has brought back the old priests, who have celebrated mass in the chapel of the Virgin. They have prepared enough holy water for a year; they have turned everything upside down. It is no longer possible to hold on, and I am determined to leave the parish without regret; there is neither God nor devil who could keep me here. In this department, there is no law, or faith, or religion. The Breton people is not made to live under a regime of liberty but rather one of slavery; its heads are too thick. Your administrative bodies deserve to be expelled; they are not worthy of having the laws in their hands. What I am telling you here I am not afraid to say in public, even to the administrators. What is more deplorable than to see the countryside desolate and that no law is respected. There is nothing but horrors, abominations . . . I prefer to seek tranquillity elsewhere.[16]

Abbé G. Moreau, curé of La Chapelle-sur-Erdre, was also worried. "There is nothing dearer to me in the world," he declared in May 1791, "than the preservation of my own existence; it is today in great danger and you are not acting vigorously against those who want to take it from me."[17]

Abbé Berceray, curé of La Chapelle-Launay, also fled from his parish early in 1792.[18] He was ordered by the directory of the department to return or be deprived of his salary.

Every Sunday at seven o'clock in Saint-Julien-de-Concelles, a non-juring Irish priest came to say mass.[19] The entire population was present, filling the church and the adjacent cemetery. For his services, he received a contribution of six livres. At ten, the bell for the intruder's mass was rung; the church remained empty: "At most, one hundred fifty people were present." To support the constitutional priest, the municipal authorities and their supporters were reduced to displaying much more religion than in the past, the informant ironically comments.

This curious situation had been going on for five months when citizen Riveron came to church for Easter. He expressed his surprise to the directory of the department: "Several patriotic citizens have asked me to denounce the situation to you, not wishing to appear as informers of the troubles created by this mass, for they fear being attacked by these fanatics, who threaten them every day."

As for the curé of Le Roussay, he wrote to the district of Cholet to express his despair: "I am insulted, mocked at the altar, pursued by stone throwing; I have neither cantor, nor sacristan, nor clerk and, to tell the truth, I don't even have parishioners."[20]

In Moisdon-sur-Sèvre, on August 8, 1791, the curé complained about a first manifestation of violence toward him: "Last night, they threw stones into my courtyard and set fire to a place where they thought I was."[21] The following September 9 he was terrorized:

Walking in my garden on Saturday, I was brutally struck by a stone on the shoulder. Yesterday, herdsmen brought their cows into my orchard, and the cows ate the fruit. I came up to drive them off. At that moment, they yelled at me: "Mad dog! rascal! scoundrel!" They ran at me to stone me and I had barely time to escape into my parsonage.

In Saint-Quentin-en-Mauges, someone went so far as to cover the facade of the church with refuse; it was ordinary practice to throw garbage in front of it.

In Vendée, the situation was such that on March 9, 1792, the directory issued a decree calling for armed force against thirty-two nonjuring priests and a sacristan:

Considering that throughout the department, the constitutional curés are daily insulted; that several of them have been obliged to abandon their duties; that a very large number are ready to leave the parishes without pastors; considering the impotence of the laws against men who abuse the mysteries of a holy religion to lead the inhabitants of the countryside astray and to stir them to repeat the frightful scenes of which the district of Challans was the theater last year . . .[22]

The law of September 20, 1792, was rapidly applied; two days after it was passed, the constitutional curés became public officials. Manifestly, most of them were more interested in the salary attached to their duties than in ecclesiastical functions strictly speaking. For example, the parish register of La Chapelle-Bassemère for 1784, found on the curé's dressing table after the departure of Caperon, was missing the sheets for the first five months which he had used to make curlpapers.[23] Given this attitude, it is easy to understand the reactions of the parishioners, who wanted only one thing, the departure of the intruder.[24]

THE REACTION OF THE POPULATION TO THE SITUATION AND THE ROLE OF THE CONSTITUTIONAL PRIESTS IN THIS CONTEXT

Contrary to a received idea, the refractory priests did not massively emigrate to neighboring countries such as England, Spain, and Portugal. Only 273 clergy of Vendée out of 768 registered submitted (35.5 percent), and 80 out of 332 in insurgent Anjou (24 percent).[25] According to the directory of Anjou, it was a matter "of implementing all the means we have used to stop the enterprises of these fanatical priests. Perhaps by removing their ability to harm, we will encourage them to withdraw either to Spain or to Rome, a step already taken in recent days by some of them here."[26]

In fact, two other patterns can be observed: the return of some priests to their native parishes, and taking refuge in the parishes in which they had served or in other parishes chosen because of particular circumstances. For many of the nonjuring priests, the return to their native parish was spontaneous, as for Abbé Robin in La Chapelle-Bassemère in November 1790: "Overcome with pain and sorrow, secretly threatened, I have come to seek safety, consolation, and peace in the midst of my family."[27] Other cases may be mentioned, for example, that of Philippe Donneux, who on May 5, 1790, declared that he was "withdrawing there to live decently, in a way befitting a priest."[28]

A return might also be tied to a deliberate policy of the departments. The idea of sending refractory priests back to their birthplaces was proposed for the first time on May 24, 1791, by the department of Maine-et-Loire.[29] The representatives of Vendée found the idea excellent. The directory of Anjou hoped by this means "to purge itself of several of these priests whose presence everywhere compromises good order and public tranquillity." This measure, later adopted and applied in Loire-Inférieure and the neighboring departments, left the priests no choice, especially because the procurator-syndics declared themselves "firmly decided to carry it out with the greatest vigor."[30]

For example, of the nine priests born in the parish of La Chapelle-Bassemère, five returned to their families.[31] The same phenomenon was repeated throughout the communes of Vendée, to the great surprise of the municipal authorities, for example, in Le Loroux-Bottereau, Saint-Julien-de-Concelles, La Garnache, and Beauvoir, among others. Indeed, 235 Vendean priests out of 561 and 196 of the insurgent Anjou took refuge in their native towns.

On their return, these priests solicited support from their families and simultaneously adopted an offensive position in the face of events. Their action was threefold. First, in the name of the legitimate curés, with whom they remained in contact, they administered the parish in parallel with the constitutional priests. Correspondence was carried out by courier. Various letters of this kind were seized by the censor.[32] In accordance with canon law, no important act, such as a marriage, was carried out without consulting the former true priest. It should also be pointed out that the Holy See and the legitimate bishops had asked the nonjuring priests to take spiritual charge of the parishes in which they found themselves because of events. As a consequence, documents in the parish registers were composed along the following lines:

> On————after the publication of canonic banns done without opposition at the sermon at mass in this parish and given the dispensation from the two other banns granted by us in virtue of the general powers delegated to us by the Holy See and the lord bishop———— exiled for the faith of Jesus Christ, we have this day affianced and married————son of————and of————natives of and domiciled

in this parish, and———daughter of———and of———natives of and domiciled in this parish, and with the agreement of the curé of this parish, exiled for the cause of Jesus Christ. Witnesses to this marriage were———.[33]

When department administrators learned of these registers, they violently attacked them, fearing dangerous consequences.[34] It even happened, for example, in Basse-Indre on November 9, 1791, that refractory priests conducted funerals.[35]

In the second place, the existing environment made it possible for these priests to revive religious fervor, beginning with their families, their friends, and their flock. Religious assemblies proliferated throughout the area on various pretexts, such as the destruction of small places of worship, the appearance of the Virgin at Chemillé on August 18, 1791, when an immense crowd gathered in La Chapelle-Saint-Laurent, and the like.[36] This resumption of control was all the easier because the region still had vivid memories of the Mulotin fathers [missionaries of Saint-Laurent-sur-Sèvre, who denounced the civil constitution] and their successors, who could be found almost everywhere.[37]

Finally, the refractory priests supported and stimulated resistance to the administration and "to changes imported from the city."[38] The fragments of speeches and writings that have been found are revealing about the violence with which the municipal governments were attacked.[39] Attempts were made to demonstrate, sometimes in a very legalistic and judicious manner, that the people had been deceived: "You were promised liberty and they imposed a constitutional priest on you. You were promised equality and voting restrictions have been restored." The Declaration of the Rights of Man and Citizen was frequently quoted. The former curé of Brignon, Abbé Dazilly, even proclaimed that the constitution and the work of the National Assembly had been abolished.[40]

At first, the authorities were surprised by this unexpected reaction. They merely denounced in writing these priests who "are using new devices to foster the credulity of country people." In a second stage, they reacted by calling on their police power. Abbé Robin, curé of La Chapelle-Bassemère, recounts in the register of 1794 the harassment to which he was subjected:

Monsieur Robin, rector of Le Pellerin and child of the parish, having always been hidden in the bosom of his family, thought that it was more prudent to maintain anonymity and to remain in order to be useful to the faithful than to show himself to scoundrels breathing nothing but murder and carnage. However, a week after Monsieur Le Mercier left, an intruder was sent, named Caperon, a wicked monk who, having heard that Monsieur Robin was in the parish and supported the faithful in their faith and attachment to their legitimate pastor, had him pursued mercilessly countless times, so that he was able to escape from those infernal minions only by a miracle, as witnessed on the day of the Holy Rosary, the first Sunday of October 1792, when measures were carefully taken; the said Caperon had the wild soldiers from Le Loroux come with Mayor Rivière des Héraux at their head, and without giving any warning to the good people of the parish, they led an armed force at four in the afternoon to the home of Dame Vivant opposite the slate cross of the little cemetery, where Monsieur Robin indeed was, and had probably been sold out. A guard was set at the door and at the corner of the little cemetery, another in the garden, and another inside the house. Monsieur Robin was in the attic hearing confession. He soon saw the danger and, not losing courage or confidence in the mother of the Holy Rosary, he left by a side door, went into the neighboring house and into the garden, which was separated by a small hedge, three feet high, from the garden with soldiers on guard, who did not recognize him but whom he recognized, and in the dress of a gardener that he had been wearing for some time, he pretended to be trimming trees and withdrew into a neighboring room, which he left that evening to return to his usual lodging. From that time on he continually worked in service of the parish.[41]

As he suspected, Abbé Robin had in fact been denounced, as indicated in a report from Rault, commissioner of the executive directory of the municipal administration of Le Loroux–Botfereau. He was convinced that he had just missed capturing Robin: "As I told you," he wrote to the department,

> I sent troops to the house where I presumed the said Robin, the curé of Le Pellerin, was staying. Almost certain informers had confirmed my belief that he was there. We went there, we searched everywhere, but in vain. He was no longer there. Someone assured me that we missed him by only a few hours, and I believe that is true. It seems that this

man is invincible. We must continue patrols day and night. I was not able to send troops there at night. The officer refused, relying on the Constitution.[42]

The situation of the refractory priests was difficult. They were obliged to live in the most complete illegality. This clandestine existence went along with the requirement that they exercise their pastoral functions. Obliged to remain in contact with a large number of people, they were exposed to the permanent danger of being informed on, which was encouraged by the revolutionary authorities, as many letters show.

Abbé Robin and his colleagues in La Chapelle-Bassemère celebrated mass in farms and in the vaulted cellar of the castle of La Vrillère,[43] the door to which was concealed by a pile of vine stems. The faithful reached it through a well.

In the country, they take refuge in the depths of the woods, in a wheat field, a deep ravine, a ditch full of water, a humble charcoal burner's hut, or a cottage. Often they even hide in dark caves or they go down into quarries and abandoned mines.

There, surrounded by little children, they speak the word of life, teach them to love God, to console their mothers, to pray for France, and to forgive. There, in a forest clearing on the bank of the Divate, in a secluded valley, they celebrate mass, usually an hour or two before the first glimmers of dawn. A table or some other piece of furniture covered with a white cloth is used as an altar, provided with the liturgical minimum . . . Often, an alarm interrupts the ceremony. The priest immediately returns to his hiding place. When they hope to avoid a visit from the Republicans, the faithful meet in a more fitting place, a house in which they choose the finest room. Then the windows are carefully blocked and they speak in low tones.[44]

This description by Peigné is poignant and no doubt quite accurate, as demonstrated by a corporal of the national guard who surprised a priest in the midst of a service in a dyer's house: "Twelve to fifteen people who did not live there had come together in the house. A table was placed along a wall and decorated with a few ribbons, a crucifix set above it, two candles on either side, two prints, several small reliquaries and winter and spring bouquets, and a plaster virgin."[45]

To avoid such risks, on May 31, 1791, the vicar-general of Luçon allowed mass to be said anywhere: "a simple barn, an attic, a cellar, and so on," with the liturgical minimum, like "the Church of the catacombs."[46] Gradually, as clandestine life went on, new habits and structures were established that made possible resistance and guerrilla movements.

The first refractory priests returned to their families as early as November 1790. The others found asylum with friends, trustworthy people who guaranteed their liberty and safety. From then until March 1793, the month of the general insurrection, they were immersed in their native setting or a neighboring one. Hidden and protected, they were constantly able to draw attention to the cleavages between Christian tradition and revolutionary principles and decisions. There then occurred a revitalization of religious sentiment among these families and worshipers. This situation very clearly explains the unshakable attachment to the refractory priests and the birth of an opposition.[47]

PART TWO

The War

SIX

The March Toward War

POPULAR REACTIONS WERE RELATED TO EVENTS AND TO DISAPPOINTMENTS created. Anger thus broke out very early. The administrations and clubs then were radicalized, pushing the Vendeans to revolt.

POPULAR REACTIONS

Popular reactions took different forms, depending on place, sensibilities, and local problems. In the first stage, a large number of municipal governments observed bitterly that the people shunned the new festivals. Even large towns like Angers were affected.[1] People refused to set up national guard units: "The people think it better to take in the harvest than to accede to the wishes of the mayors," noted Mayor Marchay of Saint-Julien-des-Touches on July 31, 1792.[2] Taxes were unpaid. The department of Maine-et-Loire seems to have been most affected.[3] In late 1791, out of 822 master lists of various taxes, only 50 had been recorded in the districts. On July 9, 1792, 58 were still lacking.

The administrations were also buried in petitions. There were protests against the closing of churches[4] and chapels and the departure of the "good priests";[5] there were demands for the abolition of requisitions, of taxes on bread, and so on. Some communes and professions, such as the bakers, refused to accept assignats.[6] In Saint-Fiacre, there were even calls for the arrest of the judge, "a vicious, seditious, and incendiary man."[7]

Some mayors and municipal agents also openly manifested their disagreement. On June 14, 1791, in Sainte-Gemme-sur-Loire,[8] they refused to take the oath and declined to promulgate the laws.[9] Others opposed legal sanctions against the refractory priests, as in Challans;[10] in Chalonnes, they insulted the patriots while publicly declaring that they supported the people in their charge.[11] In Beaupréau,[12] Jallais,[13] La Motte-Achard,[14] and Sainte-Pazanne,[15] the municipalities went so far as to resign after refusing to deliberate. This last reaction, limited at first, proliferated later, so much so that some districts were reduced to "a single man," as in Saint-Pierre.[16] Frightened, the departments tried to understand this situation, which was impossible to resolve, "two-thirds of them having been terrified by a God of fear." In Bonœuvre, they even refused to wear the tricolor cockade.[17]

To deal with this behavior, it was decided to appoint special commissioners, as in Bouvron. In Saint-Hilaire-de-Chaléons and Légé, those who had resigned were ordered to stay in office until "they had paid their share of land and building taxes."[18]

"Outlaw" mayors hostile to the regime might also conspire. In La Poitevinière on April 30, 1792, thirty municipal officers from different communes were surprised by the gendarmes at the home of the commune's procurator, an innkeeper named Courbet.[19] It seems that this meeting had the purpose of denouncing the policies of the authorities, demanding the return of the refractory priests, and destroying the Societies of Friends of the Constitution.

Clandestine meetings of the inhabitants proliferated, with or without the agreement of the municipalities, depending on their opinions. On July 10, 1791, there was a meeting in Cholet that included people who had come from as far as Poitou.[20] A special commissioner sent to conduct an investigation in the canton of Le Loroux-Bottereau noted this "sad situation":

> The illegality of the so-called deputies must no longer permit us to fear that the number of supporters of liberty is too small. They hope that your civic sense will keep you quiet. Without the participation of the municipal government, they called an assembly at the sound of the bell before four o'clock in the morning. Already, several frightened people have not dared show themselves, and they did not know the reason for the signal.[21]

The patriotic mayors were denigrated; they underwent various humiliations, were insulted in Chemillé,[22] and called on to resign in Ponts-de-Cé,[23] Saint-Julien-de-Cirils,[24] and La Chapelle-Saint-Sauveur;[25] similar cases were not infrequent. On March 19, 1792, in La Jaille, the municipal authorities met in a cabaret after vespers.[26] People furious at their presence "proclaimed that they didn't give a damn about the constitution and to hell with liberty." The municipal officers tried to restore peace, but they were attacked. To defend themselves, they armed themselves with chairs, and they fled under a barrage of stones. Similar scenes took place in La Varenne, Chaizé, Bourgueil, and elsewhere.[27] The procurator of Château-Thébaut, René Menardeau, complained of suffering "a thousand mortifications from ill-intentioned people because he enforced the law."[28]

Some brawls might degenerate into riots. The earliest occurred early in 1791. They later proliferated: on May 7, an insurrection broke out in Clisson, Vilhier,[29] and Saint-Crespin;[30] on April 25 in Apremont; on May 1 and 2 in Saint-Christophe-du-Ligneron and Saint-Jean-de-Monts. On June 22 crowds gathered in La Proutière,[31] near Sables, and on October 26 in Montrelais, on the occasion of the loading of a grain shipment.[32] In January 1792 the île d'Yeu rebelled.[33] To "purify things," three companies of the Sixtieth Regiment were enough; the same was true for fifty cavalrymen in Challans.[34] "On the other hand, on June 3, 1792, thirty dragoons and almost as many national guards were torn to pieces by the inhabitants of Saint-Joachim."[35] There was talk of nothing but pillaging: in Saint-Florent-le-Vieil, the rebels seized district papers and stole the tax collector's cashbox containing 210,000 livres;[36] the same thing happened in Bressuire and Châtillon-sur-Sèvre, where "good citizens" were robbed.[37]

The fears already voiced two years earlier were coming true; the population was on the verge of insurrection. As early as the beginning of 1790, some mayors expressed their concerns to the departments. Beginning in 1791, from everywhere came more and more pressing requests for help. Reinforcements or the maintenance of existing forces were demanded. This is the sense of a letter sent by the mayor of La Chapelle-Bassemère to obtain an increase in pay for the cannoneers garrisoned in the commune and charged with ensuring the peace:

> Given the high price of bread and meat and all provisions, the cannoneers have explained to me that they could not live in the area. Since the revenues of our commune are so little, it is impossible for us to give these gentlemen an increase in pay in order to make their life more pleasant. However, we will certainly need them for some time to come, for it seems that Saint-Julien, Le Loraux, and La Chapelle have joined together

to trouble the good citizens, and it seems they are inclined to commit foolish actions. If we did not have someone to assist us, we would be hardpressed, for they even say that they are a hundred against one. Fortunately, we will not be afraid.[38]

This general attitude was quite justified because of the procedures adopted by the authorities to carry out their policies to the end.

THE RESPONSIBILITY OF LOCAL, REGIONAL, AND CENTRAL AUTHORITIES IN THE CRYSTALLIZATION OF EVENTS

From the beginning of the Revolution, some municipal governments set themselves up as public censors and inquisitorial judges, and this was done in disregard of the laws of the nation and the most fundamental principles of the Constitution, as the district of Challans explained.[39] Ferocious excesses were followed by a climate of generalized terror. In this context, the slightest incident turned into a riot, noted a commissioner sent to Maine-et-Loire.[40] On August 27, 1792, in Les Rosiers, "some inhabitants thought they saw a gang of bandits on the other side of the river." The alarm spread, and they sounded the tocsin in every commune. The citizens immediately left their peaceful labors and came in a crowd to the levee. The national guard immediately intervened. However, the department learned "with the greatest sorrow" that in several places people had indulged in "regrettable excesses." In Beaufort, on the same pretext, the doors of the hospital were broken down and the nuns dragged from their cells into the public square and forced to take the oath. While this was going on, their dwelling was pillaged. In Saint-Georges and Jumelles, "men and women known to attend mass celebrated by constitutional priests" were dragged to the church and forced to take the oath.[41]

Patriotic excesses took various forms: refusal to provide certificates of residence, which led to loss of pensions and salaries; refusal to provide passports, which, in accordance with the law of March 28, 1792, permitted travel throughout the kingdom, and so on.[42] These abuses were denounced in the departments. For example, the procurator-syndic of Maine-et-Loire was called to account for the persecution of priests and the demolition of most of the churches of Angers, although he had received no such orders.[43] There were also protests against the "misguided patriotism of a few, the egotistical and criminal negligence of the greatest number, the illegality of decisions made against priests, which are contrary to the spirit and the letter of the constitution." The directories were accused of the greatest responsibility and "are all the more criminal because they ought to have calculated all the danger involved in this resolution. Perhaps they should have foreseen that a first violation of the law would inevitably bring about a second."

There were constant calls to order of the lower-level administrations, which, despite the oath they had taken,[44] "constantly violate the law":[45] deliberately or out of ignorance.[46] They were urged to be cautious;[47] firebrands were proscribed;[48] and they were all ordered to respect hierarchy: "get rid of any feeling of jealousy and vanity."[49] Inspectors were sent to attempt to understand the situation.[50] They noted that all populations were divided into two parties "ready to come to blows." This opposition can be explained in particular by the fact that informing had been elevated to a universal principle, in accordance with the law of June 3, 1790, requiring that all troublemakers be denounced.[51] Articles IV and IX even provided that curés and vicars refusing to mention during their sermons, "in a loud and intelligible voice," the decrees of the National Assembly, as well as anyone abusing the administration, would be deprived of all their civil rights.[52]

As a result, denunciations affected the people as well as the administrative hierarchy. Anyone might be concerned: mayor,[53] municipal councillors, or members of the district or the directory.[54] For example, René Bertrand, municipal officer of La Chapelle-Bassemère, was brought before the district on June 17, 1791, accused of having made seditious and incendiary remarks and of fomenting rebellion among the people.[55] He was accused of having said that "they were changing, overturning, and destroying religion; of trying to stir up the people on Sunday by claiming that taxes were to be increased; of spewing forth the most absurd calumnies against Bishop Minée and the department." The following July 8, the offender appeared before the department administrators under the same indictment. He was released on July 12; he had recognized his error, begged for mercy from the administrators, and promised to remedy the harm. The administration recognized that there were mitigating circumstances: his brother, a refractory priest, "had turned his head." This act of indulgence, it was thought, was more likely than punishment to bring him back to a sense of duty. The decisive influence of native priests who had returned home is here again clearly brought out.

National guards also played an influential role in this context. They were obedient in enforcing illegal decrees concerning their entry into private houses, as for example in April 1791, in the neighborhood of Les Sables-d'Olonne.[56] These searches were detested all the more because they were sometimes carried out without orders. Not only was the law not respected, but significant damage was done: shattered doors, broken closets, and the like; often, as in Cholet, the searches degenerated into pillage.[57]

On occasion, the national guard even disarmed the people, as in Armaillé, where eighteen of them went to the house of citizen Raval, the mayor, had themselves served lunch "by blatant force," and then took his rifles and six pounds of butter.[58]

There were abuses and extortions of every variety. "Have we not seen men clothed in the sacred uniform of liberty dare to engage in inquisitorial searches?" exclaimed the general council of Maine-et-Loire. In Challans, on June 26, 1791, a request was made to the district of the department for a "prompt delivery of rifles" and a reinforcement of two infantry companies on the pretext that the castle of La Proutière was bristling with cannons and the population in a state of rebellion.[59] A careful investigation revealed that the building was in ruins and the inhabitants quite calm. On September 21, 1791, in La Motte-Achard, there were loud demands for weapons and the necessary force to fight "against aristocratic maneuvers."[60]

Sometimes orders were exceeded; the general council of Vendée bought cannons, more appropriate than "any other kind of weapon" to ensure public tranquillity and disperse crowds.[61]

Sometimes the national guard killed people: in Saint-Christophe on May 1 and 2, 1791,[62] and in Angers in early July, when it "shot into the crowd," according to the directories;[63] in Le Pellerin, it had no hesitation in using drowning on the night of September 23, 1792.[64] The general council, meeting under the presidency of citizen Mainguy, found itself obliged to appoint "*fabriqueurs* as well as people to collect the corpses." This arbitrary act led to a petition being sent to the district, on the grounds that "the municipal government has no right to subject its fellow citizens to a humiliating corvée, especially at a time when the word corvée is proscribed and has become odious."

In addition to letters of protest against this "fiery zeal,"[65] confronting the gratuitous violence of the national guard, the inhabitants might be brought to turn themselves "into wolves," as in Puy-Bonet on June 26, 1792. After attending the mass of the constitutional curé, five civil guards and grenadiers were astounded to find themselves attacked in the cabaret where they had gone to drink. "Forty to fifty individuals from the country," they later explained, "had met there to foment a plot to assault them." Despite the advice of the tavernkeeper, who begged them to run away, they decided to stay. "At one point, an individual in the crowd seized a young unarmed guard by the collar, threatening him and saying that he was going to die because they were going to get the good priests to take them away; neither the Blues nor the patriots would find mercy." The guards managed to take flight, "but were pursued with sticks and stones." According to the informant, a member of the Friends of the Constitution of Cholet, they attacked especially those who were wearing the national uniform: "They were struck with large stones, their cockades were torn off, they were searched, their swords were taken and broken in pieces, and the attackers blasphemed against the Constitution."

Throughout the region, the national guards and even their families were insulted.[66] Given this state of affairs, the administrations were afraid that the situation might become poisonous. On July 7, 1791, the directory of Vihiers reported that the misconduct of the national guard in many places required close attention.[67] There was fear of the disturbances that these excesses might create. The guard had been ordered to fall into line. They had then denied the authority of the administration and went so far as to say that the national guard should give the law and not receive it. Some districts even prohibited them from pursuing priests. Nothing worked, and the context was such that a crisis was inevitable.

The situation became so difficult that some cantons, such as Paimbœuf, decided to form parallel brigades made up of young citizens between the ages of nine and fifteen.[68] Others, such as Le Croisic, "in view of the malefactors, refractory priests, and other vagabonds," created companies of gendarmes.[69] Soon, all these police forces became bounty hunters, to get the reward provided for every capture of a refractory priest, in accordance with the law of August 26, 1792. The official text is very clear:

> In consideration of the difficulties, the burdens, and the extraordinary expenses that this search, and the means used to achieve the discovery and arrest of the said priests, must cause for the national gendarmerie, it will be given an indemnity, a sum of money, the maximum amount of which shall not exceed fifty livres for each priest arrested and brought to the capital of the department, which sum shall be taken

from the funds of the public treasure as a necessary expense deriving from the execution of article IV of the law of August 26, 1792, based on the costs of arrest and transport for this purpose; a note will be made of it and a general accounting sent to the minister of the interior.[70]

Victims of this policy, two priests of Le Loroux-Bottereau, Costard and Rebion, were arrested in La Guillonnière on February 19, 1793.[71] Beaten, insulted, and bound, they were paraded through the streets of the town and then taken to Nantes. The repetition of such scenes was to affect the people, all the more because the department councils encouraged this measure by an increase in "indemnities."[72] For example, the assembly of Deux-Sèvres granted one hundred livres to citizen Beryssein, a gendarme from Corrèze, for having arrested Louis Hayer, a refractory priest, on April 5, 1793.[73]

The provocative blunders of the administration piled up. For example, the law on divorce promulgated on All Saints' Day in the district of Clisson made the situation explosive, causing many crowds to gather.[74] Other factors of discontent came into play: disappointment, aggravated by the persisting economic crisis, due to bad harvests, to injustices and arbitrary measures on the part of the administration, and to religious practices. For example, sacristans could not become mayors on the pretext "that they receive their wages from the curés." In this particular context, the opponents of innovation were the refractory priests. Having very early returned home, or protected by their congregations, they found themselves in a symbiotic relation with the country. Implacable persecution of these influential members of the community, within a geographically restricted and highly unified society, was considered a family affair.

For example, the nine refractory priests who were natives of La Chapelle-Bassemère carried with them, in addition to their families, the entire fervent segment of the parish, all of whom lived on the plateau.[75] This is where the clerical heart of the community was located. It was placed under the direct influence of the clergy, living in the town, who perpetuated attachment to Christian practice and doctrine. Under the influence of fashionable doctrines, contemporary historians have systematically minimized this purely ideological component of the attitude of the peasants of the West. The leader of Jacobin repression, General Turreau, was the first to point out the great authority of these priests, due to three reasons: the integrity of their way of life, the seriousness of their doctrinal training, and their intimate knowledge of the milieu. Most members of the clergy could have gone into exile to wait for better days. They forced themselves to live in heroic conditions, not only out of obedience, but also because they were certain of the support of the people. For their part, the people were ready to do everything for men who remained at their posts at the risk of their lives, all the more because they were relatives, friends, or confidants. On the basis of an investigation conducted by a commissioner of the National Assembly, it was observed that there were points on which all the inhabitants of the countryside were in agreement; these were liberties, particularly the liberty of religious opinion. "We ask no other favor, they say unanimously, than to have priests in whom we have confidence. Several of them," notes the commissioner, "attached such a great price to this favor that they assured us they would willingly pay double their taxes to obtain it."[76]

Finally, one of the principal demands of the *cahiers de doléances* was treated with disdain. Small peasant farmers asked for exemption from the militia a source of ruin for those in an already fragile agricultural situation. But the government suddenly requisitioned 300,000 men to be sent they knew not where, either to join troops pursuing refractory priests, or to defend a hated regime. As for civil servants and municipal officers, seen as oppressors, they were exempt from service in accordance with article XX of the law.[77] The departure of able-bodied men would leave the population even more vulnerable to the abusive power of the State, and the people were thereby pushed into rebellion. Attachment to the native soil, hostility to military service, and apprehension toward "foreign" regions, themes repeated by contemporaries and historians, are not sufficient explanations.[78]

In addition, it should be noted that the Declaration of the Rights of Man and Citizen had a significance that the members of the Assembly had not suspected, namely, resistance to oppression. The document is clear on the subject: "Any regime restricting the rights of man is abusive and must be resisted." The Vendean revolt was thus both legal and legitimate.[79]

The War Begins

THE CONFLICT BETWEEN THE LEGAL AUTHORITIES AND THE authorities that were called legitimate was expressed daily in hidden and direct ways. The standard-bearers for the legal authorities were the representatives of the central government and their supporters, and the others relied on the rest of the population. As long as local administrations had the army behind them to support them, they felt strong. When the soldiers left, the numerical proportions were reversed. From that point on, the municipal governments sensed that the latent conflict might erupt openly and violently. On many occasions they openly expressed their complaints to the central administration.[1] The government turned a deaf ear; all its attention was focused on foreign wars. Even worse, forces were reduced drastically: 1,300 men for Vendée, 50 at Fontenay and La-Roche-sur-Yon, 100 at Les Sables-d'Olonne and Challans, and 500 at Montaigu and La Châtaigneraie.[2] Similarly, artillery and artillerymen were requisitioned. Loire-Inférieure had only four 12-gauge, twelve 18-gauge, and eight 24-gauge guns.[3]

The situation of the soldiers was precarious: the volunteers of Maine-et-Loire stationed in Blain frequently complained of lacking "all cooking utensils";[4] and the Twenty-fifth Regiment garrisoned in Clisson protested against "the bad food provided."[5] From all sides, came cries of despair. "You promised us bullets and powder," wrote the mayor of Chemillé. "We have been waiting a long time. You well understand, gentlemen, that we need munitions more than ever. Hurry to our assistance and put yourself in a position to defend us by keeping your promises to us."[6] Events proved him right; at the draft lottery a few weeks later ("The electric spark that set off the explosion," exclaimed the countess of Bouère), war broke out.

THE INSURRECTION: MARCH 10–11, 1793

In an article published in 1913 Léon Maître remarks that rebellion did not break out at every point at the same time. According to him, the signal was launched from the parishes in Loire-Inférieure closest to Anjou and Vendée.[7]

In fact, all the departments were in a state of agitation. In addition to the underlying problems that have been mentioned, the people were in a state of total disarray. Until August 10, 1792, noted a commissioner, "we shot at the people in the name of the king."[8] It was still in the name of the king that the general officer, Charles de Vezion, commanding the Arvault region, informed the parish of Saint-Loup on October 29, 1789, that it would be put to the torch, and that at the same time twenty-five people would be shot if three prisoners were not freed.[9]

The closing of churches and chapels not served by constitutional priests on March 6, 1793, the law on recruitment that arrived officially on March 7, and its publication the next day, were all triggering elements. Everywhere crowds formed and more or less quickly started to take action. It is difficult to grasp the totality of events related to the military Vendée. Let us confine ourselves to the populations living along the Loire between Champtoceaux and Nantes.

Some cantons were calm, such as that of Le Loroux-Bottereau.[10] The tax collector even took advantage of Sunday, March 10, a day of rest, to go to Nantes to talk to his director about personal problems. Far from fearing danger, he brought with him only some of the money he had collected.

The pace of events was swift. In order to demonstrate their discontent, the people refused to give their names to the commissioners, with cries of "Give us back our good priests, down with the intruders." Hamlets, villages, and towns acted in concert, it seems, and had had the time to get organized since they had received the text of the law. In Beaupréau, placards had even been posted predicting misfortune to anyone advertising the militia.[11]

The inhabitants of Saint-Julien-de-Concelles proclaimed:

> What! We're going to fight for a government like this! Set off at the summons of people who have overturned all the administrations in the country, who have led the king to the scaffold, who have sold all the possessions of the Church, who want to impose on us priests we don't want, and who throw our true pastors in prison! Never! Never in living

memory has such a levy been made in the country. Our good priests and no draft![12]

In Doulon and Saint-Luce, at around four in the afternoon, after seizing Mayor Brevet and the curé Colas, 150 people invaded the town hall and tore up the department decree. In Thouaré, the scene was still more violent.[13] At the moment when Gaudriau, commissioner of the district, was about to proceed to calling up the draft, forty individuals armed with sticks stormed into the room. They made violent statements, to which the commissioner replied by calling for calm. When he read Isnard's speech and the law of February 21, which promised bonuses, he was jeered with the words "Holy liberty, sacred liberty." "They have killed our king, driven out our priests, and sold the possessions of our church; where is the money? They have taken everything; now they want our bodies; no, they will not have them." In vain, Gaudriau reminded them of the suppression of the tithe and the corvées: "All that makes no difference, we have set the liberty cap on our bell; well, if we are free we want to do nothing but take care of the work in our fields." The municipal government and the curé were ordered to withdraw.

Of the surrounding towns, only Le Loroux-Bottereau acceded to the request of the recruiters. The insurgent populace immediately attacked the representatives of the central government: the *truton* (constitutional) priest, the municipal government, and the tax collector.

Around four in the afternoon, part of the population of La Chapelle-Bassemère, which "seemed little concerned with past prejudices," stormed into the house of the constitutional curé Caperon. He believed himself to be completely safe. Confronted with declarations of insurrection and threats to make him their first victim, he remained calm, but "although recovering from a serious illness, he had enough strength and agility to climb the very high walls" of the parsonage. He claims later to have avoided countless dangers and confronted the fury "of those pagans who had long secretly planned his death." He took refuge in Ancenis, and then in Nantes.[14]

A few minutes later, the inhabitants attacked the national guard.[15] On Tuesday and the following days they seized by force the various surrounding municipalities loyal to the Republic.[16] On the morning of March 12, the men of Le Loroux, La Chapelle-Bassemère, and Saint-Julien-de-Concelles, brought together the day before by the sack of the town hall of the capital, arrived in La Bridonnière, where they were joined by men from Saint-Sauveur and La Varenne.[17] According to reports from the mayors, there were almost five hundred, wearing the traditional wool cap and in their button-holes the wooden spoon reserved for weddings. For weapons they had old hunting rifles, crosses, pitchforks, and sticks. The mayor of La Varenne, Jacques Redureau, completes the description: "Around fifty armed men, some with pikes and scythes, most with rifles, went to see the inhabitants of this commune. They forced all the men they found to join with them on pain of death. Then they went to the *maison commune*." There they broke into a cabinet, from which they removed all the laws, decrees, and other papers. In the heat of action, they tore up a tricolor flag and seized a drum and a chest full of weapons. The next day, these "brigands" had the women bring the papers into the central square and there burned them. When the troop left, they took the mayor along at gunpoint. Patriots managed to free him, but he was taken prisoner again the following day.[18]

On March 14, there were similar episodes in Mesnil-en-Vallée, Saint Florent, and Champtoceaux, which had been occupied on March 12 after par-ticularly violent battles; as in 1789, "certificates and papers" were burned.[19] According to Monlien, the procurator of Le Loroux, tax collectors suffered the same fate as patriot mayors: "On Monday, March 11, the procurator learned that the law on recruitment had created such unrest that an upris-ing was announced. He then hastily gathered his assignats in a bundle, and rode like the wind to Nantes to the revenue office, without taking the time to get a receipt."[20] He then rode back toward Le Loroux armed with a sword and two pistols. When he reached Cahéreau, in the canton of Saint-Julien-de-Concelles, he found himself in a kind of camp. Some inhabi-tants demanded his weapons. When he refused, he was pursued into a house where he hid. He was captured, and they were about to shoot him when they realized that he was a civil servant, an officer of the national guard, and in possession of a certificate of good citizenship. He was then taken to Le Loroux and imprisoned in the chapel of the Virgin. He owed his life to the protection of a citizen named Tiger-Attimont, tax collector of Carquefou, but many others were less fortunate.[21]

All these events were highly significant. From the beginning of the insurrection, the demand for freedom of conscience was linked to the revolt and persisted until complete satisfaction was given by Bonaparte. A petition sent from Thouaré to the district of Nantes on March 21, 1793, is rather explicit, in naive terms, on the subject: If the inhabitants have taken up arms, it was only because they were forced to do so. They would be glad to set them down provided each individual be left peacefully at home and that the freedom that had been taken from them, such as that of keeping their priests, be restored; they were, moreover, prepared to support the priests. "If that had been done more quickly, there would have been no revolt and there would have been enough volunteers."[22]

The young men of Maine-et-Loire, for their part, demanded primarily equality of conscription: "We do not refuse to leave; on the contrary, we are ready to go, but we want the purchasers of *biens nationaux* [confiscated property] . . . and those who are in charge and paid by the nation, with no exceptions, to march at our head, or else we will not go; it is just that those who are enjoying the fruits of the nation be the first to defend them." There followed a number of recommendations: "We know, gentlemen, that you want to search our parishes and seize all our iron tools, which have cost you nothing and which we need for our work. We beg you, gentlemen, to do nothing of the kind, but if you make an attempt in any parish, you will have to deal with all of them."[23]

In addition to driving out the constitutional priests, the inhabitants attacked the symbols of a hated government: the national guard and its flag; the tax collector, his books, and his cashbox;[24] the municipal governments, which they could make into "a kind of rampart";[25] and the registers and administration buildings, which were burned in Machecoul and Challans.[26] These various institutions housed the patriots who were "supporters of the Revolution," and who were also intelligence agents and therefore future instruments of repression.

The same scenes occurred everywhere, noted Esnault, a government commissioner: "Everywhere their sacrilegious steps carry them they leave traces of their wickedness. In one place they burn the municipal offices, in another they destroy civil records . . ."[27] Churches and parsonages occupied by *trutons* were burned, as in Miré. There were few communes, such as Bressuire and Bouaye, that remained apart or regretted having rebelled. The former had already experienced ferocious repression after an uprising in August 1792; the latter feared possible reprisals and promised to restore order on condition that the army not be sent.[28]

The bells in almost every parish in Vendée sounded the tocsin; war had begun. The region was at once abandoned to the insurgents. Bold municipal governments were imprisoned or put before a firing squad.[29] Members of municipal councils and patriots fled for their lives. They turned up in large cities such as Orléans and Blois,[30] or in neighboring republican communes. More directly targeted, the *truton* priests went into hiding; Abbé David, the vicar of Orvault, stayed under a haystack for four days.[31]

Statements made by the insurgents spoke volumes. In Montfaucon, they even declared that they "wanted neither nobles nor bourgeois and that they would share the land" after a "complete victory."[32] The Republic had few men to offer resistance: no more than about 200 in Loire-Inférieure and 1,400 in Vendée. What is more, this armed force was hardly reliable, because it was ill equipped and in an ambiguous position.[33]

Despite all this, lists of names of conscripts, corresponding to those who were supposed to be called up, are to be found in the archives of Nantes and La Roche-sur-Yon.[34] How were they established? How was the lottery carried out? By the authorities in retreat in the capitals? Whatever the case may be, and contrary to a widely held belief, the Vendeans as a whole complied with the conscription, even in relatively high numbers: for example, 33 percent in the Clisson district and 53 percent in Les Sables-d'Olonne. There were, however, differences among locations: Martin-Lars and Chazelou sent 44 of the 49 men called; La Jaudinière 27 of 33; La Chapelle-aux-Pies 14 of 25. There were few communes that, like Saint-Julien-de-Concelles, refused all conscription. Clearly, those who accepted were supporters of the Republic or feared reprisals.

The opposition between Republicans and "counterrevolutionaries" corresponds, to a certain extent, to an opposition between social strata. In La Chapelle-Bassemère, for example, this was particularly evident between artisans and sailors on the one hand, and peasants on the other.[35] This was expressed in a struggle between the town and the valley where the Republicans lived and the rest of the commune. But distinctions must be made that apply to the countryside, the town, and the valley all together—a single family might be internally divided. The members of the bourgeoisie were also divided: the notary Vivant gave moderate support to the Revolution, while the two surgeons sided with the insurgents. Here, too, there were internal divisions in families, since the notary's mother effectively protected the refractory priest Robin. The most expressive criterion, at least locally, was geographic: the twelve men out of twenty-four who answered the call came from the valley and embarked on the ships of the Republic.[36]

The administration, lacking military resources, very soon felt the situation slipping from its grasp. An address from the department of Loire-Inférieure to the "inhabitants of the countryside" is eloquent. It begins by recalling the benefits of the Revolution, the freedom from feudal obligations, and the sharing of communal land.

Men who have not yet felt any of the benefits of the Revolution, artisans who have received only the requirement of being regulated, rich men who could purchase the capacity to harm you, to wall themselves up in castles in order to make you pay feudal taxes; all these men fought so that you would be exempt from tithes. Their blood flowed so that you would no longer be thrown into prison on such barbarous pretexts as killing a hare or a partridge, so that you would have the right to have justice done to the rich landowner who ravaged your field with his horses or his hunting hounds. They risked their lives so that the means of conserving your life would be independent of the rapines of an avaricious miller, so that you would have the right to have your grain milled by an honest man. They sacrificed a part of their fortune so that yours would be increased by the rents and the tolls that had been taken from your means of subsistence.

Now, you may live in happiness in your country; you have been delivered from those legal leeches who swallowed up your possessions, the family tribunals; justices of the peace secure for you without cost, or with modest cost, the inner calm that expensively prolonged trials used to rob from you and your unfortunate descendants. You are still the cherished care of a tender mother; the nation at this moment is engaged in having you enjoy the sharing of communal property and you . . . ingrates, blind citizens, have not yet done anything for her. We pity you because peasants are in our eyes infinitely estimable, because we love you, because we wish you to be happy.

The document then praises the military victories of the Republic in the north and the east. "A few more months . . . but help us, let us go and relieve our victorious brothers in Argonnes, Spire, and Jemmapes. At this moment they are capturing towns from our enemies, they have just taken two fortresses from the Dutch, and while they are fighting for us, we are destroying ourselves."[37]

Incidentally, this military description was deliberately erroneous. The massive return of the volunteers of 1791 and their arms and equipment after their two years' enlistment had put an end to the first French offensive. The Austrians took advantage of this to return in force; the Prussians had already resumed their campaign, bringing on the sieges of Mainz, Condé, and Valenciennes and the need for mass recruitment in 1793. The address then promised "the enjoyment of lasting calm after a few efforts lasting a few months." Finally, it exhorted citizens not to shirk their military duty—accommodations were possible.

Citizens, let us join together, let us imitate the eagerness of the peasants who are close to the enemy. You would be surprised to learn that near the borders there are no young men who have not borne arms for liberty, no smallholding and no farm that does not contain defenders in the army. Citizens, you will remember with indignation the weakness that, keeping you cowardly at home, counterbalanced your zeal. Citizens, on the march. The sooner the effort is made, the easier victory will be.

Peasants have been told only about the draft lottery; several have testified that they would willingly chip in to purchase men and that it is possible to find men of good will among them. Two have already come forward in Cordemais.[38]

It is therefore necessary to inform them, following this address, about their freedom with respect to the method of recruitment.

But the address was psychologically hugely inept with respect to religion. To reassure the faithful, it used exactly the arguments that troubled them concerning the marriage of priests, divorce, and the persecution of the refractory clergy, unfaithful to their promises and agents of feudal abuses.

You cry out that religion is lost. Your sorrow on this question, citizens, proves that you do not know this divine religion. What do you find that is unjust in the regulations that you believe are related to it? Is it the way of recording births, marriages, and deaths? But, citizens, do you regret that, instead of entrusting to a single man, often corruptible, the interest of your legitimacy and your rights of inheritance, recourse has been had to measures which make it impossible for your claims to be unknown? Is it the ability to divorce? Were the legal separations of the old regime anything other than divorces? And because the law anticipates individual disagreements, because instead of exposing the secrets and the faults of families to public ridicule and curiosity, because it has called on relatives to reconcile you by gentle means, you exclaim that the law is impious! Citizens, think about it. Is there impiety in softening the condition of men, in preventing them from spending unhappy days in quarrels, reproaches, and all the dissensions created by mutual incompatibility? Is it allowing priests to marry? Eleven of the twelve apostles were married. Priests were still getting married four centuries after Jesus Christ. Is it the oath required of them? Is it their expulsion? But, citizens, could we maintain any confidence in men who were unwilling to promise to do nothing against the laws, through which you are exempt from tithes, exempt from paying feudal taxes, exempt from submitting to rapacious prosecutors, against laws, finally, through which you are free? Citizens, we think too well of you to believe that you will remain in your blindness. Come to us, we will teach you; you may confide your conscience to us; we will never deceive you!

But it was precisely because of their faithfulness to their sacerdotal promise and as opponents of revolutionary abuses that the people admired the priests; the misunderstanding was thus blatant. After conferring together, encouraging the hesitant, and drawing up plans to "blow up the districts,"[39] the recalcitrant agreed on codes and signals, like the traditional cry of the screech owl. But effective conduct of a subversive popular war presupposes a different level of organization.

The Organization of the Insurgent Population: March 13 – October 18, 1793

This organization was noted by a certain number of patriot mayors.[40] Generals spoke of well-prepared counterrevolutionary plans carried out by experienced men. In any event, it is indisputable that the military Vendée, the entire region, rather than the province alone, never suffered from hunger during the wars. Indeed, as Turreau observed, "the Vendeans were in plenty and their neighbors in shortage; this is what brought many converts to the royalist party."[41]

The Organization of the Parishes

It seems that this organization was almost the same everywhere. Populations were divided into three groups. The first and second contained the men old enough to bear arms; that is, from thirteen on.[42] Officers were freely elected: a commander for each parish, at least two captains, and various commissioners, with elected generals at their head.

The first group was charged with the defense of the communal territory against an always possible Republican invasion. For example, all the parishes on the banks of the Loire were organized in relation to the river and the woods that provided natural protection. This obstacle was so substantial, that if the Blues were to cross it in small numbers, they would suffer considerable losses. The soldiers of this group were also to guard the noncombatant population: women, children, and old men. In La Chapelle-Basse-mère, this section was divided into five posts in which "one hundred fifty men watched day and night."[43] They had various functions: to warn the population in case of danger, to hunt down Republicans in the area, to resist a possible attack from the Blues by diverting their attention chiefly to the banks of the Loire, where a flotilla was permanently stationed. Sailing on light barks, the "guys from Le Loroux" evaded enemy surveillance.[44] They sometimes advanced as far as the Republican camps set up on the other side of the river. On 16 prairial (June 6) they landed on the île du Haut-Bois and seized a sizable herd of cattle intended to supply the garrison in the castle of Aux. A few days later, there was a similar expedition on the île Moron, opposite Le Cellier. On the night of May 12 in Thouaré, they came close to capturing the ship *Le Républicain,* armed with two cannons and two small artillery pieces. The ship's commander called for another gunboat to be sent immediately.

The villages along the river were turned into veritable armed camps; they were supplied with cannons able to respond to fire from the Republican positions. In a letter dated May 14 sent from Mauves, Aubinet reported the interview between his lieutenant Aubin and one of the leaders from Le Loroux on the tip of the île Harrouys. "They are determined," he said, "to fight to the death; nothing will be able to defeat them but fire and sword. Besides, they threaten to attack us with very superior forces."

Unable to dislodge the Vendeans, Aubinet at least attempted to protect himself from attacks from the land. For this purpose, he coordinated his movements with the commanders of detachments in Nort and Ancenis. In late April, an expedition divided into three columns entered the forest of Le Cellier, which it searched in every direction without result. The operation was repeated three days later with no greater success.

On the other side of Mauves, the posts of the castle of Clermont, Le Cellier, and Oudon, commanded by Meuris, were constantly on the alert. Coming from La Chapelle, La Varenne, and Champtoceaux, Vendeans daily tried to communicate with the groups in Ligné, Saint-Mars, and La Forêt.

Mills also played a major role in this defense. According to an old tradition, their elevated position made it possible to survey the neighboring territories from which danger might come, and to warn the people. Windmills had been used, for example, to announce the death of the miller or one of his relatives.[45] In the case of serious illness, they were stopped as the last rites were carried by and then turned toward the house of the dying person. Based on this custom, a code of various signals was worked out: the sails "in quarter," that is, in a cross of Saint Andrew, indicated calm; "at the end of the foot," following the axis of the mill, a gathering; "dog's left leg," the lower sail to the left of the entry, imminent danger; "dog's right leg," danger avoided.[46] It took the Blues some time to discover this code. Thereafter, following orders, they did their utmost to destroy systematically all wind- and watermills without distinction, because they were suspect.

The signals were supplemented by a team of messengers, on foot or horseback, who warned the people. The messengers ran to the town and set the bells ringing or sounded a horn. Inhabitants unable to fight scattered through the countryside while attempts were made to slow and block the march of the Blues by any means: felled trees, broken wagons, and the like.[47] The Vendeans never allowed themselves to be taken by surprise. Woods, sunken lanes, and haystacks, veritable traps, served as hiding places.

In addition to these skirmishes, the people had to support countless battles—shocks, they said modestly, as if they were speaking about the sudden collision of two large carts full of sticks or cabbages on the way home to the farm in the evening. As Jean Yole has pointed out, "The experience was so new to the peasants that they lacked terms to express it. They had no choice here as well but to borrow words from their work as they had already taken weapons from the same source."[48]

The counteroffensive came at first from the Loire, from which "more than seven thousand cannon shots were fired," according to Abbé Robin. "We pick up bullets and grapeshot by the handful on our islands."[49] However, he notes, "all these battles have caused few losses."

The third group, that is, the noncombatant part of the population, was charged with working the land and maintaining the cattle. In the case of necessity, it might take an active part in battle. Some women, as Emile Gabory has noted, occasionally cheerfully shared the life of the troops "where they were even more serious than the men."[50]

This organization, which was to be very effective, was established spontaneously in the days following the uprising. How can this rapid reaction be explained? By a conspiracy? The answer is both simpler and more complex. The old society had its particular structures: first, the rigorously hierarchical and disciplined family; then the *fabrique*, an organized, structured, and elected body. Before the departure of the municipal government, or immediately afterward, it went back to work under the leadership of the curés or others. Lacking that, structure was imposed by the superior council of Châtillon on August 7. A circular was then sent out:

> We, the officers of the superior council, sitting provisionally in Châtillon-sur-Sèvre, on the good and praiseworthy report that has been made to us of the persons———all inhabitants of the town and the parishes of———and of their attachment to religion and to the king, have appointed them as follows: the said———president, and the said———officers of the local council of the said parish of———and charge them to well and faithfully fulfill the duties given to them, not to cease or interrupt them for any reason whatever, even in case of the assembly of the soldiers of the royal Catholic armies, in which they may not be included;
>
> Therefore, we order them to meet without delay and to form themselves into an administrative council.
>
> We enjoin them, in the exercise of their duties, to obey our rules and decrees and to choose a secretary.
>
> For these purposes, we have delegated to them, in the name of his most Christian majesty, all the authority necessary for them to effectuate and carry out these presents.
>
> We mandate and order to all that they are obliged to recognize their status and to grant them the respect and obedience that is due them.
>
> In witness whereof we have delivered to them these presents, to which we have affixed the royal seal.
>
> Done in the superior council in Châtillon-sur-Sèvre, on——— 1793, first year of the reign of Louis XVII.

Signed, Michelin, Le Maignan, Boutellier, Coudray, Michel des Essarts, Bodin, Duplessis, and the bishop of Agra.[51]

In all the communes of the military Vendée, these parish organizations formed the basis for the Vendean army. Following a disappointing municipal experience, they came out of the crisis strengthened.

"Military service" existed under the Old Regime, as we have already said. Hence, in each of these parishes, there was a significant number of men skilled in handling a rifle, even the nonsoldiers. Most of the time, they were very experienced hunters; the high price of ammunition forced them to be economical with it. And we should not forget that people living on the Loire had been hunting in their territory for a very long time. Their skill with the slingshot was also remarkable. Indeed, in his memoirs, Turreau expresses his surprise: "No known people, however warlike or tactically skilled, draws as much benefit from firearms as the hunter of Le Loroux and the poacher of the town."[52]

Former soldiers trained the others. They themselves were commanded by former officers and career soldiers, such as Lyrot de La Patouillère from Basse-Goulaine and Poulain de La Vincendière from La Barre in La Chapelle-Bassemère, both of whom were knights of the Order of Saint Louis.[53] As a rule, the nobility had disappeared or emigrated; it therefore played only a secondary role in this organization.

The Great Fear [of 1789, caused by rumors of foreign invasion] and the various resulting uprisings had provided the opportunity for a first mobilization of the countryside. This produced major local repercussions that strengthened community bonds in the face of danger. From the beginning of the insurrection in March 1793, two movements are notable: on the one hand, the reconstitution of veritable military units by already trained soldiers; on the other, obligatory training for all other men. This took place in specially designed camps, such as that of La Louée in Haute-Goulaine. These two movements occurred at the express demand of those involved. The first weapons of the inhabitants were "the *gourdins à reboule*" (sticks) taken up at the time of the draft lottery. Once in full revolt, those who had hunting rifles picked them up. Lacking those weapons, they took pitchforks, put handles backward on scythes, and made swords out of sickles. As in all jacqueries, the first weapons of war of the peasants were thus those that came immediately to hand.[54]

The rebels also took care to requisition all the weapons scattered throughout the parishes. Thébault de La Monderie, owner of the castle of Barbechat, had his rifles stolen;[55] following that adventure, he took refuge in Nantes with his entire family. The case was not unique. Later on, a number of weapons, including cannons, were taken from the Blues and triumphantly carried into the parishes.[56]

Organization and Tactics of the Vendean Army

On this question as well there are a number of prejudices. The Vendean army was well organized, trained, and ready for battle. Indeed they also conducted battles in open country, with massed forces on each side of between twenty-five and forty thousand men. This was the case at Saumur, Cholet, and Entrammes, where the army of Mainz was wiped out in a crushing victory. Military training showed itself in all these encounters and demonstrated the superiority of the Vendée forces over those of previous jacqueries, as Vaton, captain of the Seventieth Demibrigade of Cerisay, explains: "The brigands we dealt with fight methodically; they have many skirmishers on foot and on horseback and a large infantry platoon marching in good order with drums at its head. The horsemen are almost all elegant and fight very well . . ."[57]

In addition to testimony from soldiers, two reports contribute to knowledge of this army. The first is from Jaudonnet de Laugrenière, dated December 27 and 30, 1793, that is, shortly after the defeat of Savenay.[58] This Dominique-Alexandre Jaudonnet was lord of the parish of Moustiers-sous-Argenton; a former musketeer and officer of dragoons, he was thoroughly familiar with the countryside and the inhabitants, who had set him at their head. The second report is from commanding general Beaufort, who seems to have composed it on the basis of questionnaires.[59] The Catholic army, as it was constituted by August 7, 1793, can be divided into the standing army and the supporting army.

1. The Standing Army. It is difficult to estimate its size, which varied with needs and availabilities. At its head was a headquarters staff, the superior council made up of a commander-in-chief, Cathelineau, who was succeeded by d'Elbée, La Rochejaquelein, and Fleuriot; a second-in-command; generals; major-generals; and various subordinate officers.[60] Among the latter, Amissant was governor of conquered territories; Rouarain directed attacks; de La Roche Saint-André took on the composition of addresses to the people; La Trémouille commanded the cavalry; Obenheim and Bernard de Marigny the heavy artillery; and Grellier the light artillery. There were in addition officers responsible for garrisons, munitions storage, and so on.

Medical provision was a matter of particular concern. It was decreed that all royalist and Republican wounded would be transported to Saint-Laurent-sur-Sèvre and treated by the community of the Sisters of Wisdom. Surgeons were to follow the army.

A chief treasurer, Beauvollier, was appointed quartermaster, in cooperation with the superior council. Various measures were taken to procure some clothing and shoes and to establish stores of wheat and stables for the cattle necessary for feeding the troops. According to Jaudonnet, the army never lacked anything; all kinds of provisions arrived in abundance: wheat, wine, sheep, calves, cattle, brandy, and even fodder for the animals. The greater part of the conquered territories spontaneously offered its goods. "'I have seen,' he went on (a unique occurrence in social history demonstrating the wealth of the peasants), 'fifty tenant farmers beg that we take their cattle . . . and even cry when they were refused . . . because we did not need them . . .'"

In case of urgent necessity, generals requisitioned supplies at the expense of nobles, large landowners, and émigrés. Individuals, moreover, were required to reserve their cattle and crops for the army "on pain of a fine of one hundred écus and confiscation the first time, and death in the case of a second offense . . ." Again according to Jaudonnet, "The peasant was so up in arms that he would have given everything he had." He received compensation in the form of vouchers; at first they used the money found in the chests of the Republican army of Fontenay, 900,000 livres; in a second stage, from September 20, 1794, on, they turned to paper money in the form of assignats with a "secret mark." For this purpose a production facility managed by Colonne and Saint-Merrys was established. The vouchers issued, of different denominations, earned interest at the rate of 4.5 percent until reimbursement by the royal treasury, to be paid in peacetime. They were signed by the marquis of Donissens, the prince of Talmont, the curé Bernier, and Beauvollier.

Political and administrative affairs were managed by another council presided over by Abbé Guyot de Folleville, known under the name of bishop of Agra. He was seconded by the marquis of Donissens, former gentleman of honor of Monsieur the count of Provence, and father-in-law of Lescure; Desessarts the elder, the count of Bouthillier; and Abbé Bernier, former curé of the parish of Saint-Laud in Angers. A lawyer from Fontenay named Carrière was appointed procurator of the king for the administrative council, and Le Jagaut, a former Benedictine monk, was secretary-general.

The army itself had three core elements. The vanguard, containing the parishes along the Loire in the neighborhood of Saint-Florent-le-Vieil, was commanded by Bonchamp and Stofflet. The army of the center under d'Elbée was made up of men from the areas around Cholet, Beaupréau, and Mortagne. The rear guard, led by Lescure and La Rochejaquelein, controlled the cantons of Clisson, Les Aubiers, Saint-Aubin-du-Plain, and Echaubrognes.

The parishes in the neighborhood of Montaigu and Vieillevigne marched under the orders of Royrand, and those of the Marais and the coast under the orders of Charrette, both of whom were relatively independent. Each section was subdivided into four brigades of approximately three thousand soldiers, making for twelve to fifteen thousand men per division. The infantry was not divided into regiments but into companies organized by the parishes, which fostered a greater degree of rivalry. Brothers, relatives, friends, and comrades were together under the orders of the curé or the captain. They all wanted to distinguish themselves, in comparison both with one another and with the neighboring hamlet or parish, or even with another family. The system of naval classes under Louis XIV had had a similar spirit.

The cavalry was made up of four divisions of one thousand to twelve hundred men, totaling approximately five thousand horsemen. Westermann mentioned it frequently in his dispatches: "Everyone knows that this is where the enemy has the advantage of us." Boutillier de Saint-André described it marching by: "The cavalry came after the artillery which followed the *Grande Armée*. Among the horsemen one was surprised to see rope harnesses, men without boots wearing round hats and no pistols, often having a sword and a rifle over the shoulder for their only weapons."[61] This matches the description of Madame de La Rochejaquelein: "The horses were of all sizes and every color. You saw many packsaddles instead of ordinary ones, ropes instead of stirrups, wooden shoes instead of boots. The cavalrymen, like the infantry, wore all kinds of costumes, pistols at their belts, swords and rifles attached with string; some had white cockades, others black or green ones."

After the battle of Doué on June 6, 1793, the cavalry was significantly reinforced by several regiments of hussars and dragoons who had deserted to the victor. At first, the cavalry was made up largely of the divisions of Montfaucon, Cerizay, Le Loroux-Bottereau, Cholet, Argenton-le-Château, Châtillon, Beaupréau, and Chemillé, parishes considered to have more resources than the others. Each one of them was required to supply fifteen mounted men. Later, the ranks were swelled with renegades and German prisoners of war, who received good pay. A number of Bretons, particularly from Rennes, mercenaries or unpaid volunteers, also joined up.

The artillery was made up of about 180 cannoneers divided into four companies commanded by former sergeants, under the overall command of former major Pérault.[62] A company of light artillery was later set up, led by an officer named Grélier. There were about fifty cannons, and a few artillery pieces, the largest of 12 or 8 gauge, most of them of 4, along with eighty crates of ammunition. The command was assigned to de Marigny, former ship captain and knight of Saint-Louis. The artillery stock and manufacturing facilities were placed in Châtillon, and the ammunition factories in Mortagne and Beaupréau, which, according to Jaudonnet, turned out sixty and even eighty pounds a day.

2. The Supporting Army.   Two groups should be distinguished, the first of which were the regulars, who made up the bulk of the army.[63] Most of them were peasants who returned to their land once a battle was over. Their assembly could be contingent on immediate local circumstances or ordered, in accordance with the decree of Fontenay, by a printed notice prepared by the central command in the following terms: "In the Name of the King . . . We, commander-in-chief and general officers of the army, order the inhabitants of the parish of———to go to———with their weapons and to bring bread. At———on———the second year of the reign of Louis XVII."[64] At least forty-eight hours before the date set, this circular was carried by a member of the standing army to leaders of districts and from there conveyed to parish commanders. "Immediately," wrote a soldier to the minister, "all the men leave their houses or usual refuges, to which they return after the expedition."[65]

The first to be called were those on the lists established by the parish councils. For example, Jallais owed one officer and forty-eight men; Beaupréau, one and thirty; Sainte-Christine, one and twenty-five; Segré, one and forty.[66] Able-bodied men who refused the call were punishable by a fine ranging from ten to fifty francs. Companies of about fifty men, paid ten sous per day, were thus set up. The two or three commanding officers called the roll at least once a day and saw to the proper distribution of provisions. Nine companies made up a battalion with flags and drums. Whenever the men called up lacked weapons, the wounded and ill were obliged to surrender theirs.[67]

The second group was made up of "occasionals": deserters from the Republican army and inhabitants of newly conquered territories, as General Beaufort explained.[68]

The army marched methodically. In the vanguard were companies of skirmishers (around three thousand men) and part of the cavalry, escorted by three artillery pieces. Then came the bulk of the army with the artillery "in battle order." Baggage and supplies followed with the rear guard, made up of almost all the cavalry, the rest of which was always stationed on the flank to protect against possible attacks.

When this army went into battle, it marched in a single column. "At the head," according to General Beaufort,

> are set two artillery pieces. Preceding them, there are a few cavalrymen, and to put the enemy off the track, the rebels are very careful to have the infantry occupy a very large space of ground. Behind the head are found the true attack forces. The artillery mixed with the cavalry is usually set in the center. Most frequently, this artillery consists of ten pieces, one 12 gauge, two 8, and the others 4. The right and left sides try to skirt the Republican army and take it on the flank.
>
> Their success in battle always depends on the initial attack, especially the movement of their wings. They believe they can intimidate our troops by loud cries, but they have not been using this stratagem for some time, because it has been forbidden by their commanders.
>
> In the thick of battle, the wings are most heavily supplied, and the center almost completely deserted. If our forces were to concentrate there, it would very easily be broken because it is guarded only by the cavalry armed with muskets and fighting on foot.[69]

The general recommends the intervention of the Republican infantry and observes: "Every time that the center has been attacked, the rebel enemy has been beaten; witness the memorable days of Luçon. The generals opposing them who have not used this tactic were considered by them lacking in knowledge and even in courage." Vendean tactics surprised the Republicans, heirs of the old military tradition of the eighteenth century, the bases of which were maneuver and pitched battle.[70] Turreau was astounded by it:

> Let us now speak of the Vendeans, let us speak of these truly extraordinary men whose political existence, their rapid and remarkable progress, and especially their unprecedented ferocity, will mark an epoch in the annals of the Revolution; of these Vendeans who are lacking only humanity and another cause to defend in order to embody all the characteristics of heroism. A way of fighting hitherto unknown and perhaps inimitable insofar as it can only be used in this region and is tied to the spirit of its inhabitants; an unbreakable attachment to their party; a boundless confidence in their leaders; such great loyalty to their promises that it can replace discipline; an indomitable courage that withstands all kinds of danger, fatigue, and deprivation: this is what makes the Vendeans redoubtable enemies and must place them in the first rank of the warlike people of history.

The vanguards, always made up of the best troops, attacked the enemy head on and immobilized it, while the body of the army fanned out around it and surrounded it without being seen. Then this invisible circle would tighten, fire from hedgerows, and attempt to lead the Blues into a sunken path or a crossroads, the better to "strike" them. In other cases, the Vendean soldiers used the tactics later followed by the French army. They relied on the heroic courage of the infantryman who approached the enemy as closely as possible to fight hand to hand. When they went into battle, the Vendeans always looked behind them to make certain that they were not cut off from the rest of the troops.

An inhabitant of Le Loroux-Bottereau, witness to most of the battles, recounts the way of proceeding:

> Our army is made up of peasants like me, wearing jackets or coarse clothing, armed with hunting rifles, pistols, muskets, sometimes with farm implements, scythes, sticks, axes, pruning knives, or roasting spits. It is organized by parishes and districts, under the orders of an individual leader. We march straight at the enemy and, after kneeling to receive the blessing of our priests, we begin at point-blank range with

a fusillade, no doubt irregular, but strong and well-aimed. As soon as we see Republican cannoneers about to fire, we fall to the ground. When the shot has gone by without touching us, we get up and run with the speed of lightning at the batteries, which we seize before there is time for the cannons to be reloaded. For commands, our officers merely yell: "Scatter, my boys, here are the Blues." At this signal, we spread out and form a fan to surround the enemy.[71]

The Vendeans thus always faced the enemy head-on with no trenches, "trusting in their God and in the force of their arms," General Beaufort ironically commented. "The vanguard, mustering all their confidence, feel the greatest security in the remainder of their troops. The losses are very small. If, to the cry of 'who goes there,' you answer 'royalist,' you could force the guard and seize everything." The Vendean army was not without its weak point, for, again according to General Beaufort, the aftermath of victory could change into defeat:

> These brigands do not keep watch at all. They have the habit of pursuing very far and with determination. When they come back, they are very tired. At that point it would be urgent for the defeated general to remove from the battlefield a rather large body of infantry and cavalry, that each horseman take an infantryman on his horse, and that an hour after the battle this body go by roundabout roads to harass these brigands; they would surely defeat them by nightfall.

In any event, the Vendean army long had the advantage, especially when it followed the tactics of guerrilla warfare and ambush. As Victor Hugo said so well, at home, the Vendean is a smuggler, laborer, soldier, shepherd, poacher, sharpshooter, goatherd, bellringer, peasant, spy, assassin, sacristan, and creature of the woods. Vendée was a veritable maze of thickets and sunken paths. Only the inhabitants knew its secrets. In his *Mémoire sur la guerre de Vendée*, Kléber complains:

> It is an obscure and deep labyrinth in which one can walk only by feeling one's way; through this system of redoubts and natural fortifications, one has to find tortuous paths. As soon as you leave the main roads and wish to go into the interior of the territory, there are nothing but impassable defiles, not only for the artillery, but for everything that

does not have the narrow span of the carts of the country. And even the main roads offer no advantage but that of greater width, for they are bordered by the same system of enclosures. The places where some kind of deployment could be ordered are extremely rare.[72]

The woods provided great advantages both for attack and for retreat. It is easy to explain that, outside their own country and despite their courage, these same soldiers experienced defeat at Dol, Quiberon, and Savenay. It is a mistake to see in these reverses, as some have done, disarray or nostalgia created by absence from their native soil. These soldiers had already served properly under the Old Regime, as we have explained.

Another characteristic of this army was the familiarity between officers and soldiers. Traditional relationships in the tenant-farming system had already been characterized by great simplicity. When owners invited farmers to visit, they had them sit down and served them themselves. In his *Guerre de Vendée*, Crétineau-Joly points to this ease on the part of the soldier:

> He sits at his general's table. He wants to take part in councils, and of course to come forward on the day his bravery will be called upon. In this self-assertion . . . we should not look for a trace of pride. The peasant of the West, when he knows that he has been warned of danger, is more sure of himself. Uncertainty troubles his courage, and in his suspicion he always has at the back of his mind the idea that he might be betrayed. Free and sincere, he hides the truth neither from himself nor from others. If a gentleman has shown weakness, "What you have done is not good for a noble," he tells him with brutal frankness. They have even been heard saying to their general, "You were a little cowardly in that fight"; and no one can charge these judgments with injustice or thoughtlessness. The volunteers have seen and judged their officers on the field of battle.[73]

A certain equality came out of this relationship, as Napoleon wrote in his memoirs: "The Vendean armies were themselves dominated by the great principle that had just invaded France and against which they were fighting every day." This eagerness for battle and rivalry were supported by certain songs, which amount to so many pamphlets against the national guard, the *trutons,* the *patauds* [the Blues], the municipal agents, the administration, and the robbers of ecclesiastical property. Peigné collected some verses from old soldiers of Le Loroux-Bottereau:

1
National drummers
Sound the retreat;
National guards,
Surrender your flags.

2
Let's drive out our intruders
who are schismatics,
robbers and thieves,
burners of houses.

3
You have driven out
all our good bishops,
vicars and curés
and all the clergy.

4
Your shameless women
wear the cockade,
You will be hung,
you and your intruders.

5
You have sold
the goods of the Church;
Have you paid for them,
Notorious thieves!

6
You have lifted
your sacrilegious hands,
with no power,
up to the censer.

7
You have driven
many Catholics
to follow your steps,
villainous scoundrels!

Another
Down with the Republic,
Long live the king! Long live the
    king!
Down with the Republic!
Long live the king! We want a king.

Another
It is our philosopher
Who is still making plans;
France is in agony,
her subjects are immolated
our pompous doctors,
to lose us for ever,
want a republic,
the grave of good Frenchmen.

2
Strike, strike your breast,
finally open your eyes.
It is the most foul doctrine
that makes you so unhappy.
Come see a people of brothers
professing the same faith,
singing like our fathers,
Long live the Church and the king!

3

Finally, God abandons them
these men, feeble mortals,
all robbers of the crown,
destroyers of our altars.
Long live the king, the nobles,
the clergy, our good Frenchmen;
Let us all live in joy
and never be divided!

4

Let us go forth,
despite all the envious;
the citadel is open
we will be victorious;
but if the enemy advances,
we will make our moves;
we will all be heroes
of the eighth regiment.

5

Let us all face the artillery,
the entire regiment;
let's not fear the infantry,
run straight at the cannoneers

soldier, watch the bomb
which must burst on you,
and, at the moment it falls,
let us all cry, Long live the king![74]

For their part, Vendean leaders and officers had songs written by cleverer pens. Among others may be quoted the following (according to tradition, it was composed and sung by Charrette himself):

1

French people, people of brothers,
Can you see without shaking in horror
crime flourish the banners
of carnage and of terror?
The breath that an awful horde,
of assassins and of brigands,
soils with its fierce venom
the territory of the living.

2

What is this barbarous sloth,
hasten, sovereign people,
to send to the monsters of hell
all those drinkers of human blood.
War on all the agents of crime,
pursue them unto death,
share the horror that drives me.
They will not escape us.

3

Oh, may they perish, the vile ones!
and those devouring cutthroats,
who bear deep in their souls
the crime and the gall of tyrants.
Plaintive shades of innocence,

4

See already how they tremble,
the scoundrels dare not flee!
the trace of the blood they spew
would soon uncover their steps.
Yes, we swear on your grave,

be calm in your tombs,
the belated day of vengeance
finally makes your killers suffer.

by our unhappy country,
to make only a sacrifice
of these odious cannibals.

5

Representatives of a just people,
O you, human lawmakers,
whose august countenance
makes your vile assassins tremble,

follow the path of your glory,
your names dear to humanity,
fly to the temple of memory,
in the bosom of immortality.

One of the ruses of war was for the soldiers to sing something to the tune of *La Marseillaise.* From a distance, not understanding the words, the Blues thought these were their men and fell into the trap. The most famous incident was the battle of Le Pont-Charron, near Chantonnay, on March 19, 1793. The small regular army of General Marcé, which had come from La Rochelle, was beaten by peasants who had been enlisted a few days earlier. The soldiers, hearing the tune of *La Marseillaise,* thought the peasants were a column that had come from Nantes to meet them.

The strength of the resistance is thus explained by the conjunction of all these factors: new religious faith; love of freedom; rational organization, making it possible, among other things, to continue farming during fighting; perfect knowledge of the terrain; and popular solidarity.[75] We can therefore better explain what caused the astonishment of contemporaries and later scholars; Napoleon's admiration for the Vendée, "that people of giants"; and finally the failure of the invincible armies of the Republic that had brought the kings and peoples of coalition Europe to capitulation. Unfortunately, the Convention found no way out but the single and terrible solution of an order for systematic extermination.

The Confrontation Between Legitimacy and Legality in the Same Territory

WE CAN DISTINGUISH FOUR PHASES IN THIS PERIOD. FIRST, THE Republic geographically confined the cancer; then departmental authorities, with the help of the Convention tried to take the situation in hand. Under attack, the Vendeans consequently felt compelled to retreat to the other side of the Loire, abandoning the territory to the triumphant administration. The local population, desperate from having suffered so many outrages and repressive measures, rebelled again.

CONFINING THE CANCER

A report from Adjutant General Beysser, prepared on April 11, 1793, in Rennes and sent to citizen La Bourdonnaye, commander-in-chief of the coastal army, is explicit on the subject.[1] Charged with an "important mission related to recruitment for the army and for defense of the coast, and going through Vitré," he found the citizens in an uproar: "A crowd of armed peasants was advancing on the town. The outposts were retreating into the suburbs. All the residents were armed but unorganized, and they wanted to remain on the defensive." Beysser then took charge of the national guard, "defeated the enemy," and went to Rennes after taking the necessary measures "to prevent more gatherings and to make the town safe from attack."

The situation in this part of Haute-Bretagne created the same alarm as in Vitré: "communications were almost all intercepted," and terror "chained" some of the troops to their garrisons. Beysser then took command of the Thirty-ninth Regiment and of the national guard and began a long circuit that took him from Redon to Guérande, passing through Rieux and La Roche-Bernard, and returning through Le Croisic, Pontchâteau, and Savenay. The column, originally 1,200 strong, was soon reduced to 340 because of the need to leave soldiers in insurgent towns and villages (thirty in Rieux). The general was perfectly aware of his numerical weakness, but "in the kind of war in which he was involved, he had always believed, and experience had always shown him, that boldness is the true strength, and that victory always followed the banners of the most intrepid."

The means used were both effective and expeditious. After reorganizing the national guard and integrating them with his troops, Beysser spread terror by prohibiting the taking of prisoners, sharing the booty among the victors, and taking hostages. In Séverac, thirty or forty captured brigands were condemned to immediate execution by a military commission set up on the battlefield. In La Roche-Bernard, an inhabitant accused of assassinating the district procurator-syndic and another citizen had his head cut off by an ax on a cannon breech. "This terrible example," Beysser commented, "inspired salutary terror and contributed a good deal to peace," to the return of legal authority, and to the restoration of conscription.

On occasion, cannons were fired at churches, as in Campbon, or a few houses were burned.[2] These methods were designed to calm Breton peasants who were very sensitive to their material interests: "The death of a man is soon forgotten, while the memory of a house burned down lasts for years."

Beysser concludes his report by swearing that he had saved the Republic. In any event, this energetic attitude in the face of widespread disorder prevented the whole of the West from revolting. It also allowed the public authorities to implement the means necessary to take the situation in hand. In a few weeks, in accordance with the decree of the provisional executive council of March 23, the seaports were occupied and passages on the Loire guarded to prevent communications. New divisions were installed in Doué, Puy-Notre-Dame, Montreuil, Thouars, Ponts-de-Cé, and Saint-Georges, and along the Layon,[3] and columns set up "to follow the course of the Loire to Angers" in the north and "at the same time in the other direction into the department of Vendée to put the rebels in a crossfire . . ." Towns such as Niort, Angers,[4] and Nantes[5] were transformed into veritable armed camps.

Their fortifications were restored and strengthened, costing 51,886 livres in Niort.[6]

THE ADMINISTRATION'S ATTEMPT, TIMID THEN BOLD, TO TAKE THE SITUATION IN HAND (APRIL 1793–JANUARY 19, 1794)

The early victories of the Vendean army produced in the insurgents a euphoria barely troubled by the Republican initiatives, which had two objectives: to prevent at any cost an alliance between territories north and south of the Loire, and to surround the military Vendée in a slowly closing vise. There does not seem to have been an overall plan, but rather a series of converging personal and local initiatives, on which were grafted departmental measures.

Immediate Measures

To protect against the danger threatening them from every direction, the representatives of the people took several steps:[7] they dissolved the general councils and administrative bodies of the departments at war; they established cannon foundries in the major cities, as in the Cordelier cloister in Nantes;[8] they gathered all scattered weapons, pikes, scythes, iron-tipped staffs, axes, and other "offensive tools";[9] they made contracts for manufacturing ammunition;[10] they collected saltpeter; they arrested suspects;[11] they established committees of surveillance; they created two criminal tribunals; they ordered the immediate execution of the condemned. For this purpose, by April 7, 1793, Niort had ordered five decapitation machines.[12] The districts also decided to send a battalion of the national guard commanded by the tinsmith Meuris to threatened areas on the right bank.[13] Posts set at intervals between Nantes and Ancenis contained the flow of rebels from the north and confronted those from the south trying to cross the Loire. By the beginning of April, Thouaré had received 100 men, and then another 150; the mill of Auray, at the top of the hill of La Seilleraie, 200; Mauves, 250; the castle of Clermont, 50; Le Cellier, 130; and Oudon, 200, with the headquarters staff. These troops constructed "earthen fortifications" to protect themselves.

Aubinet was in command of the camp in Mauves and all the posts located downstream. On his arrival, he immediately disarmed suspect inhabitants. The operation was relatively easy on the right bank, particularly in Thouaré and Mauves, where the national guard seized the church bells. The people of Sainte-Luce, Doulon, and Carquefou offered more resistance and refused to enlist. The tenant farmers subject to onerous corvées to bring supplies to military posts, subjected in addition to requisitions of all kinds, protested indignantly. Soldiers, ill-fed and often without pay, wandered through the countryside, robbing and pillaging the farms and molesting the inhabitants. Even the municipalities most loyal to the district authorities made their complaints heard and protested against the long occupation by troops which threatened to starve the area.

On the other bank the situation was more complex. On April 3, a Republican column under the command of General Ferrant provisionally restored the municipal government of Le Loroux-Bottereau. The inhabitants had rallied to the army of Anjou and Poitou and deserted the village. But, isolated and with too few troops, the Republicans soon had to retreat.

On June 15, Aubinet crossed the river and marched to Mauves, in an attempt to put an end to repeated attempts by the local inhabitants to cross the river.[14] The Vendeans, wishing to facilitate the march of their principal army, decided to destroy or capture the posts protecting Nantes. Sheltered behind trenches on the banks of the Loire and supported by several artillery pieces, they opened a punishing barrage against the Republicans, whose forces consisted of merely 250 men of the Eleventh Battalion of Seine-et-Oise, 100 men of the old regiment of the Ile-de-France, and the detachment from Mauves; in addition, 250 national guards were stationed on the heights of Le Moulin-Cassé (d'Auray) two kilometers away, in order to prevent a diversion by the Vendeans through the valley of Gaubert. Meuris replied to the fusillade with his two cannons. They were too light and had a short range, thus doing no damage to the Vendeans, and nightfall put an end to the battle. The next day, an 18-gauge artillery campaign piece on a gun carriage was set up facing the trenches on the opposite bank, and Meuris waited for an attack that did not come.

In his report to the district, Meuris did not conceal his worry at the progress of his opponents. Foreseeing the need to evacuate Oudan, Le Cellier, and Clermont and to retreat, he planned to set up camp with his large artillery pieces on the heights of La Seilleraye, on the other side of Gaubert. His light artillery went along the neighboring hill and raked the Vendeans trying to cross the marsh to take him from behind. "There," said Meuris, "we will defend the approach to Nantes to the last drop of our blood." The approach of the Vendean army, on march toward the city, gave him no time to react. Two days later, his battalion headed swiftly north where he held up Cathelineau's vanguard for twelve hours.

On June 20, General Beysser returned to Le Loroux-Bottereau and occupied the canton with 2,400 men.[15] He and his troops were subjected to military tactics similar to those used against Meuris. The inhabitants scattered before them and constantly set ambushes on the road back to Nantes. The troops were attacked from every direction in the meadow of Les Places, between Cahérault and Bois-Courant, from trenches and the woods; the rout was complete. Many men were massacred, and some drowned trying to cross the Loire. In the southern part of the rebel departments the situation was as confused and catastrophic.[16]

Departmental and Regional Measures

At first, departmental and regional initiatives were limited to calling for help from neighboring departments. Only five of these responded favorably to requisitions for grain, which made possible the distribution of 13,500 quintals in six districts of Nantes.[17] Shoemakers and gunsmiths were constantly required by the army.[18] The workers in the munitions factories, including the one in Nantes, were exempt from military service.[19] Recruitment, according to the representatives of the people in Deux-Charentes, "surpassed expectations."[20] However, the results of recruitment were limited by the general anarchy, verbal exaggeration, and lack of coordination. The situation was particularly aggravated by the lack of munitions and the cowardice of troops who were capable, as in Machecoul, of rebellion.[21] On June 22, 1793, Guy Coustard, general of a division, made distraught by the cowardice of his men which had prevented him from recapturing Saumur, demanded to be reassigned to the army of the Alps.[22] For the same reason, General Laval refused to defend Nantes on July 14.[23] In an official letter of July 22, the administrative authorities of Nantes complained, "We know not through what fatality all our troops are infected by the contagion of panic fear; we need a miracle worker to save us."[24]

The situation was identical in the south. On May 8 the battalion from the Var refused to head for Parthenay and turned toward Saint-Maixent "with the flag."[25] The coastal army in La Rochelle behaved similarly. "For a long time," its general wrote, "desertion has been frightful and some of the cowards who have abandoned their flags have been arrested and imprisoned. We are certain that most of these soldiers are misguided rather than traitors to the country, and we are sure that, if we showed a good deal of fraternity for them, they would return from their errant ways . . ."[26] Generals were even accused of "seeking to disgust in every way the citizens who had been drafted . . ."[27] In a letter of June 26, 1793, to Bouchotte, the minister of war, Cottet, a commissioner of war, advised mistrust of volunteers, particularly those from the army of the North, who claimed "that there was injustice in sending them back to what they called butchery . . ."[28]

Moreover, the numerically reduced forces lacked everything. On June 18, 1793, Goupilleau, representative of the people for the army of the Coasts, called for uniforms, shirts, and shoes.[29] Some officers observed that because they had left in haste they had been unable to take their equipment and had been forced to abandon their horses or sell them cheaply. In May 1793 in Saint-Père-en-Retz Major Poulain noted that his detachment was in no condition to march; he even took it upon himself "to leave the soldiers lying rather than to see them perform their service naked as the day they were born . . ."[30]

This dramatic situation occurred because the workers attached to military stores had left their posts, some claiming the inadequacy of their wages, others demanding to be paid in hard currency.[31] The state of affairs was aggravated by the refusal of local populations and authorities to collaborate.[32] According to the generals, the people spread discord in the army and caused many desertions. The fearful local authorities were obliged to obey the committees of surveillance established on March 21, 1793, whose areas of responsibility were constantly growing.

In short, it was a state of total anarchy, which brought about a multitude of abuses:

> The soldier who does not do his duty is necessarily at loose ends; he comes out of one cabaret only to go into another, and he has soon spent all his pay. Once that is gone, he looks for expedients, and the first one that occurs to him is to sell his equipment. He soon finds that he lacks everything. Then he makes demands, and when he is refused, he pillages.

Official requisitions were doomed to failure because grain had become scarce and expensive: "all the fruits of the earth" were intercepted by the "brigands" who controlled the roads.[33] Concrete measures were taken: maximum prices were established, surpluses had to be sold, and the like. They failed, particularly for lack of wagons: the Vendeans had removed the wheels.[34]

The Vendean main army, in the meanwhile, had had a number of victories, but it was defeated before Nantes on June 19: "The whole population was armed[35] and Republicanism[36] enthusiastically cheered . . ." Cathelineau was mortally wounded. According to Napoleon, the Vendeans thereby lost the opportunity to carry off a decisive victory for all of France and to win the war. The public authorities profited from the opportunity to regroup and get organized; they consolidated fortifications, energized the army, and took a number of coherent measures by calling on new and "effective" men such as Carrier.

The decree of the National Convention of August 1, 1793, fit in with this logic.[37] Military forces were strengthened thanks to the army of Mainz and the obligatory requisition of conscripts[38] and volunteers from sixteen to sixty, in return for payment of thirty livres per man.[39] The only ones exempt were workers, and certain suppliers such as millers, bakers, gunsmiths, bomb makers, and the like; otherwise, "citizens armed for the defense of the nation would lack provisions, shoes, and other objects of the greatest necessity."[40]

Headquarters staff and the commissioners were purged, to be replaced by general officers and commissioners "of pronounced patriotism." Deserters, runaways, traitors, and those who threw away their weapons and sold their uniforms were punished. The organization of companies, foot soldiers, and workers was accelerated. Significant financial resources were devoted to this: 3 million francs in August 1793, to which were added voluntary subscriptions and new taxes. The principles of terror articulated by Beysser were already being applied. The same decree provided for sending combustibles of every kind to burn down woods, thickets, and shrubs (article VI), cutting down forests, destroying the hiding places of rebels, and seizing the harvests for the army. Measures were also taken to ensure a good supply of weapons, ammunition, and food.

This reorganized army was ready to march on the Vendée. Roux, the curé of Champagne-Mouton, noted that the general goodwill could not be doubted:

> The children of the Charente await only your orders to exterminate those brigands who are tearing the bosom of our dear nation. You, citizens, steady at your posts, watch for traitors and conspirators; never forget that as long as you nourish vampires and vultures within the walls of

this town, in reward for your indulgence they will one day drink deeply of the blood that has preserved them from the vengeance due to their offenses.[41]

On June 17, General Salomon set forth the tactical means to be used. "It is," he said, "a war of brigands, and we must all be brigands. At this moment, we must forget military rules, we must fall in a mass on these scoundrels and pursue them without mercy; the infantry must rout them out of the woods and shrubs and the cavalry crush them on the plain. In a word, we must not give them the time to rally."[42] Despite the scarcity of available means, this general plan was immediately implemented. In addition to troops, supplies were seriously lacking until September. Nantes, Angers, and Saumur had only 7,280 quintals of hay, 3,750 of straw, 14,040 of oats.[43] As for weapons, Nantes and La Rochelle had only 74 artillery pieces, 494,287 bullets, 75 caissons, and 399,901 flints, "a pittance," according to the generals.

On the other hand, a substantial medical service had been set up. It was made up of two stationary hospitals, one in Saint-Jean-d'Angély and the other in La Rochelle, and nineteen field hospitals, totaling 10,700 beds, in addition to local ambulances.[44] In order to supply them, the possessions of émigrés were centralized in departmental capitals and distributed.[45]

According to Abbé Robin, following the defeat of Cholet on October 17, "to avoid an army of cannibals coming to put everything to fire and the sword, we crossed the Loire in great numbers to form on the other bank an army of more than twenty thousand souls."[46] The priest was referring to the army of Blois. In La Chapelle-Heulin, its grenadiers had received precise orders from Carrier to disarm the entire population of the left bank of the Loire, from Nantes to Saint-Florent-le-Vieil. In reality, the number of Vendeans who crossed the Loire appears to have been greater than Robin's figure. According to contemporaries, more than eighty thousand used ships or the ford at Saint-Florent. They thereby accomplished an engineering feat that astonished Napoleon and can only be explained by the army's organization.[47] But the time of success had passed, all the more because soldiers operating in unknown territory were troubled by the mass of women, children, and old men accompanying them.

It is interesting to note the hostile role played by some towns and communes in Brittany and Normandy. In a report sent on 14 messidor of the year IV (July 2, 1796), the mayor of Saint-Georges-de-Reintembault boasted of having on many occasions resisted the assaults of "brigands" and even of

having marched against them at the siege of Granville.[48] The same thing
was true in Gahard, in the northern part of Ille-et-Vilaine.[49] The glorious
symbol of the tricolor atop the church was a reminder. The case was not
uncommon and can be explained primarily by the constant fear of pillage.
The departmental authorities of Ille-et-Vilaine, aware of their role, were
not inactive: "We must exterminate, pulverize the remnants of those impious hordes who massacre and burn as they flee."[50]

The body of Republican troops consisted of approximately twenty thousand soldiers: five thousand for the Westermann vanguard; three brigades
of five thousand for the Muller division; three thousand well-trained men
of the Tilly division (the army of Cherbourg); five to six thousand for the
Marceau division, made up of the coastal army of Brest and the reserves of
Klingler and Kléber.[51] Villages did not hesitate to sign up en masse. All
patriots were urged to arm themselves with rifles, swords, scythes, pitchforks, pikes, and other weapons, to collect four days' provisions, and to go to
the place designated by the army leaders. The men were paid according to
their rank: eight livres for the head of a division, seven for his adjutant, six
for a battalion leader, five for his adjutant, five for a quartermaster, a division
surgeon, and a captain, four for a lieutenant, three for a second lieutenant,
two for a sergeant, one livre and fifteen sous for a corporal, and one livre and
ten sous for a simple soldier—a windfall for many of these men who were
in a state of extreme poverty.[52] To this were added bonuses for "heads cut
off" (*sic*) and weapons found. At the same time, everyone charged with failing in his civic duty was disarmed and imprisoned. Women were drafted to
make cartridges, workers to "repair" swords and rifles, and bakers to bake
bread.[53] The houses of émigrés were even opened up in order to collect
mattresses and bedclothes, and the demolition of potential refuges, fortified
castles such as Combourg, was immediately stopped.[54]

As for the defeat of Granville, aside from the fact that the Vendean
army was decimated and worn out and the English absent, it was explained
by the fact that the forts had been strengthened and rearmed during the
months of April and May 1793, at a cost of nearly twenty thousand livres.
The expedition to the other side of the Loire was a veritable butchery, as the
generals themselves, such as Westermann, admitted. "Without stopping for
an instant," he wrote in his description of the Vendée campaign,

> I followed the enemy on the road to Laval where hundreds and thou-
> sands of brigands died at each step. They scattered in the woods, aban-

doning the army. The local citizens hunted them down and brought them in by the dozens. All were cut to pieces; I pursued them so closely that princesses and marquises abandoned their carriages and splashed through the mud. It was over heaps of corpses that I reached Laval on the evening of the 24th [December 14] with my cavalry and my artillery. The enemy had passed through and left the town in haste, so much so that women had disarmed the laggards. I followed the enemy to Craon, and from there to Saint-Mare [Saint-Mars-la-Jaille]. Each step, each farm, each house became the grave of a large number of brigands.[55]

"Hunger, fatigue, and sorrow," wrote Mme. de Lescure in her memoirs,

had disfigured all of us. To protect against the cold, as a disguise, or to replace worn out clothes, everyone was covered in rags. I was dressed as a peasant, wrapped in an old blanket and a large piece of blue cloth attached to my neck with strings. I was wearing three pairs of yellow woolen stockings and green slippers held on my feet by small ropes. Monsieur Roger Moulinier was wearing a turban and a Turkish costume, which he had taken from the theater in La Flèche. The Chevalier de Beauvilliers was wrapped in a lawyer's robe and had a woman's hat over a woolen cap.[56]

The recruits were undisciplined, drunk with blood and pillage, and some of them even lacked clothes. The representative of the people delegated to the armies reported: "We meet a large number of them barefoot in the mud and cold . . . risking having their courage held back by illness."[57] A letter from Division General Marceau, provisional commander-in-chief of the army of the West, to the minister of war is without ambiguity. It describes the attack on Le Mans, to which the Vendean army, exhausted and beaten by Tilly, had withdrawn:[58]

Dawn had barely broken when the light vanguard of the division asked my permission to make a bayonet charge, which I granted. A dismal silence, interrupted by the cries and moans of the dying, told me of the success of the venture. This truly Republican boldness disconcerted the enemy, who evacuated the houses en masse and thought only of seeking safety in flight. Then abandoning their baggage and throwing their rifles aside, they took the road to Laval. Our soldiers butchered

them horribly in the town and pursued them so relentlessly on the road
that they soon overtook not a few stragglers but the entire rear guard. I
had just ordered Westermann to take to horse with his entire cavalry;
the speed with which he acted did not give the enemy time to go very
far; he caught up to them, and charging them with the boldness you
know he has, he spread such terror among them that they thought only
of making an about-face to fight him off. Soon, the whole road was
covered with the dead. The infantry, following swiftly on the cavalry,
killed all those who had been left behind, as well as the men who tried
to escape their blows by leaving the main road. Despite the harassment
they suffered, our troops covered eight more leagues, constantly mas-
sacring and amassing huge spoils. We seized seven artillery pieces, nine
caissons, and countless women (three thousand were drowned at Pont-
au-Baux).[59] Many crosses of Saint Louis and Malta told us that we had
killed many ci-devants . . . If one of us had had the power of Joshua to
stop the course of the sun, it would have been the end of the brigands,
none would have escaped our blows. Some thought they could find
refuge in villages away from the road; the energy of the peasants must
have been a great surprise to them, for they showed the fighters no
mercy. I evaluate their losses for the day as at least seven thousand men
of their best troops. You will have trouble believing that ours amounted
to no more than twenty dead; it is true that we have one hundred fifty
wounded . . . Each man, on this decisive day, did his duty, and I would
have to name for you every individual if I wanted to name all who distinguished themselves . . .

"A delirium of blood and sadism," writes Gabory,

took hold of the soldiers; they kept the most distinguished women and
the nuns as spoils of war. They stripped corpses of their clothing and
carried them on their backs; they called this operation "unlimbering."
According to de Béjarry, "They went so far as to place cartridges inside
the bodies of victims and then to light them . . ." "Prisoners," said Abbé
Deniau, "old men, women, children, priests, were dragged to Ponthière
to be shot. An old and infirm priest was unable to keep up, so a soldier
stabbed him with his bayonet and said to one of his comrades, 'Take the
other end'; they carried him until the poor man gave up the ghost." A
man carting off corpses, according to a witness, stuck the victims on a

pitchfork and piled them in his cart. The Blues cut down victims without stopping: "I saw [corpses]," wrote Representative Benaben, "by the side of the road, a hundred of them, naked and piled on top of one another, a little like pigs being prepared for salting . . ." Twenty-seven Vendean women, with their children, brought back in carts from Bonnétable, were killed on the place des Jacobins by the *tricoteuses*. "This is the finest day we've had in ten months," exclaimed Prieux.[60]

On returning from this painful adventure, many Vendeans, seeing familiar country on the other side of the Loire, separated from the army and tried to return home. After going through Brittany, Mont-Saint-Michel, Normandy, Maine, and Anjou, the army returned to Ancenis on December 15 in order to attempt to recross the river. "But," according to Abbé Robin, "the enemies of God and religion had, like Pharaoh, intercepted all means of crossing by removing all boats and lining all the banks from Nantes to Orléans with armed cannon boats."[61]

In accordance with Rossignol's orders, Carrier himself had organized this defense. He explained to the Convention on December 20, 1793:[62]

> The affair of Le Mans was bloody, so deadly for them that from that town to Laval the earth is littered with their corpses. One gang of these scoundrels headed for Châteaubriant and the other for Ancenis . . . I took the promptest and most effective measures to prevent the crossing of the Loire and the Vilaine . . . The next day, I was informed by the captain of an armed ship that I had stationed on the left bank of the Loire that the Brigands, in large numbers, who had headed for Ancenis were trying to cross the river with barges, boats carried on wagons, and barrels they had taken from Ancenis and nailed on planks; but he told me at the same time that the artillery of our armed ships, destroying these boats, had killed and drowned them all. Indeed, all the crews did their duty so well that only very few brigands were able to cross the Loire. "The river was destined to be their grave," exclaimed Marceau.[63]

On December 28, Westermann and Adjutant General Hector entered Ancenis. "They dreadfully butchered the brigands; the streets of the town are littered with the dead . . . On the 29th, Westermann marched to Nort . . . he found three or four hundred brigands there and massacred all of them . . ." Abbé Robin made a similar observation:

A large part of the army perished while trying to cross and the other withdrew in small detachments toward the north and Savenay under the command of General Jacques-Nicolas de Fleuriot de La Freulière. A very small number survived by disappearing in the countryside. Abbé Robin was among them; he made a raft out of barrels and crossed under cover of darkness. He then hid in the parish.[64]

The Vendeans who reached the left bank of the Loire thus avoided the disaster of Savenay, which put an end to the Vendean epic on December 21. Indeed, Westermann, the great victor, boasted of it when he wrote of his joy a few days later to the Committee of Public Safety:

> There is no more Vendée, Republican citizens. It died beneath our free sword, with its women and its children. I have just buried it in the swamps and woods of Savenay. Following the orders you gave to me, I crushed the children beneath the horses' hooves, massacred the women who, those at least, will bear no more brigands. I have not a single prisoner to reproach myself with. I exterminated them all . . .[65]

A letter sent to Carrier confirmed the victory:

> Finally, the destructive core that came out of the Vendée has been destroyed. Westermann has purified the free soil between Savenay and Montoir, on the borders of our district. Individual reports tell us that the brigands lost seven thousand men, three thousand killed and four thousand prisoners. Only two hundred horsemen escaped from their captors. They will not escape from the pursuit of the Republican cavalry and the other forces surrounding them. We will further express our satisfaction, citizen, that at our demand, our communes have enlisted en masse, at least the greater number of them, and have headed for the posts assigned to them by the general. They have thus proved that their rallying was sincere.[66]

The head of the Fourth Brigade of the garrison in Angers boasted of "cooperating in a general destruction of the brigands." "Patience," he wrote to his fellow citizens of Niort, "we have them, and I assure you that we are making them dance the *carmagnole* in that town . . . They are often brought to us in groups of one hundred or one hundred and fifty. I have already given orders to different detachments of my brigade to lead them by torch at night to Ponts-de-Cé where, I believe, they are made to take baths."[67] Those who had taken refuge with their families fell, perhaps, from Scylla to Charybdis, because the triumphant administration was waiting for them. A war of unbearable barbarity, which nevertheless remained a war, was followed by a cool organization of genocide.

The Triumph of the Administration and Its Policy of Repression

"All men and women captured on returning from the Loire are led to Nantes and inhumanly massacred," wrote Abbé Robin.[68] This systematic killing was added to that organized by the patriots. The countryside, abandoned by the bulk of the population, was reoccupied, and inhabitants who had stayed behind or had not wanted to leave were massacred. The Republicans, representatives of legal force, then took revenge for the humiliation they had suffered. They too knew the country and could therefore guide the armed forces in complete safety to the hiding places of the fugitives.

The first roundups were so large that any form of trial was given up. There followed mass executions, which, it was believed, corresponded to the wishes of the Convention. Carrier wrote to the Convention about this on 30 frimaire (December 20), in order to secure its approval: "The defeat of the brigands is so complete that our posts kill them, capture them, and take them to Nantes and Angers by the hundreds. I ensure that they suffer the same fate as the others."[69]

"As for me," wrote General Bard,

I have ordered a hunt all around my headquarters, and on my shopping list I have asked that my hunters offer me twenty brigands' heads every day, all for my amusement. So far, the gift has been given me, but the game is beginning to grow very scarce. I will soon be forced, given the scarcity, to reduce the number agreed between my brothers and me. The last twenty that were presented to me were surprised in the middle of the woods in the midst of a ceremony for the tyrants.[70]

The guillotine, nicknamed the "mill of silence" or the "national razor," operated without interruption.[71] Vendeans arrested in possession of weapons were taken to department capitals and held in prisons called "antechambers of death" by Carrier. Everywhere, they were executed on the spot, without trial.[72] Because "holy mother guillotine" (an expression of Francastel) was too slow (in Cholet, it was reserved for important figures such as nobles, Vendean leaders, priests, and rich bourgeois),[73] use was made of more radical and effective means, as a citizen explained to a representative of the people named Minier:

> My friend, I inform you with pleasure that the brigands are thoroughly destroyed. The number brought here in the last week is incalculable. They come at every moment. Because shooting them takes too long and would use up powder and bullets, we've decided to put a certain number in large ships, to take them to the middle of the river, a half a league from the town, and to sink the ship. This operation is carried out daily.[74]

The procedure was simple: the human cargo was piled into an old fishing boat fitted with scuttles; once the boat was out in the water, the scuttles were shattered with ax blows, water flowed in from every direction, and in a few moments all the prisoners were drowned. Those who escaped were immediately put to the sword (hence the term *sabrades*, coined by Grandmaison) by the executioners watching the spectacle from their light ships. A witness at the trial of Carrier, Guillaume François Lahennec, testified as follows:

> At first, the drownings were done at night, but the revolutionary committee soon became familiar with crime; it only became more cruel, and from then on drownings were done in daylight . . . First, individuals were drowned with their clothes on; but later the committee, led by greed as much as by a refined sense of cruelty, stripped the clothes from those it wanted to immolate to the different passions driving it. I must also speak to you of "Republican marriage," which consisted of tying together, naked, under the armpits, a young man and a young woman and throwing them into the water . . .

A woman named Pichot, the twenty-fifth witness, who lived at la Sècherie in Nantes—that is, just opposite the drowning place—declared that on 2 brumaire she had seen carpenters make holes in a barge; the next day she learned that they had drowned "a large number of women, several of whom had children in their arms," and that another day sixty prisoners were found dead, suffocated in a fishing boat; they had been "forgotten" for forty-eight hours.

Carrier boasted to the inspector of the army, Martin Naudelle, "of having put two thousand eight hundred brigands through it," in what he called "vertical deportation in the national bathtub," "the large glass of the churchgoers," or "patriotic baptism." In fact, 4,800 people were swallowed by the Loire, "that revolutionary torrent," in the course of the autumn of 1793 alone.

At the conclusion of the trial against the proconsul, Carrier's lieutenant, Goullin, declared cynically:

> This tribunal should know that at the time the prisons were full of brigands and that the intent to sacrifice all prisoners was sufficiently justified by the circumstances, since there was talk of nothing but conspiracies. I maintain that these measures, however extreme they may appear, were inevitable. Parisians! if you thought the day of September 2 was necessary, our position was even more delicate than yours; these drownings, however revolting they may seem to you, were no less indispensable than the massacres which you carried out.

Many documents from municipal authorities, including those of La Tessoualle and La Chapelle-Bassemère,[75] in particular from Mayor Rivière des Hérys, reveal the active role played by councillors, "those localist patriots,"[76] in the denunciation and arrest of rebels. For example, on 29 nivôse of the year II (January 17, 1794), the newly appointed municipal agent, a native of La Chapelle-Bassemère, boasted of having himself brought about the capture of ten insurgents.[77] Just as municipal authorities participated in the repression and served as intelligence agents, district authorities went even further. On 4 brumaire of the year II (October 27, 1794), the national agent of Clisson, while hoping for a rapid return to prosperity in the country, wrote to the department: "The brigands who have returned will never repent of their error, they are fanatical and cruel. It is a crime that will end only with their lives."[78]

This policy was experienced as a great injustice by the people who, as the mayors themselves admitted, wished only to submit: "We warn you that there are many insurgents of our parishes who have returned from Ancenis and gone home. Those who had taken up arms have deposited them in our common house. All have promised never to take them up again against our brothers and have said that they submit to the laws, in accordance with the decree of the Convention of 2 nivôse."[79]

This first wave of repression was all the more pitiless because, according to the decision of the generals and commissioners, the bodies of the prisoners belonged to those who had denounced or arrested them.[80] So the inhabitants concluded that they had nothing more to lose, that they had to risk all.

The Uprising of the People and Its Final Crushing by the Legal Authorities: January 20 – May 1794

1. The Uprising of the People. Shattered, desperate, the target of incessant and murderous military actions, "on January 20, 1794, the elements of the royal Catholic army rallied and revolted a second time." They killed a "large number of scoundrels who had mistreated old men, women, and children who had remained in the region," according to Abbé Robin.[81]

These were essentially reprisals against representatives of the government, including municipal authorities.[82] The latter had indeed, by the law of 21 frimaire, been given the responsibility of applying measures for general security and public safety (article VIII), with the theoretical requirement of reporting to district authorities every ten days. The Vendeans were courageous, but they recognized that it was useless to surrender, as the government had urged; all those who had given up their weapons and begged for mercy from the Republic had been pitilessly massacred, despite official speeches promising them peace and security:

> It is time . . . for the French to be a single united family. Your population has disappeared, your commerce has been annihilated, your agriculture has been devastated by a disastrous war; your misdeeds have caused many evils and you know it, but the National Convention, great as the people it represents, forgets the past and forgives. A law of 12 frimaire decrees that all persons known as rebels of the Vendée and Chouans who give up their weapons within a month of its publication will be neither troubled nor pursued for their act of rebellion. This law is not a pretense of an amnesty; charged with carrying it out, bearing words of peace and consolation, we come, in the name of the National Convention, to speak to you the language of clemency and humanity.

If the bonds of blood and friendship are not entirely broken, if you still love your country, if your return is sincere, our arms are open, let us embrace each other like brothers.[83]

Other declarations offered assurance that the generals were charged with enforcing this order.[84] These were treacherous speeches, since the infernal columns (*les colonnes infernales*), launched on January 17, were beginning to ravage the country. Since the people were confronting almost certain death, their only hope for survival was an uprising, for this spontaneous action might help the resistance that still existed in the southern part of the region. Consequently, a second repression was organized.

2. The Second Repression Organized by the Legal Authorities.　Passions had been so stirred during the year 1793 that chemical weapons were even considered. A pharmacist from Angers named Proust invented a ball containing, according to him, "a substance able to poison the air of an entire region."[85] The idea was to destroy the Vendée by means of infection; tests on sheep, however, showed it to be ineffective. Carrier then proposed poison in the form of arsenic in the wells. Westermann had a similar but more treacherous idea: he asked for the shipment of "six pounds of arsenic and a cartload of brandy" which the Vendeans would be allowed to capture. It is not known why this plan was not followed. Probably, as Simone Loidreau suggests, there was uncertainty about the discipline and sobriety of the Republican troops and fear that they would secretly drink the brandy. On August 22, 1793, Santerre asked the minister of war for "mines! . . . powerful mines! soporific and poisonous smoke!" Following him, Rossignol asked the Committee of Public Safety to send the chemist Fourcroy to the Vendée to study possible solutions, as Santerre explained: "With mines, fumigations, or other means, we could destroy, put to sleep, asphyxiate the enemy army."

Ideas proliferated. Some even seem to have been acted upon, as this letter from Savin to Charrette on May 25, 1793, shows: "We were truly astonished by the quantity of arsenic that we found in Palluau at the beginning of the war. We were even constantly told that a foreigner, who they had with them and who was killed in this affair, was charged with carrying out the plan for poisoning."

To achieve their ends, the Republicans then decided to use the infernal columns, the flotilla, whose activity is almost unknown, and civil commissioners. The aim was to turn the Vendée into a "cemetery of France," "to transform the country into a desert, after having taken from it everything it contains."[86] The idea was already partially articulated on April 4, 1793: "The war that we have to carry on," the generals declared to the Convention,

> is all the more disastrous because the positions occupied by the brigands are of a kind to cause many losses if we do not use extraordinary means. Only one seemed to us likely to spare the blood of fathers of families who have left their homes to support the cause of liberty: burning the woods into which the brigands will retreat when pursued; demolition of all the mills set up in occupied territory that we traverse without being able to hold it also seemed to us a way to defeat them . . .[87]

In July, Barère went further and proposed a plan of "total destruction":

> The inexplicable Vendée still exists . . . It threatens to become a dangerous volcano . . . Twenty times, the representatives, the generals, the Committee itself have announced the imminent destruction of these fanatics . . . The brigands of the Vendée had neither powder, nor cannons, nor weapons, and not only the English, but our troops, sometimes by their defeat, sometimes by their flight, have supplied them with artillery, cannons, rifles . . . To the general mobilization of the Vendeans, we have opposed the general mobilization of the entire country . . . Never, since the wave of the Crusades, had there been seen so many men spontaneously coming together as there were suddenly beneath the banner of liberty to extinguish the long-burning fire of the Vendée . . . Panic terror struck all, frightened all, dissipated all like a puff of smoke . . .
> The Vendée is the hope of external enemies and the rallying point for internal enemies . . . That is the target that must be struck to strike them with the same blow. Destroy the Vendée! Valenciennes and Condé will no longer be under the control of the Austrians; the English will no longer trouble Dunkirk; the Rhine will be freed from the Prussians; Spain will be taken apart, conquered by the men of the South . . .
> Destroy the Vendée! and Lyon will no longer resist, Toulon will revolt against the Spanish and the English, and the spirit of Marseille will rise again to the heights of the Republican revolution . . . The Vendée is still the Vendée, this is the political coal burning up the heart

of the French Republic; this is where we must strike . . . We must bring desolation to their very endurance.[88]

The Convention adopted the decree on August 1, 1793, and ordered in article VI that

> the ministry of war will send combustible materials of every kind to burn woods, thickets, and shrubs; (art. VII) that the forests will be cut down, the hiding places of rebels destroyed; harvests will be cut by companies of workers to be taken to the rear of the army; and the cattle will be seized; article XIV, that the possessions of the rebels of the Vendée are declared to belong to the Republic: a portion will be taken to indemnify the citizens who have remained loyal to the nation for the losses they have suffered . . .

"The Vendée must become a national cemetery," exclaimed Turreau.[89]

By August 16, Representative Momoro was ready to go into action, taking a solemn oath:

> We will execute the decrees of the Vendée, we will burn down all the hiding places of the brigands, we will send the women, the children, and the old men to the rear of the army and we will shoot all the others. We will never be done with them otherwise, all these villains are fanatics. The minister of war is sending us large supplies of incendiaries.[90]

As Simone Loidreau has written, these documents for the moment were without effect: "It was infinitely easier to say than to do."[91] The Republican troops suffered reverses both in the Mauges and in the department of Vendée. "The inexplicable Vendée still exists," Barère bitterly admitted on October 1. There was an attempt to revive the idea after the battle of Cholet; but ten days later the Vendeans crushed the army of Mainz at Entrammes.

Throughout 1793 there were cases of destruction and massacres, but generally in connection with battles. The army of Mainz was not above reproach; on leaving Nantes, it was preceded by cartloads of sulfur and it destroyed several villages. Westermann lost no opportunity to burn and massacre, and his nickname, "butcher of the Vendée," preceded the battle of Savenay. Various massacres may be mentioned, such as the one in Noirmoutier from January 3 to 6, even though Haxo had given his word that all those who surrendered would be unharmed. Nor should we forget the burning of Machecoul by the men of Adjutant General Guillaume on December 17 or 18, 1793, because of "the troops' lack of discipline"; the destruction of Saint-Christophe-du-Ligneron on January 7; and of the area around Légé on January 11. In a letter to the Convention, Representatives Choudieu and Bellegarde admitted, as early as October 15, that the army of the Republic was everywhere preceded by terror: "fire and the sword are the only weapons we use."

The program of total destruction was in fact applied only following the proposal of the plan by Turreau, new commander-in-chief of the army of the West.[92] As soon as he arrived in the Vendée after the battle of Savenay, he wrote to the Committee of Public Safety to set out the plan he intended to follow and to ask for a document to cover him: "I ask you for express authorization or a decree to burn all the towns, villages, and hamlets of the Vendée that are not on the side of the Revolution and that constantly supply new support for fanaticism and the monarchy." There was no reply. When Carrier himself was informed, he refused to cover Turreau with a decree; he had made a similar request on December 28.[93] Further, the deputies on mission, Louis Turreau and Bourbotte, wishing to avoid any responsibility and any compromise, had themselves recalled to Saumur on the pretext of illness "resulting from the fatigues of their long mission."

General Turreau reiterated his demand, however, on January 17:

> My intention is certainly to burn everything, to preserve only the points necessary to set up camps needed for the annihilation of the rebels, but this great measure must be prescribed by you. I am merely a passive agent . . . You must also decide in advance on the fate of women and children. If they must all be put to the sword, I cannot carry out that measure without a decree covering my responsibility.

The same day, after heading his paper by hand with the slogan "Liberty, Equality, Fraternity, or Death," Turreau sent the following instructions to his lieutenants: "All the brigands found with weapons, or convicted of having taken up arms, will be put to the bayonet. The same thing will be done to women and children . . . Nor will persons who are merely suspect be spared. All the villages, towns, woods, and everything that can be burned will be consigned to the flames." Still worried by the silence from Paris, he

sent a new petition to the Committee of Public Safety: "The military promenade that I am considering will be finished on February 4 or 5. I repeat that
I consider it indispensable to burn towns, villages, and farms, or else I will
be unable to guarantee the annihilation of this horde of brigands which
seems to find new resources every day." From Cholet (Maine-et-Loire), on
January 31, he had expressed "the state of perplexity in which he was left."

It was not until February 8, 1794, that the Committee sent its agreement
through Carnot: "You complain, citizen, of not having received from the
Committee a formal approbation of your measures. They seem to it to be good
and pure, but, removed from the theater of operations, it awaits the results
before pronouncing judgment: exterminate the brigands to the last, that is
your duty . . ."[94] Turreau acknowledged receipt as early as February 11:[95]
"I have received with pleasure the approbation that you have given to the
measures I have taken . . ." He confided to Representative Bourbotte on February 15: "You know that without any authorization I adopted and carried
out the most rigorous measures to end this frightful war. The Committee of
Public Safety has granted its sanction to them, but I was calm, I relied, if
I may say so, on the purity of my intentions."

The same day, the Committee of Public Safety wrote to Representative Dembarère: "Kill the brigands instead of burning the farms, punish the
deserters and the cowards, and totally crush the horrible Vendée . . . Agree
with General Turreau on the most certain means of exterminating the en-
tirety of that race of brigands . . ."[96] One can see from reading this proclamation that the responsibility of the Committee of Public Safety was total.

On January 17, General Grignon, leader of the first column, harangued
his soldiers in these terms: "Comrades, we are entering rebel country. I give
you the order to put to the torch everything that can be burned and to put to
the bayonet every inhabitant you encounter on your way. I know that there
may be some patriots in this country; no matter, we must sacrifice them
all."[97] On January 19, Cordelier prepared instructions for his corps commanders concerning the execution of orders given by Turreau. The general
is "to concern himself personally" with the right bank of the Loire.

> Every day and in turn there will be a picket of fifty men with its
> officers and noncommissioned officers, which will be ordered to escort
> the road workers and to do their duty. The officer commanding this
> picket will take orders from the general every day before leaving and

will be responsible to him for their execution. To this end, he will act militarily with those road workers who attempt not to carry out what he orders and will have them put to the bayonet.

All brigands found in arms or convicted of having taken them up to rebel against their country will be put to the bayonet. The same will be done with women and children. Nor will those who are merely suspect be spared, but no execution can be carried out without previous orders from the general.

All villages, farms, woods, thickets, and generally everything that can be burned will be put to the torch, but only after removing from those areas all the provisions they may contain; but, we repeat, these operations may not take place until the general has ordered them. The general will designate those objects that are to be saved.[98]

Armed with this program, the Republicans stationed in the Vendée split into two armies.[99] The first, extending from Saint-Maixent to Ponts-de-Cé, was under the command of Turreau from Cholet; the second, from Les Sables-d'Olonne to Paimbœuf, was given to Haxo. The entire military Vendée was thus surrounded. The two armies each included six divisions: Dufour in Montaigu, Amey in Mortagne, Huché in Luçon, Grignon in Argenton-le-Château, Cordelier in Le Loroux; Beaufranchet, Grammont, Dalliac, Commaire, Charlery, Caffin, and Chalbos were set at intervals from the east to the west of the department of Vendée. Each of these divisions contained two columns broken down into twelve corps, supposed to advance toward each other, from the east or northeast, and from the west or southwest. In fact the second army had only eight columns, each of approximately eight hundred men, not doubled, and full of new recruits.

The rebel country had to be crossed in six days. And the route to be followed was specified in detail as well as the destination to be reached. The departure was set for January 21, anniversary of the execution of the king, and the arrival for January 27. As a result, the troops had to march "sometimes by day, sometimes at night."[100] It is difficult to provide a general narrative of "this military promenade." Some passages from daily reports sent by division commanders to their commander-in-chief need no commentary.[101]

On January 25, 1794, Caffin wrote to Turreau from Maulévrier: "For the good of the Republic, Les Echaubrognes is no more; there is not a single house left. Nothing escaped from the national vengeance. As I write, I am having fourteen women who were denounced to me shot . . ." The same day, the leader of another column, Grignon, who was operating a little farther on in Deux-Sèvres, wrote from Ceizay: "I am still continuing to have provisions removed, to burn and kill all who bore arms against us. It is going well, we are killing more than a hundred a day . . . I forgot to tell you that a dozen fanatics were arrested . . . they will go to headquarters."

On January 26, Caffin wrote again from Maulévrier:

> A detachment of one hundred fifty men left in La Tessouale evacuated and burned all the farms on the road to Saint-Laurent . . . I hope to have two hundred bulls and cows before this evening. All the cattle are scattered through the fields. Yesterday I had all the mills that I saw burnt . . . Today, with no risk, I can burn three-quarters of the town of Maulévrier.

On January 27, Cordelier wrote from Jallais: "I had ordered that all the scoundrels encountered be put to the bayonet and that all the farms and hamlets neighboring Jallais be burnt; my orders have been promptly executed and, at this moment, forty farms are illuminating the countryside . . ." On January 31, Caffin wrote yet again from Maulévrier:

> I must inform you that the entire village of Yzernay was burned yesterday, with no man or woman found in it. There were still four windmills which I am having burnt this morning, not wishing to leave a single one.
>
> This morning, I have had all the remaining houses in Maulévrier burnt, not leaving a single one, except for the church where there are still a number of things that it would be appropriate to send for later . . .
>
> The village of Toutlemonde was burned the day before yesterday.

On February 1, Caffin wrote again, from Saint-Laurent:

> At noon I write you again from Saint-Laurent . . . Since I absolutely intend to go to La Verrie this evening, I fear I will be unable to burn everything as I had wished . . . I had thirty-two women who were in the convent taken to Cholet . . . I found about twenty men left whom I had shot before leaving. If I find others on my way, they will suffer the same fate.

On February 3, in La Verrie, Caffin concluded: "I must inform you that tomorrow morning, with my column, I will go to burn this village [La Gaubretière]; to kill everyone I encounter without consideration, as the refuge of all the brigands. Everything will be put to fire and the sword . . ."

Turreau was not to be outdone, as he explained in his reports to the Committee of Public Safety and the ministry of war. On January 22, he wrote, "Our troops are sacrificing to the shades of our brothers the scattered remnants of that execrable army." On January 24, he stated, "My columns have already accomplished wonders; not a rebel has escaped from their pursuit . . . If my intentions are well supported, within two weeks, there will exist in the Vendée neither houses, nor food, nor weapons, nor inhabitants. All the woods and tall forests of the Vendée must be cut down." Turreau wrote on January 31:

> They [the columns] have put to the bayonet all the scattered rebels who were waiting for a new signal to revolt . . . We burned farms, villages, towns . . . You cannot imagine the quantity of grain and fodder we found in the farms and hidden in the woods.
>
> I have given the most precise orders that everything be removed from this accursed country and carried to the storehouses of the Republic. This morning a convoy left for Saumur that was almost two leagues in length.

Subordinate officers, often disgusted, also provided accounts. "Amey," according to a report by a police officer named Gannet,

> has the ovens lit and when they are hot enough, he throws the women and children into them. We protested to him; he answered that this was how the Republic wanted to bake its bread. At first, brigand women were condemned to this kind of death, and we did not say very much; but today the cries of these wretches have provided so much amusement for Turreau's soldiers that they intend to continue with these pleasures. With no royalist women left, they are going after the wives of true patriots. Already, to our knowledge, twenty-three have suffered this horrible torment and they were guilty only of adoring the nation . . . We wanted to interpose our authority, but the soldiers threatened us with the same fate . . .

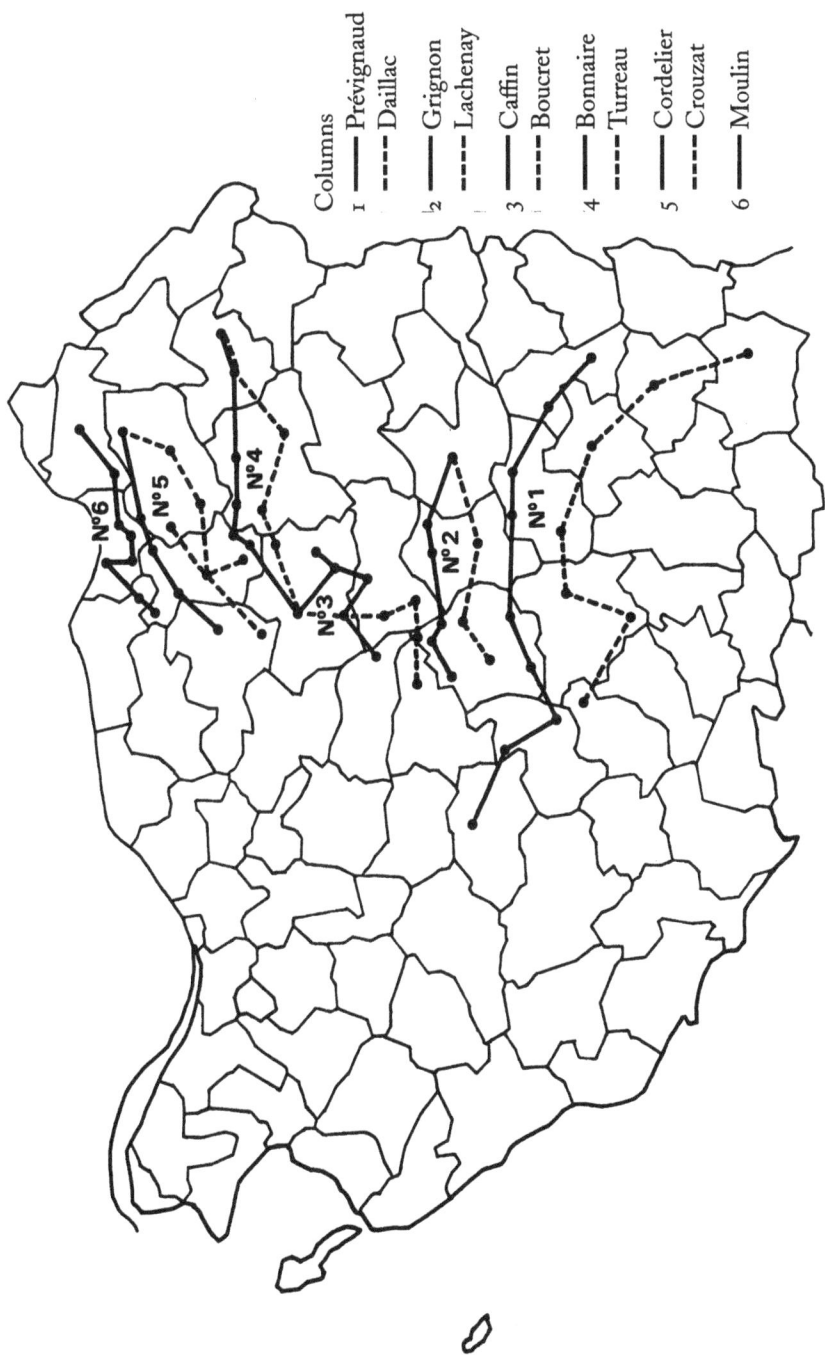

Columns

1 ——— Prévignaud
  ------ Daillac

2 ——— Grignon
  ------ Lachenay

3 ——— Caffin
  ------ Boucret

4 ——— Bonnaire
  ------ Turreau

5 ——— Cordelier
  ------ Crouzat

6 ——— Moulin

Map 8.1. Plan of the first "promenade" of the infernal columns (January 21–27, 1794)

The president of the district expressed his surprise on January 25: "Your soldiers, who call themselves Republicans, indulge in debauchery, dilapidation, and all the horrors of which even cannibals are incapable." Captain Dupuy of the "Liberté" battalion sent two equally explicit letters to his sister on 17 and 26 nivôse (January 1794):

> Down dreadful roads our soldiers cross the drear deserts of the Vendée . . . Everywhere we go we bring fire and death. Neither age, nor sex, nor anything else is respected. Yesterday, one of our detachments burned a village. A volunteer killed three women with his bare hands. It is horrible, but the safety of the Republic urgently requires it . . . What a war! Every person we see, we shoot. Everywhere the earth is littered with corpses; everywhere flames have brought their devastation . . .

"Offenses are not limited to pillage," wrote Lequenio.

> Rape and the most outrageous barbarity show up at every turn. We have seen Republican soldiers rape rebel women on stones piled on the sides of the main roads and then shoot and stab them when they leave their embraces; we have seen others carrying nursing babies on the point of a bayonet or a pike that had run through mother and child in a single stroke.

And a surgeon named Thomas wrote: "I have seen women and men burnt. I have seen one hundred fifty soldiers mistreat and rape women, girls of fourteen and fifteen, and then massacre them, and toss from bayonet to bayonet tender infants left next to their mothers stretched out on the ground."

Baudesson, general manager of military supplies who had followed the Bonnaire division from Doué to Cholet, made the following statement: "The road from Vihiers to Cholet was littered with corpses, some dead for three or four days, others having just expired. Everywhere the fields next to the main road were covered with victims with their throats cut . . . Here and there scattered houses were half burnt . . ." In ventôse of the year II, General Avril rejoiced in having "put down the rebels of Saint-Lyphard to the number of one hundred. A number of them were roasted when all the houses in town were burnt."[102]

The action of the infernal columns lasted in fact for four months, from about January 21 to May 15, 1794.[103] Only the first "promenade" had a precise plan. Turreau encountered only two minor problems: General Duval, unable to march because of a wound received at the battle of Moulin-aux-Chèvres, had to put his division under the command of battalion chief Prévignaud; and in Saint-Florent, General Moulin, although "as good a patriot as his colleagues," could muster only a small column of 650 men: most of the soldiers had already been sent to Basse-Vendée.

By February 2, each column had reached its intended destination after carrying out the program to the letter. Simone Loidreau points out that there were varying degrees of cruelty, sadism, and sacrilege. It can be said that columns two and five were particularly noteworthy, whereas Prévignaud, temporary commander of the first, and particularly Bonnaire, general in charge of the fourth, though great burners of houses, seem to have killed much less.

The first column was made up mostly of inadequately armed conscripts, which explains its moderation, which was in fact only temporary. Moreover, the commander was disappointed in his itinerary, the southern border of the military Vendée, for, he said, "All the places I have passed through are inhabited by patriots." That did not prevent his adjutant, Daillac, from committing a horrible massacre in La Châtaignerie, while the town at the time boasted of "hunting rebels day and night like wild beasts," nor Prévignaud himself from destroying by fire the village of La Vendrie near Tallud-Saint-Gemme.

Grignon, commander of the second column, crossing the Vendée from east to west, from Argenton to Les Herbiers, achieved hideous notoriety in most of the towns he went through. According to his own expression, he had lit many "bonfires." He told the story himself in a report sent to Turreau from Bressuire:

> "I have just arrived with my column, after crossing from right to left the woods and hamlets from Argenton to Bressuire. I have had many farms burned, particularly around the town of Saint-Aubin-la-Plaine, where I found a black and white flag in the church. The men and women that were there were all put to the bayonet . . . I would have burned more farms if I had not found a good deal of provisions . . . I have heard no news from the columns to my left and right: I am waiting for them

to come parallel with me; but that will not stop me from burning what is near Bressuire . . ." In Etusson, in the villages of Longueville, Le Breil, La Charbonnière, and Laval, Grignon seized twenty-four old men, women, and children and had them shot in a field. In Chambroutet, he ordered that a large number of inhabitants have their throats cut.[104]

He expressed his joy on January 24: "The soldiers break their weapons when they kill the brigands they encounter in the woods and thickets; wouldn't it be better to kill them with gunshots, which could easily be done?" On January 26, Cerisay was put to the torch: "I've had a castle belonging to Lescure burnt, and two or three others. Yesterday cost the lives of perhaps three hundred rebels; among them was a chevalier of Saint Louis who was fleeing on horseback with his servant; I am sending you his decoration."

The same day in La Pommeraie, he "burned and broke heads as usual." On January 27, he entered La Flocillière. Chapelain, the mayor and captain of the national guard, tried to intercede with him to save his "unhappy town." Grignon threatened to have him shot and ordered that the whole population have its throats cut. He did not hesitate to kill even Republicans. "I know that there are patriots in this country," he noted. "No matter, we have to sacrifice all." A patriot and his maidservant were cut to pieces. "When everyone was sacrificed in La Flocellière," according to Mayor Chapelain, Grignon decided to go to Pouzauges: "In vain, former Representative Dillon, curé of Le Vieux Pouzauges, tried to plead the cause of his fellow citizens; in vain. Grignon put it to the torch. At this time, followed by his staff, he went up to the castle and had the fifty odd people inside shot." Then he headed for La Meilleraie, caught several families from the town of La Vinatière and other neighboring hamlets, and carried out a "frightful massacre."

The inhabitants of the town who had been given certificates of loyalty had stayed home, full of confidence. Abbé Rabillé, a constitutional curé and an "excellent patriot," according to Lequinio, was among them. Grignon had them gather in the church, and no one suspected his plan. There they were searched, their gold and silver were taken, and they were pushed outside one by one and shot in the cemetery. Only one managed to escape, a man named Pain de La Godinière.

Then Grignon marched on Le Boupère where he found the national guard in arms. He hesitated to charge them but did manage to disarm them. Nineteen prisoners had their throats cut; three thousand bushels of wheat, eight hundred thousand of hay, and three thousand pounds of wool were put to the torch. In the village of Les Combes, *sieur* Vende was horribly mutilated. In Bois-Rousseau near La Bonnelière, Abbé Gaudin, curé of Saint-Germain-l'Aiguiller, was murdered. Seventy people were shot in the castle of Saint-Paul.

On January 31, Grignon arrived in Ardelay, which suffered the same fate. A report drawn up by the revolutionary committee of Fontenay, printed in *Le Courrier républicain* (no. 364, p. 32), recounts the terrible experience of citizen Marianne Bastard, from the commune of the little town of Les Herbiers:

> When the volunteers of the Grignon division came to her house, she went to meet them to show them a certificate she had from General Bard and to offer them refreshment; they raped her and then set fire to the farm. These monsters then wanted to burn her with her cattle, but she managed to escape, running to her mother's house; she found her mother with an arm and her head cut off.

In Les Herbiers, Amey, Grignon's faithful lieutenant, was charged with applying the Convention's plan. On the night of February 1, the town was put to the torch. "No house was spared," he wrote to Turreau. "The municipal authorities were obliged to give me a list of the inhabitants who had been brigands and borne arms against us. I had them put in prison. On the way, they rose up against the guard, who fired on them."

The third column also demonstrated unprecedented savagery. Its route, south of Cholet, led Boucret to La Tessoualle, which he burned; all around were fields of broom plants where terrified women and children had taken refuge. When the column arrived, they were mercilessly killed. From there he went to Moulin-le-Temple, Mallièvre, and Châtillon; everywhere he burned, and cut the throats of all he encountered. He proclaimed his satisfaction to Turreau: "All the territory I have covered has been minutely searched, there is nothing left to ask for, nothing has escaped from my watchfulness." From there he headed to Saint-Amand and then to La Boissière; he next reached Les Epesses, "where he put everything to fire and the sword."

Caffin, his second in command, settled in comfortably in Maulévrier, where he directed operations. By January 22 there had been massacres in the towns of Toutlemonde, Le Grand-Pin, Les Nillères, Les Guyonnières,

Les Jahaudières, and Lala. On January 23 it was the turn of the town of Les Echaubrognes, where he boasted of not leaving a single house intact. Material destruction, thefts, and human losses piled up.

The two columns of the Fourth Division, in the center, which followed the commander-in-chief, led by Bonnaire, carried out the plan of burning, but committed fewer excesses against the inhabitants than the two preceding columns. But they did pile up ruins: the first division burned all the villages around Concourson and Vihiers; the second set fire to the castle of Bitaud and destroyed all the houses on the road to Les Cerqueux and as far as Coron. It even tried to burn the forest of Vézins, but it was January, it had rained a good deal, and the trees did not burn.

Anjou was reserved for the fifth column, commanded by Cordelier. His lieutenant, Crouzat, ravaged on his way Gonnord, Joué, Chemillé, Chanzeaux, and Melay. His method was familiar: first he searched the houses, taking out the women, children, old men, and the sick, whom he forced to witness the pillage of their homes and of the church, then he put everything to the torch. Then he lined up the inhabitants and shot them.

Cordelier owes his reputation to his unutterable cruelty and his frightful exploits. Having set out from Brissac, like Crouzat, he attacked Beaulieu, whose inhabitants he did not spare even though he called them "good people," then he went to Saint-Lambert-du-Lattay, where he killed patriots and "royalists" indiscriminately and amused himself by dragging some victims who had been tied to horses' tails. He stayed two or three days in La Jumelière, where he had "operations to carry out in the area": burning five castles and sending one column against Saint-Lézin and another against Neuvy "with orders to put it to the torch and to put all the inhabitants to the bayonet." At the same time, he hunted down brigands hidden in the woods between La Jumelière and Chemillé. "Everything was promptly carried out," he noted with satisfaction. He was less pleased with his march on Jallais. "It is with regret," he wrote, "that I inform you that we encountered nothing."

Moulin, in charge of the sixth column, not finding the men he needed, did not leave until January 24; but he had only a short distance to cover in the northern part of Mauges. He burned Mazé, devastated the towns of Saint-Laurent and Sainte-Christine, and complained of "impassable" roads and the rain that kept the woods from burning.

For the two or three days following their arrival, the columns stayed put. They used this apparent rest to spread out from the towns serving as garrisons in order to pillage, burn, and kill in remote farms. When Grignon and Lachenay joined forces in Pouzauges, the town and its surroundings lived through an atrocious nightmare. This was also the time when a detachment under the command of battalion chief Chaud left Cholet to reconnoiter in Chemillé; the bloody traces of this column could be found in all the farms along the road.

Cordelier also took advantage of this respite to search the area around Jallais and to "put to the bayonet all the scoundrels he might encounter and burn the hamlets and farms." Daillac went through the parishes of Sainte-Hermine, Saint-Simon-la-Vineuse, La Réorthe, and Bazoges-en-Pareds.

Other "promenades" followed, but as Turreau himself explained on February 8, "Since the enemy has no plan, it is impossible for me to make one myself."[105] To protect against any possible problems, Vimieux, the general in charge of operations, sent out various instructions:

> We must have fortified camps, and as a consequence I require that they be surrounded front and side by a circular ditch eight feet wide and five feet deep; earth thrown into it will form a kind of parapet. Roads wide enough for the cavalry to pass four abreast will be built on the sides of each camp and blocked, as much as possible, by chevaux-de-frise or tree branches . . .[106]

This fortification, simple but sufficient to protect from surprise, could be supplemented with others by generals in charge of the camps if the locality or the small number of troops required it.

> What I recommend particularly to the care and attention of the generals is the advantageous position of a camp, the appearance of the tents, their perfect alignment, the intervals maintained between battalions, the order of stacks of arms, the cleanliness of the streets, the tents of general officers aligned and set according to rank, the kitchens to the rear, the front always completely free, finally the most complete execution of the camp regulations.

The guards were not forgotten: "Sentinels should be placed so that a ring surrounds the camp and no one, officer or soldier, can pass through it without express written permission from the general officer in command." Troops in camp had to be kept continuously active:

Strong detachments will go out daily for fodder and to break up gatherings that might take place in the area and particularly to protect the work of the sappers engaged in scouting the country ahead, on the sides of the camp, and along the main roads. Those who may be nearby and who are not on duty or in a picket will exercise at least once each day, and the generals will pay close attention to their training.

Communications between camps should be regularly maintained: "Commanders will take care to have couriers always a little to the rear to prevent their being intercepted." In order to prevent any Vendean from escaping, Turreau ordered the beefed-up national guard border posts "to watch by day and light up by night all passages in order to arrest anyone who might come by." He also decided to place Moulin in command of the division that he left in Cholet. As for the other columns, Turreau re-formed only eight, which were always to "march in parallel" so as to be able to come to one another's assistance. According to Division General Robert, on April 2, 1794, the army comprised 103,812 soldiers, 95,735 infantrymen, 4,108 cavalry, 3,809 cannoneers, and 160 artillerymen. These troops were divided into three centers: the coastal army of Brest, the coastal army of Cherbourg, and the army of the West, smaller than the two others.

Repression remained as bloody as before, as Turreau wrote to Huché on March 1: "Courage, comrade, and soon the environs of Cholet will be cleaned out of rebels. If each general officer or superior officer killed them by the hundreds as you do, we would soon be at an end."[107] This was a reply to a letter from Huché, who boasted on February 27 of having dispersed the Vendeans in a

fine way . . . More than five hundred, men and women, were killed . . . I had the bushes, ditches, hedges, and woods searched; and that's where they were found huddling. Everyone was put to the sword, for I had forbidden that ammunition be used if they were found like that. When I arrived in La Verrie, I put to the bayonet everyone I found.

The better to define what happened at the local level, we will take the example of Le Loroux-Bottereau, the canton of which was particularly affected. A column of 1,870 men from the interior of the country, reinforced by 800 fighters from the North, struck La Chapelle-Bassemère twice (on

March 10 and 17). Disorganized, the inhabitants, who had prepared a plan of defense based in the woods on the banks of the Loire,[108] were backed against the river, which was patrolled by ships of the Republican navy. A manhunt took place, supported by foot soldiers conscripted in the patriotic communes, where local people served as informers, and even by trained dogs. Women were not excluded because, according to Turreau, "they are more than ever involved."[109]

On the morning of Sunday, March 9, three hundred inhabitants of Le Loroux-Bottereau tried in vain to stop the column coming from Vallet.[110] After a two-day massacre in the canton capital, during which Cordelier made "the rebels dance a complete *carmagnole*," the column went through La Chapelle to go to Saint-Florent-le-Vieil.[111] "An infernal army reappeared a few days later, on March 10, and put everything to fire and the sword. All who had escaped from the first fell beneath its blows."[112] In speaking of a first army, Abbé Robin was alluding to the five thousand Blue prisoners released by Bonchamps in Saint-Florent-le-Vieil on October 18. After proclaiming their gratitude to "their liberator," they devastated La Chapelle and assaulted the population of women, children, and old men who had stayed behind.

The column of General Cordelier went through Beauchêne, then arrived in the town, which it put to the torch.[113] According to tradition, only the town hall and the parsonage, used as a prison, escaped from the disaster. The church burned. In this fire, "the ornaments and all the sacred vessels that Abbé Robin had hidden when the persecution began" disappeared. Thereafter, many inhabitants took refuge in the forest of Léppo, in Montrevault.

However, the column was merely passing through the commune. It left, going through La Guillonnière and Le Bois-Guillet, leaving behind at least seventy-two corpses. After five days of killing in Saint-Florent-le-Vieil, the same troops took the road back to Nantes. They stopped again at La Chapelle on March 17 and spent several days there. The soldiers, dead drunk, were not content with destroying and killing only what they found on their way; they spread terror throughout the communal territory. One hundred eighteen "massacres" were counted, but "these figures are far from being complete," Abbé Robin explained. The population defended itself energetically, particularly in Le Grand-Champ and La Mouchetière, which, according to tradition, were covered with corpses.[114] Peigné and the abbé provide horrible descriptions of the killing:

There were poor girls, completely naked, hanging from tree branches, hands tied behind their backs, after having been raped. It was fortunate that, with the Blues gone, some charitable passersby delivered them from this shameful torment. Elsewhere, in a refinement of barbarism, perhaps without precedent, pregnant women were stretched out and crushed beneath wine presses. A poor woman in that situation was cut open alive in Bois-Chapelet, near Le Maillon. A man named Jean Lainé, from La Croix-de-Beauchêne, was burned alive in his bed where he was confined by illness. A woman named Sanson, from Le Pé-Bardou, suffered the same fate after being half massacred. Bloody limbs and nursing infants were carried in triumph on the points of bayonets.

A girl from La Chapelle was taken by torturers who raped her and then hung her, head down, from an oak. Each leg was attached separately to a branch of the tree and separated from one another as far as possible. In that position they split her body with a sword all the way to her head and cut her in two.[115]

In the castle of La Vrillère, the Blues seized two girls and tried to take them away as prisoners. One of them clung to her crippled mother's chair. A soldier, furious at being unable to make her let go, unsheathed his sword and cut off her hand.[116] In other cases, women were thrown out of windows onto bayonets pointed in their direction.[117] There were many more atrocities on that March 17, which Peigné called the day "of the great massacre." "In the village of La Trônière," he writes,

> you can still see today a little street where the corpses were piled up and from which flowed a stream of blood as far as Le Guineau. In La Pironnière and in several other places, children in their cradles were pierced and carried still breathing on the points of bayonets . . . In La Grange, a commune of Le Loroux-Bottereau, they saved the life of a child who had been torn from the breast of his mother whose throat had been cut and on whom her already livid lips were still fastened . . .

Inhabitants of La Chapelle still speak of the "damsels' hole" on the road to Le Guineau. Girls were thrown into it and then drowned.[118] If they did not drown, they were "led behind the house"—that is, shot. Some villages were more affected by repression than others. This was the case for Beauchêne, the residence of the family of Abbé Robin. The killing there was systematic. On March 10, twenty-six inhabitants were massacred, including eleven women, nine children younger than eleven, and three babies less than a year old. On March 17, the goal that had been so long sought was reached: the abbé's own sister, the widow Bontemps, was captured and taken as a prisoner to Nantes with two of her daughters, Françoise-Marie, born March 26, 1770, and Mathurine-Jeanne, born September 6, 1774. One of the brothers, François, who had returned wounded from the war, aged twenty-two, was killed.[119]

Two days later, on 28 ventôse, the three women were incarcerated in the women's prison of the Bon-Pasteur. On 21 floréal of the year II (May 10, 1794), they were tried by the military commission presided over by Lenoir. There was no appealing the verdict. It

> declares the widow Bontems [*sic*] fanatic and an instigator, protecting refractory priests and evidencing decided devotion for the counterrevolution under the veil of patriotism, having supported her children in brigandage and having made them change according to circumstances, considering the acts of patriotism that she performed for some Republicans only to find the means to escape from the law; the Bontems daughters, fanatics, influenced by their uncle Robin, a refractory priest, and by their mother, have heaped scorn on the sacred principles of the popular constitution and the misfortunes of their fellow citizens of the same commune and even displayed their fanaticism by wearing little standards in processions. [It] condemns the widow Bontems to death and her daughters to detention until the coming of peace.

The sentence was carried out within twenty-four hours. The younger of the survivors, Mathurine-Jeanne, died in the hospital on 13 fructidor of the year II (August 30, 1794). The elder, Françoise-Marie, married her jailer, François-René Fleurdepied on 22 nivôse of the year III (January 11, 1795).

The attack on Saint-Julien was even more dramatic. According to Pétard, it took place in the middle of the night, around three in the morning:

> Barges landed on the bank and bands of soldiers rushed into the valleys, swords and torches in hand. Cordelier, for his part, sent his troops across the fields, with orders to kill all and massacre all. The inhabitants, surprised in the middle of darkness, fell to the number of several hundred. Entire families disappeared.

Fire broke out everywhere. The entire town was in flames: only four houses were spared, among them the presbytery, intended for use as a military storehouse.

A few inhabitants managed to flee in the darkness. They hid in thickets, behind hedges, in grain silos, wherever they could find refuge. After the Blues had gone, they ran to put out the fires and save some of their possessions. It is said that fire was set four or five times in the Bois-Adam house; each time an old farm woman managed to put it out and to save the home of her employers. [120]

Testimony about atrocities committed is plentiful. In Clisson, mutilated corpses and still living people were thrown into a well of the castle;[121] forty-one people were drowned in Bourgneuf-en-Retz.[122] In Angers, the skin of the victims was tanned, to make riding breeches for superior officers. "The man named Pecquel, surgeon-major of the 4th Battalion of the Ardennes," explained a witness, Claude-Jean Humeau, in a declaration to the tribunal of Angers on November 6, 1794, "skinned thirty-two of them. He tried to force Alexis Lemonier, a leather worker in Ponts-de-Cé, to tan them. The skins were transported to the house of a man named Langlais, a tanner, where a soldier worked them. These skins are at the home of Prud'homme, a sleeve maker . . ."[123] Another witness, the shepherd Robin, recounted that the corpses "were skinned to the middle of the body because they cut the skin below the belt, then along each thigh down to the ankles, so that after it was removed the breeches were partially formed; all that remained was to tan and sew . . ."[124] A soldier confessed to the countess of La Buère that he did the same thing in Nantes and sold twelve skins in La Flèche.[125] In this, these men were merely following Saint-Just, who, in a report to the Commission of Extraordinary Means dated August 14, 1793, declared: "In Meudon, they are tanning human skin. Skin coming from men has a consistency and quality superior to chamois. That from feminine subjects is suppler, but it has less strength . . ."[126]

In Clisson again, on April 5, 1794, soldiers of General Crouzat burned 150 women to extract fat from them. "We made holes in the ground," one of them testified, "to place cauldrons to catch what fell; we had put iron bars above and set the women on top . . . then above them was the fire . . . Two of my comrades were with me for this affair. I sent ten casks of it to Nantes. It was like embalming fluid; it was used in hospitals."[127]

The popular societies, the directories, and town councils were not far behind, as in Angers, which made a decision "apt to strike the popular imagination":

On 16 frimaire of the year II of the French republic, one and indivisible, the medical officers, following the command of the representatives of the people, were invited to go to the common House so that they might participate in the decree of the said representatives providing that the heads of all the brigands who died under the walls of this town will be cut off and dissected and thereafter set on the walls. The laboratory of the School of Surgery of this town has been selected to do this work.[128]

However, the medical officers do not seem to have been very eager to respond to the summons, because three days later the general council was obliged to rescind its decision, not knowing what to do with the heads:

Citizens Pinval and Chotard, charged with ascertaining from the representatives of the people what should be done with the heads deposited in the storehouse of citizen Delaunay, that the medical officers had neglected to take for dissection as they had been commanded to do, and that smell very bad, report that the representatives have decided that they should be buried. It has therefore been decided that they will be immediately buried . . .

On the other hand, these excesses seem to have troubled some inhabitants of Nantes. Some women adopted a substantial number of children who had been transported to the town to be shot with their mothers. Prisons were so full that the representatives of the people asked the municipal authorities of Nantes for new premises, "secure and spacious." The coffee warehouse, a very large building, was selected.[129] Because of the deplorable condition of the premises and the bad diet, a typhus epidemic broke out causing massive deaths. Four hundred prisoners died in a month, as indicated in a report by the "charitable" commissioners, Allard, Louis Cheptel, and Robin, entitled "Work for the Inhumation and Interment of Dead Animals."

A few days later, Turreau summed up his campaign: "In this march, we have destroyed at least two thousand five hundred brigands whose terror had caused them to hide in various places." In a report to the ministry of war on March 18, he was even more precise. He declared that he had set up camp on March 14 under the cannon of Saint-Florent, where he had joined up with Cordelier: "We marched in parallel in five columns, carrying out the revolutionary measures that experience had convinced me were the only ones likely to annihilate the Vendée war."[130] This form of repression lasted until November 1794. The columns were then replaced by the regular army, whose numbers for the whole of the military Vendée, according to Vimeux's report, amounted to sixty-two thousand men,

There were various reactions during and after this "crusade for liberty." Some soldiers stubbornly refused to fight; they were afraid of the brigands, wrote Dubois-Grancé, "as children are afraid of mad dogs."[131] In Cholet, flight began as soon as battle was engaged. In places, there was not a single soldier, and many profited from theft in imitation of their generals.[132] Instead of protecting convoys, they pillaged houses in their path; in villages and towns, they found all kinds of goods that no one prevented them from taking: wine, food, money. Each expedition, according to Simone Loidreau, was an orgy and a means of seizing money. Those who thought they were rich enough took advantage of the first bend in the road to slip away; others feigned illness. To pillage at leisure, a large number wandered through the countryside, and when Vendeans encountered them they shot them. The columns thus shrank, and those that remained moved sluggishly, loaded with unaccustomed wealth. The leaders were no better. At each defeat, they blamed someone else; their letters are full of complaints and denunciations. On February 15, Dutruy, commander of one of Haxo's columns denounced to the Committee of Public Safety "rivalries among generals and the recklessness of some of them." He also complained that the brigands, "playing hide and seek," managed "always to escape between columns composed and commanded as they are."

A few generals, however, were disgusted by all this blood. This was true of Brigade General Danican: "For a year," he wrote to Bernier on October 20, 1794,

I have been crying out against all the horrors of which I have been the unhappy witness. Several citizens have taken me for a madman . . . but I will say and I will prove to anyone who asks that I have seen old men massacred in their beds, children with their throats cut on their mothers' breasts, pregnant women or women who had just given birth guillotined, that I have seen the burning of immense storehouses of grain and provisions of all kinds . . . Overcome with labor and worry, it is impossible for me to provide a detailed account, but if I were called as a witness, it would take me only a week to prepare a memorandum in which I would reveal to all the true friends of the Republic the intrigues of this war about which there have been constant lies, the crimes of Bouchotte and of all the jokers he set at the head of our armies to make them fight. I will prove that drownings took place not only in Nantes, but that this kind of torment was practiced at thirty places upstream on the Loire. The atrocities that were committed before my eyes have so affected my heart that I will feel no regret in dying . . . I will speak in the face of the cannibals.[133]

Inhabitants of Nantes, for example a student named Baudry, were scandalized: "Carrier had thousands of men drowned without trial."[134] General Haxo, leader of the incendiary second army, managed to save Challans, La Garnache, and Sallertaine by passing them off as "military posts."[135] The department of Angers called for and adopted a decree against pillage.[136] Conversely, officers like Francastel regretted their lack of resources: "There are still twenty thousand men left to slaughter in this 'unhappy country.'"[137] On May 9, 1794, Vimieux wrote as follows to Turreau: "Reflection and my experience support the observations I have made of this war to persuade me more than ever that the total end depends absolutely on the resources you will determine."[138]

Some generals and other officers hostile to the war were justifiably accused of moderation: Haxo, abandoned by his troops, committed suicide; Grignon had to retreat because his soldiers, influenced by their officers, refused to fight on the pretext of exhaustion. Moderates gathered denunciations against their leaders, most of whom were bloodthirsty. Huché, constantly drunk, scandalized his colleagues: "He has the habit of appearing at the head of the troops overcome with wine and he makes improper remarks."[139] Turreau also complained of inadequate support; if it were adequate, "within two weeks, there would remain neither houses, provisions, weapons, nor men in the entire Vendée except for those hidden in the depths of the forests. This was because, according to the general, they could not be burned."[140] He proposed to have the forests cut down and sold at auction and to require that "those who buy them vacate the country within a definite time."

Some even asked whether it was useful to burn. This was true for Le-quinio, who was asked by the Committee of Public Safety to give his views on ways to end the war:

> To burn the cottage of the inhabitant of the countryside is to break his strongest link to society, to force him to withdraw to the woods, and to make him a brigand out of necessity. To burn the clay and the equipment of the artisan is to deprive him of all resources, to break the bonds that might join him to the social order, and to force him as well to become a brigand in order to survive.
> What has happened to the cattle has happened as well to fodder and grain. We have killed without quarter, corpses have needlessly been left as prey for dogs and carnivorous animals.
> Loyal spies paid by some generals have been shot by patriots who, surrendering with unfortunate haste to the just desire for vengeance, have thereby deprived themselves of one of the most essential elements for our success.
> In a word, it seems that the malevolence of several patriots and the fecklessness of the majority have cooperated, in the most thorough possible way, with the perfidy of the enemies of the Revolution in the prolongation of this war . . .[141]

The action of the troops was supplemented by that of the fleet. "The soldiers of the gunboats sailing on the Loire completed the ruin of our parish," Abbé Robin sadly noted.[142] Measures taken to organize policing of the river did not become really effective until late 1793, and particularly from March 1794 on.[143] River patrols, consisting of a few units, did not yet have their own administration. Until 1772, they had depended on the Corporation of Merchants and Sailors, then on the Corps des Officiers des Turcies et Levées, and finally on the Roads and Bridges Administration.[144] At the beginning of the Revolution, the administration hesitated over the organization of the service. Civil, maritime, and military authorities each had their mission. In order to simplify and unify such a complex service, a committee of navigation was created in April 1793; it was presided over by a naval officer, G. Berthault, and one of its duties was gunboat service. This new authority immediately set to work. Its principal goal was to increase the number of men in service, to make them capable of dealing with events, and to resolve various problems: to support the columns operating on the banks of the river; to maintain free circulation of convoys on the Loire, particularly those intended to supply the towns and the armies of the Republic in a country in open rebellion; and to intercept to the extent possible any movement from one bank to the other of isolated individuals or troops.

In March 1793 a plan for an armed ship was presented to the Central Committee of the department.[145] It was approved on April 5, 1793, and twice put out for bids. Because of the difficult situation, the administration had no time to construct new vessels and decided to organize and equip several other ships. After using whatever came to hand—barges, pinnaces, coasters, and store ships—the department recognized the need to carry out requisitions and charterings. The prolongation of the war led to substantial modifications in large ships built for peaceful purposes. First, they were provided with railings: flat sides were raised by planks with strong pegs; fascines and sandbags or old mattresses were then used to reinforce this construction and make it more effective against enemy fire. Openings with scuttles were constructed.[146] Four- or 6-gauge artillery pieces with their carriages were set on platforms. The construction of special carriages soon turned out to be necessary in order to fire at targets located on high slopes and to avoid recoil effects. To protect the men from bad weather and to make these ships habitable, since some of them had no bridges, tents and other shelters were used.

The ships had one or more masts with replacements, a set of square sails, oars, poles, boat hooks, various rigging, boarding hooks, firewood, anchored landing planks, and so on.[147] Thus fitted out, they could move only with the wind behind or with a little quartering wind against the current; otherwise, they had to use oars or tows. Their tactical role in those circumstances was nonexistent. Each one was escorted by a railed towboat and a small dinghy. These light ships were usually equipped with a small-caliber artillery piece called a *pierrier*. Constantly patrolling the length of the Loire, they ferried back and forth between the banks and the armed vessels, stationary or sailing as a fleet.

Opposite the station of each cannon boat and serving as a support base was a small fort armed with cannons and surrounded by stockades, embankments, and ditches. Forces soon turned out to be insufficient, for a large number of conscript sailors failed to respond to the call. On April 16, 1793, one month after the beginning of the insurrection, the central government was forced to react. It required that ship captains and masters of wood transports immediately report to the navigation office for enlistment. Crews

Table 8.1. Ships stationed on the Loire in the year II from Angers to Paimbœuf

Names of Ships	Location of Stations	Names of Captains	Size of Crews	Artillery				
				18	8	6	4	3
1st Division								
La Carmagnoie	La Pointe	Boisson	30				4	
Le Duquesne	Lambardiere	Baguideau	30			4		
Le Montagnard	Chalonnes	Bachelier	30				4	
Le Scipion	Aux Noyers	Breton jeune	30				4	
Le Sans-Culotte	Montjean	Rodrigue	30	1		3		
Le Thémistocle	La Maison Blanche	Magré Comt de la Don	30				4	
Le Citoyen	Ingrandes	Degounor	32			4		
Lapeyrouse	Cul de Boeuf	Barbier	30					3
Le Vengeur	Montrelais	Etienne	30				4	
Le Pompée	Mont-Glone St. Florent	Fauvet	30		4			
Le Cassart	Isle Moccard	Darricaud	30				4	
L'Annibal	Isle Paulard	Viaud (André)	30				4	
Le Ça-Ira	Anetz	Bautet	30			2	2	
Le Jean-Bart	Ancenis	Viaud (Louis)	30				4	
Le Fabius	La Rompière de Drain	Racault	30					4
Le Républicain	Champtoceaux	Boutet	30				4	
2d Division								
Le Trouville	Isle Dorelle	Gallais	30				4	
L'Invincible	Le Cellier	Lefevre	30				4	
Le Caton	Moulin Lampitaux	Boutet	30				4	
Le Ruithers	Isle à Tulo	Lartigue	30				4	
Le Patriote	Mauves	Thibaud	30				4	
Le Colomb	La Subuette (Chebuette)	Rolland	30					4
Le Duguay-Trouin	Thouaré	Braheix	30				4	
L'Intrépide	Belle Rivière	Garret	30				4	
Le Cook	Grand Bouge	Giraud Benjamin	30				4	
Le Protecteur	Saint-Sébastien	Hardy	30				4	
La Batterie no. 2	Richebourg	Mauclerc	18					2
La Batterie no. 1	Pont de Primil	Couillaud	18			1		
Le Fort	Isle Patriote	Le Roux	18			2		
Le Forbin	Prée au Duc	Villain	18					3
3d Division								
La Catherine-Elisabeth	Isle Cheviré	Abautret	26				4	
L'Imposant	Haute Indre	Lafloury	26				1	3
La Prévoyane	St. Jean de Boiseau	Arnaud	26			6		2
La Bonne Intention	Le Pellerin	Chauveau	35					
Le Courageux	La Martinière	Villenave	26	2			6	
Le Brave	Etier de Buzay	Bouyer	32				4	
Le Fanfaron	Etier de Vue	Bonamy	26				2	2
Le Furieux	Champ-Neuf	Demolière	26				4	
L'Actif	Le Migron	Opoix	26				4	
L'Argus	Pierre Rouge	Genehete	20				2	4
Le Surveillant	Paimbœuf	Fouassier	20				4	

Pierriers	Miscellaneous Weapons				Kind of Ship	Distance from Nantes
	Pikes	Swords	Rifles	Blunderbusses		
3	6	6	16	2	Bateau	54 *milles*
3	6	6	16	2	—	51
3	6	6	16	2	—	47
3	6	6	16	2	—	43
3	6	6	16	2	—	39
3	6	6	16	2	—	37
3	6	6	16	2	—	36
3	6	6	16	2	—	34
3	6	6	16	2	—	32
3	6	6	16	2	—	30
3	6	6	16	2	—	29
3	6	6	16	2	—	26
3	6	6	16	2	—	24
3	6	6	16	2	—	21
3	6	6	16	2	—	18
3	6	6	16	2	—	15
3	6	6	16	2	—	13
3	6	6	16	2	—	12
3	6	6	16	2	—	11
3	6	6	16	2	—	10
3	6	6	16	2	—	9
3	6	6	16	2	—	7
2	6	6	16	2	—	6
2	6	6	16	2	—	5
2	6	6	16	2	—	4
2	6	6	16	2	—	2
>>	6	6	8	>>	Batterie	1
>>	6	6	8		Batterie	Nantes
>>	6	6	8		Hollandais	Nantes
>>	6	6	8		Hollandais	Nantes
2	6	6	12		Hollandais	2 *milles*
4	6	6	12	2	—	5
2	6	6	12		—	8
4	6	6	20		—	9
2	10	6	12		—	11
2	6	6	12		—	12
2	6	6	12		—	15
2	6	6	12		—	16
2	6	6	6		—	18
2	6	6	6		—	21
4	6	6	6		—	24

constituted in this way were given regular pay of thirty sous a day in June 1793; pay was higher for officers according to rank. Regular distributions and ration tickets took care of subsistence. If there was not enough, the crews resorted to pillage.

In principle, each ship had an average crew size of thirty. According to a report from the commander-in-chief of the station of the Loire and the Erdre, five of them had the permanent duty of transporting flour from America between Nantes and Orléans.[148] Discounting the wounded, the sick, and the supply personnel, there was an average of twenty men for service: steering the cannon boat, patrolling night and day in the towboat, and often fighting or skirmishing. From the military point of view, the service was definitively organized in the year II of the Republic (1794).

From Angers to the sea, the river had three divisions: the first went from the village of La Pointe at the mouth of the Maine to Champtoceaux; the second from the île Dorelle to south of La Prairie-du-Duc, including Nantes and the stations on the Erdre; the third from the île Cheviré to the sea.[149] The action of these ships became particularly violent beginning in April and May 1794; the routed Vendean army had left the way open for them.

In a report to the Directory of April 21, citizen Mahouhet, captain of *Le Républicain* and commander-in-chief, summarized the action conducted between Champtoceaux and Thouaré.[150] At the beginning, Commander Berruyer asked for assistance in besieging Champtoceaux and La Patache. He had to withstand two attacks lasting an hour and a half, the first opposite Le Cellier, and the second in La Chapelle-Bassemère. In the course of these confrontations, he estimated that he killed about one hundred brigands who were trying to seize his ships, fifty-two of which were heavily laden. Among other things, he was transporting the bells of Champtoceaux. Completing the convoy were seven or eight prisoners, including the servant of M. Couault, the owner of a barrel of powder and four sacks of lead. In the course of this skirmish, the battalion lost three sailors and a rifleman. In Mahouhet's estimate, the Vendean forces consisted of about eight hundred soldiers in Champtoceaux and five hundred opposite Le Cellier and La Chapelle-Bassemère.

On April 16, the commander of *L'Intrépide* received the order to convoy seventeen ships assembled at La Pointe. He set out without delay for Nantes and was not a little surprised to see the hills of Drain and Champtoceaux "lined with brigands and the white flag flying in several places." The reports from ships stationed along the valley of Saint-Julien-de-Concelles and La

Chapelle announced that three days earlier the former guard had resumed its activity. On April 17 the commander of *Le Patriote* was charged with protecting the debarkation of 120 soldiers at La Pierre-Percée to take on fodder. He reported in a summary that *Le Patriote* was moored very close to the land and responded with its artillery to the fire coming from the houses in the hamlet. The battle lasted for two hours. Several Republicans were wounded and nightfall prevented a landing.

On April 25 General Delage sent a request to the commanders of the ships stationed at Mauves and Thouaré for a projected landing in the valley. The operation was fully successful. General Robert's column arrived soon thereafter, cut the insurgents to pieces, and made it possible to load hay on the ships. He was greatly surprised to realize that there were still "so many rebels after the passage of the infernal column." Several attacks on the post at the mill on the island caused the death of fourteen inhabitants of La Chapelle.[151]

On May 24, 1794, the cannoneers of the Loire were responsible for the killing of René Jousseaume, the memory of which has been preserved by the local population.[152] This seventy-five-year-old man was ordered by the Republicans on pain of death to chop down the statues of the Saint-Simon chapel. He refused and had his throat cut at the foot of the altar.

The launches carried out brief and rapid operations. They frequently pillaged the country and took the inhabitants captive:[153] "a large number of women and especially of young girls were made prisoner and shot in Mauves"; four on April 25, near L'Arche; and two on May 25, near La Barre.[154] Following this general repression, the corpses of men and animals were so numerous that the administration had to take urgent precautions to prevent contagion.

On 29 nivôse of the year II (January 18, 1794), the departmental Committee of Loire-Inférieure required that "all citizens be expected to cooperate in continuing the work of burying corpses." This decree was justified: "The number of these infamous people is unfortunately too great and it is important that they be buried with the greatest precaution, so that after their death they do not cause us even greater harm than during their life."[155] In Paimbœuf, 253 livres taken from the "booty chest" were spent to bury those who had been shot, the others "having been buried by women who had remained behind."[156] In Couëron, "one hundred eighty human corpses and ninety-seven animal corpses were buried." Soon thereafter, these measures became general. "Considering that the air is more and more tainted," the general administration called for "the exercise of the most continuous and most active watchfulness over the burial of corpses in public cemeteries as well as in other places where they might be buried."

All the districts of the insurgent Vendée were required to make a careful search for all unburied corpses. They had to be buried in deep ditches and covered with quicklime and a layer of earth at least three feet deep. If corpses were found at the edge of a forest, they were to be burned. Commissioners were even appointed to supervise these burials.[157] On February 5, 1794, Doctor Terrier, charged with assuring the burial of "corpses dead because of the war," reported to the departmental administration that there were still many "unburied or badly buried," infecting the air. Several times, he asked for one hundred casks of lime "to throw on top of them.[158]

The armies were supplemented by civil commissions, called commissions of subsistence, created by the departmental capitals on 1 brumaire of the year II (October 22, 1793), the object of which was to collect on behalf of the nation all proscribed and abandoned personal property in order to strike "the final blow."[159] As a result, these commissions, following the regular army, maintained another army of agents (there were several thousand, wrote Hervieux on 20 messidor) who seized all the grain, fodder, and cattle.[160] Soldiers and prisoners,[161] in accordance with the decree of 6 germinal of the year II, were even encouraged to pillage by the offer of rewards.[162] These seizures, calling for "all the solicitude of the army," were to complete, even more quickly than "the war[,] the annihilation of that horde." "Immense resources," wrote Beaudesson, managing inspector general of supplies,

> were buried in the Vendée; they are being discovered today. You know the order of the commander-in-chief and his inclinations: there is nothing closer to his heart than to save from the flames that must pulverize this vast region all manner of provisions. He has even reiterated the express prohibition against burning any kind of provisions, and depots will be set up in various hamlets and farms . . . placed at the rear of each column . . . You will deploy all your energy and all your efforts to serve the Republic. Our needs are great and the large communes are asking for help. Hasten to come to get it in the Vendée.

Various recommendations followed:

> You will be careful to see to it that the fodder be carried for three days; each citizen will take on one or two portions according to the strength of his horse or mule. You will also take good care that a man be in charge of leading two horses. Now or never is the time to say that the execrable Vendée is nearing its end. One more effort and we will have peace and plenty.[163]

The representatives of the people themselves drew up a balance sheet in the form of a poster:

> What cruel effects a moment of aberration has produced! Of how many evils has it not been the source? Cast an eye on what has happened, see your country slaked with blood, your furrows littered with corpses, brothers mercilessly tearing each other apart, fertile plains now presenting nothing but the odious picture of sterility; famine or death arise beneath each of your steps; your fathers, your mothers, your sisters, your children wander from field to field, without shelter, without rest, constantly tormented by the fear of death that they are reduced to hoping for or by the horrors of the famine that threatens them from every side. That is the heartbreaking picture of the position of your country.[164]

In Couffé, twenty-two cartloads of grain were seized, and it continued.[165] By the end of 1794, according to Turreau, the mission assigned seemed to have been accomplished: "This rich region, which fed several departments and supplied cattle in quantity for Paris and horses for the army, is nothing but a heap of ruins."[166] This dramatic phase was followed by a long period of instability.

PART THREE

The Period of Instability

NINE

Political Incoherence

THE COUNTRY WAS MILITARILY OCCUPIED, WITH ALL THE RESULTING
abuses: pillage, lack of safety for the inhabitants, and so on. From headquarters in La Chapelle-Bassemère on 29 brumaire of the year IV (November 24, 1796), General Caffin sent a report on the occupation to General
Hoche.[1] On his arrival, he found the second regiment of the 171st Demibrigade leaving for La Chapelle-Heulin in the greatest disorder. Following
an episode of pillaging, it was carrying off cows, bulls, tethers, thread, and
all manner of things. The inhabitants were so terrified that they brought
their "wheat" themselves.

For concrete reasons, explained Guillemot, the wish for peace expressed
on many occasions by different governments was without effect:

> To end the war in this country, it would be necessary, if it were possible,
> to change the great majority of the troops who breathe nothing but mas-
> sacre and pillage, in particular the volunteers,[2] to increase their numbers,
> and to supply them with weapons, which are lacking to seven-eighths of
> them in some battalions; to punish generals such as Grignon, Caffin, and
> Guillaume, who are "absolutely incompetent," because they seem to be
> proceeding in the monstrous direction that has just been abolished.[3]

The lack of continuity in policy and the accumulation of blunders and
repressions were very prejudicial to the central administration. Far from restoring a certain balance, the central administration definitively discredited
itself in the eyes of the population. At the same time the Church and the

149

fabrique continued to carry out their traditional functions. Some excesses were demonstrated on either side.

During the phase following the war, the central government adopted a succession of policies whose essential characteristic was incoherence. The Thermidorian Convention, in reaction against the policy of terror conducted by Robespierre, very early demonstrated its willingness to restore peace and took several steps in this direction. All the decrees of the former Committee of Public Safety were invalidated. Generals Carpentier, Turreau, Huchet, and Grignon were arrested by decrees issued on September 29 and 30, 1794, as were Carrier and some members of the Revolutionary Committee of Nantes. This was the occasion for a solemn proclamation from Carnot on December 2:

> For two years, your regions have been prey to the horrors of war. These fertile climates that nature seemed to have intended for the so-journ of peace have become places of exile and carnage. The courage of the children of the nation has turned against the nation itself, flames have devoured your dwellings, and the earth, covered with ruins and cypress trees, refuses to provide to the survivors its bountiful substance.[4]

There followed a whole series of measures likely, it was thought, to restore the Vendée "to the bosom of the nation." Among other things, prisons were partially opened following a decree carried out by eleven representatives who, according to Crétineau-Joly, applied themselves zealously to their mission:

> In Nantes, Rennes, Saumur, Niort, Vannes, Fontenay, and Laval they went themselves into the houses that liberty had turned into dungeons. These houses were jammed with a crowd of men and women suspected of royalism, of probity, and of virtue; a number of them were liberated unconditionally. The possessions of most of them had been confiscated by the nation or sold by abuse of power; they let it be known in veiled terms that measures of reparation would be taken in order that justice be done to all citizens. Certificates of amnesty and loyalty were offered to those who declared or had it declared that they had participated in the insurrection. This was to open the Vendée to all the women, all the children,

all the wounded, who, after escaping from the disaster of Savenay, had hidden in Brittany or were wandering without refuge.[5]

At the same time, the Vendée was moving in the direction of peace. A few days later, Hoche was given the task of negotiating with the Vendean leaders. The tone was, of necessity, one of understanding:

> Considering that French blood has been flowing too long in the departments of the West; that to defeat the Vendée and the Chouans by force, Republican blood will have to flow and we will have to annihilate a population of at least six hundred thousand individuals; that the reign of Robespierre, Carrier, and their accomplices has come to an end; that justice is the order of the day.
>
> That fires, rape, pillage, and other atrocities that have been committed in the Vendée have embittered the spirit of its misguided inhabitants; that confidence is beginning to be restored and that this feeling which can be encouraged but not commanded can be spread only with principles of justice and gentleness.
>
> Considering that the current position of the armies of the West, of the coasts of Brest, and of Cherbourg, and the political situation of the departments in the areas of those armies requires the most immediate remedies; that the scarcity of food, the total shortage of fodder, and the near impossibility of providing them create the greatest anxiety.
>
> That the energy with which the Chouans have organized in setting ablaze the former Brittany, a portion of the former provinces of Anjou, Maine, and Normandy, means that the communication routes between the major towns are broken and hence the arrival of provisions suspended; that thefts and murders are proliferating and that the Chouans seem to be acquiring strength the progress of which it is important to stop . . .[6]

The meticulously prepared treaty was signed with Charrette in La Jaunaye on February 17, 1795. It included favorable conditions for the Vendeans: general amnesty; freedom of worship (article I: Every individual and every group of citizens whatever may worship freely and peacefully); quiet possession of the country; exemption from any conscription or requisitions. The same day, the Vendeans were also given the opportunity to enlist in the army:

Considering that the return of the inhabitants of the Vendée to the bosom of the Republic, by providing to agriculture and commerce the manpower that has been lacking, leaving men without position or profession no means by which to subsist, and that it is their duty to assure their subsistence and to make them useful to their fellow citizens, the department decrees:

1. The Vendeans who have no profession or position are free to enter the armed forces of the Republic.
2. Those among them who have no profession and were inhabitants of the Vendée before 93 will be organized in territorial guards and soldiers paid by public finances.
3. These guards will not exceed the number of two thousand and will be subject to the established civil and military authorities.
4. The representatives of the people will organize them in companies that will be distributed to all points of the French territory known as the Vendée and may not be stationed elsewhere.
5. In case of conscription, the inhabitants of the Vendée will remain in their department in order to restore agriculture and to revive commerce and industry.

Reimbursement for vouchers signed by the rebel leaders and 2 million francs in indemnity completed these guarantees.[7] In order to ensure that publication of the decree was really carried out, each commune received a minimum of six copies, which were required to be posted.[8]

For personal reasons, Stofflet had a disagreement with Charrette and halted the negotiations. He brought with him the inhabitants of the district of Clisson and resumed the war in March and April 1795. Various skirmishes followed: his army vigorously fought to prevent General Caffin's column from crossing the Layon and subjected it to withering fire in the village of Les Tailles on April 1; a few days later, a Republican convoy of provisions and ammunition on the way to Chemillé was almost completely destroyed in an attack.[9] On May 2, the treaty of Saint-Florent-le-Vieil, signed by the commander-in-chief, put an end to the dispute. He had obtained conditions analogous to those given to Charrette. In addition, he was granted the liberation of imprisoned Vendeans and the return of those who had been forcibly conscripted by the Republicans.[10]

The Convention then proclaimed the definitive return of the Vendée to the Republic. It had made many concessions. The secular state, which "no longer paid the expenses or the salaries of any cult," abolished in practice the Civil Constitution of the Clergy and placed refractory and constitutional priests on the same footing. The desire for peace was accompanied by a return to tolerance: freedom of worship and the reopening of churches on January 21 and May 30, 1795. The administration was thereby following the will of the Convention.

Pillage was prohibited by a decree issued by the departmental authorities. Brigade General Le Bley even required, each time a force set out, that it be joined by an ad hoc military commission of five members and five alternates to provide for immediate judgment of looters and perpetrators of atrocities. He regretted this war "which is not ordinary and in which the soldier does not keep in line, obliged to run throughout the countryside so that officers of every rank can only observe the smallest part of them. How many soldiers will continue to escape from just punishment?"[11]

Some municipal authorities, troubled by the poverty they saw, carried out small distributions of wheat: for example, two and a half pounds for five days in the region of Saint-Père-en-Retz.[12] This was not much, in the eyes of the inhabitants, particularly those of Arthon and Chauvé, who began to agitate again. Probably in order to avoid possible difficulties, the district decreed that every ten days an adequate portion of threshed wheat would be provided for the people of Frossay, Vue, Rouans, Chemiré, Arthon, Chauvé, Les Moutiers, Pornic, and Paimbœuf.

However, the central administration delayed in living up to its commitments, such as returning Louis XVII to the Vendée by June 13, 1795. Even worse, the Blues committed many infractions of the treaty. For example, on March 2, a Republican column surrounded fifty-two people (forty men and twelve women) in the church in La Gaubretière.[13] The besieged, led by a man named Bizon, defended themselves with remarkable energy for eight hours. From the top of the belltower, from the windows, and from loopholes in the walls, they shot at the patriots. Keeping up their courage by singing hymns, the women loaded the rifles. For lack of ammunition, however, resistance soon became impossible, and the Blues charged and broke down the church doors; they found twenty-three of the besieged, eight of them women, and immediately shot them at the Grand Henry bridge. Several weeks later, on April 9, General Gaffin besieged the church tower in Chanzeaux, where twenty-nine inhabitants had taken refuge.[14] The fierce battle ended with the church being burned down, ten fighters killed, and the nineteen survivors imprisoned. As a result, relations grew ever more tense, and grievances on either side more frequent. On May 16 (27 floréal), a band of royalists threatened the mayor of Chemiré and seized his rifle.[15] On June 2 (14 prairial), Pierre Legeay, a notable of Brains, was assassinated.[16] For their part, the Republicans seized Allard, one of Charrette's lieutenants and a former aide-de-camp of La Rochejaquelein, in the middle of his troops and tried to imprison the commander-in-chief.[17] Soon, on the pretext of thefts and murders committed in the communes of Arthon and Saint-Père-en-Retz, Adjutant General Cambray ordered Captain Biré to carry out a reprisal expedition.[18] On the night of June 14, he seized a dozen rifles and, despite their passports, arrested three Vendeans of Guérin's division at their homes.

The commander-in-chief responded to this ambiguous policy with a solemn declaration published on June 22:

> It is with sorrow that I take up arms again; but the Republicans have vowed our death, and we can avoid it only by fighting. Dispatches from the princes inform me that one of them is to lead the great expedition that will give such strength to our armies. These events will not occur in our land, but they must be seconded. A diversion is necessary; I am counting on your zeal, it will not fail me.[19]

On June 26, at the announcement of the death of Louis XVII and to cries of "Long live Louis XVIII, king of France," Charrette took up arms again. War was once more declared. Clashes proliferated, especially after the shooting that took place in Quiberon from July 30 to August 4 became known. On December 28, 1795, the commander-in-chief of the coastal army, considering "that the advances of the enemies of the State in the departments of the West are more troubling every day . . . and that it is his duty to liberate the inhabitants from an odious yoke that they detest," decided, first, that all the large towns were declared to be in a state of siege; attached to each one of them was a mobile column charged with providing supplies and keeping off the Chouans. Second, he decided to establish, independent of the troops of the interior, a disarmament cordon. The only commune exempted was Mueil, whose inhabitants "have often withstood the attacks of the brigands with truly Republican energy."

In short, the treaty of Saint-Florent-le-Vieil was violated every day until the death of Stofflet on February 25, 1796, which was an irremediable loss for the movement. No one thereafter was able to secure massive sup-

port from the peasants. Indeed, the population was in no position to respond to the 40,000 Republicans moving through the region. Charrette
was captured in turn and shot on the Place Viarme in Nantes on March 29,
1796. According to commentators, this event electrified the entire Republican army. The news arrived in Paris at eight in the evening, and the five
directors greeted it with cries of joy. They immediately had the news announced in all the theaters as if it had been the capture of a capital or a
kingdom.[20]

General Hoche, confirmed in his post as head of government armies,
was nevertheless able to win the respect of the conquered by his generosity
and his words: "Flee us no longer, we will be able to respect your weakness.
Restore your cottages, pray to God, and work your fields. I come to restore
you to rest and offer you the olive branch of peace."[21] A prudent administrator, he exhorted the directory to make large concessions: "The Vendée
region loudly calls out for civil organization; military rule is no longer suitable
for it; it is not robust enough to support constitutional government." In a
confidential dispatch to the five directors, Hoche was more explicit: "Patriot
refugees never get along with royalist peasants. I conquered the peasants by
gentleness united to force, but the refugees will ruin my work. They have
hatreds to assuage and revenge to carry out; I fear that they will let no opportunity go by."

Hoche was convinced that, as new owners of the land that the nation
had sold to them at very low prices, the patriot refugees could never play
the role that the nobles had for the peasants: "They will respect neither
religion, nor the priests, nor the memories of another time to which the
Vendeans are attached." The solution would be to have the region administered by the former inhabitants and even by royalists who had willingly
made peace with the Republic. For Hoche, the Vendean was hostile to the
revolutionary principle and it was therefore necessary to accommodate
him. He was convinced that if there was another external war, the region
would rebel again:

> It is a contained volcano, but it is still smoldering and new lava can
> erupt. Therefore, give the patriots the least authority possible. Inspire
> confidence in the Vendeans by measures that may even be a little counter-
> revolutionary; gratify their religious ideas; grant concessions to their
> monarchical fanaticism and above all to the intense desire that they all
> have not to lose sight of their village steeple.

For Hoche, the Vendée was nevertheless a good land whose fine fruits would be gathered by the Republic:

> Its children have honor and courage. The Revolution was wrong to ignore it; be just enough to correct errors that, in early days, could be spread through France in order to excite enthusiasm; but you may be sure that everything I have accomplished will be futile if you continue the system followed until now. The Vendée is an exceptional region; it must thus be allowed to govern itself with exceptional laws, for a war like this one, were it to recur in a few years, would sink the government.

As Crétineau-Joly points out, these prophetic words addressed to the government fell on deaf or indifferent ears. By the law of August 24, 1797, the directory theoretically proclaimed amnesty and the return of a measure of religious liberty. In fact, the Vendée was left to the hateful, arbitrary power of local authorities; it was persecuted with fierce tenacity.

On 7 thermidor of the year IV (July 25, 1796), the municipal council of Le Loroux-Bottereau prepared an address to the inhabitants of its district. It regretted "the disasters of anarchy," promised "the safety of persons and property and a soothing of evils . . . Surrounded by your confidence, your administrators are going to take care of people and things." The document disavowed the preceding regime and characterized it as "disgusting anarchy that perpetuated vice and demoralized the people." The whole conclusion is an exhortation to forget the past and to practice fraternity, in terms evocative of gospel morality. It ends like this:

> Men are all brothers and we must look on them as such. Finally, follow these beautiful maxims that should be engraved in every heart and are one of your principal duties:
> Do not do unto others what you would not have others do unto you.
> And always do to others the good you would like to receive from them.
> Therefore, rally around us, help us with all your might, and you will always find us at the honorable post in which your confidence has placed us.[22]

Almost all communal authorities used similar official language:

> Return to yourselves, the nation holds out its arms to you, take advantage of its clemency, do not wait for more crimes to make you unworthy of its forgiveness, go into the bosom of your families to depict the horrors of war and work with them for the return of all to peace and happiness; do not wait for the consummation of your crime by turning arms against your brothers, your friends with whom you have so often achieved such glory by sharing so many dangers. No, you will not thus be the enemy of your honor, of your repose, and of your nation; the blood of your companions in arms that you would shed would spatter you, and you would never erase the stains with which it would cover you; their relatives and yours would one day call you to account and you would have only tears to offer them. These counsels, do not doubt it, will have their effect; men will disappear, your abandoned tyrants will leave your hearths and you will soon be delivered from war.[23]

Unfortunately, these fine declarations to the inhabitants of the military Vendée and its surroundings were signed by the same men who had directed the brutal repression of the preceding months. They were thus hardly taken seriously by the still watchful people. Later events were to justify their fears and insecurity was to take hold again.

To begin with, the administration resumed the sale of church property.[24] This measure could only be wounding to Catholics after the condemnation by the pope. Priority was given to sales of churches, chapels, and presbyteries. These buildings were usually sold to people from outside the communes.

In the second place, Vendeans were supposed to receive indemnities for real and personal property that had been destroyed.[25] In fact, the indemnities were restricted to patriots, especially to inhabitants of Nantes, to the great indignation of the majority of the population.[26]

In the third place, in pluviôse of the year V (January 1797), the administration dared to celebrate with great ceremony the festival of the just punishment of the last king of France, followed by the solemn oath of all the officials and representatives of the communes: "I swear hatred to royalty and anarchy, and attachment to the Republic and to the constitution of the year III."[27]

On 17 brumaire of the year VI (November 8, 1798), the municipal councils of the various cantons decided to celebrate a festival of peace. In order to give this ceremony all the requisite pomp, the armed forces in full uniform were present, along with various public officials. The procession, joined by male and female citizens wearing cockades, passed through all the central streets of towns and villages, arrived in the church squares, renamed for the occasion, and planted the tree of liberty to the sound of Republican songs. "Fraternal" banquets, balls, and fireworks ended the day. Similar ceremonies took place for July 14, August 10, and 9 and 10 thermidor, which "mark the fall of a second throne erected by a mad tyrant on the ruins of the first and watered with the blood of his fellow citizens."[28]

A special program was established for each of these ceremonies, in order to give them the "pomp and ceremony" that they deserved. Everywhere, in ceremonies and in speeches, one was

> to strive to make the constitution and the laws loved, by retracing before the assembled people the pictures of the countless abuses of which they had so long been the victims . . . At the ceremony of July 14, one will make them go back in their minds to the times when the will of a single man was the supreme law, when privileged castes shared wealth, employment, and honor; at that of August 10, one will show them the ineptitude of the throne and the vices seated at its side; at that of 9 and 10 thermidor, one will point to those hypocritical patriots who shackled the French while speaking to them of nothing but their rights . . .

Nantes even celebrated the victory over the royalists on June 29, 1793.[29] In Niort, a *decade* ceremony was organized that imitated a religious procession.[30] The citizens, "gripped by righteous indignation," after breaking the saints and the tabernacles of the temple of the Mountain (formerly Saint-André church), "and armed one with a saint, another with a Virgin, one with an infant Jesus, another with a reliquary, at four o'clock set out for the champ de Mars."

Central schools were not forgotten, and municipal authorities such as those of Niort frequently attended prize ceremonies with the same pomp— that is, escorted by a detachment of national veterans and preceded by the orchestra of the national guard.

While waiting for the young students to be ready for the exercise in the form of an argument which was to precede the distribution of prizes, the orchestra performed several pieces appropriate to the circumstance; it also played the tunes beloved of Republicans and through a sweet symphony prepared the audience for the feelings that such a touching ceremony was capable of inspiring. After the music, the argument composed by the students who were part of the ceremony took place; the following question was the subject: what is the most appropriate way to consecrate the glory of the defenders of the nation? This question was treated under four different headings, namely: history, eloquence, poetry, and finally public monuments . . . The four orators displayed great talent, to the repeated applause of the audience; the one playing the role of the commissioner, in a long and luminous conclusion, expressed all his preference for poetry. Finally, the tribunal, made up of three students, determined that the most appropriate way of consecrating the glory of the defenders of the nation belonged to history.[31]

These ceremonies were greeted with little enthusiasm, however, by the people of the Vendée.[32] The mayor of Guérande even declared that he was distressed to "see almost no one present and to encounter sadness everywhere."[33] The canton of Brious sadly observed that "almost all its citizens are wallowing in shameful indolence and despicable lack of concern, seeming to take hateful pleasure and to make a criminal game out of contravening the expression of the general will."[34] Consequently, the authorities took steps to have that will respected by everyone, even if that meant using informers.

Thereafter, the administration began again to levy taxes, calling for back payments, and even the Convention decreed a war tax,[35] a forced loan,[36] and threatened to generalize the progressive tax to which the rest of France was subjected. On 20 nivôse of the year IV, Hoche publicly justified this policy:

At least you will not deny that it is just to make you pay for the expenses caused by your thoughtlessness, or rather your rebellion. You are the ones who from now on will be principally charged with providing maintenance and pay for the many legions that you dare to fight; you will be discharged from this burden whenever you like. When you fight, the charge will increase because of more troops being sent;

by laying down your arms, by obeying the laws of the Republic, by paying the contributions you owe to it, we will return to the new limits of the Empire, and you will enjoy peace like the rest of your fellow citizens.[37]

To the municipal administrations of the cantons of Bressuire, Saint-Varent, Argenton-Château, La Chapelle-Tireuil, Saint-Pardoux, Secondigny, Armailloux, and Verruyes, who claimed the right to certain exemptions, the administration replied curtly:

> You must believe, citizens, that we have not lost sight of the disasters that you have suffered; they are the object of our constant concern, but you would strangely misunderstand the rights given by misfortune if, in the hope of securing considerable relief through the exemptions that we intend to grant to you, you were to conclude that you ought to cease all work related to the tax base for this year's contribution . . . This work is indispensable in order to bring your region out of the anarchy in which it has too long existed . . .[38]

Missions were sent to the districts to exhort them to pay up as soon as possible:

> We are finally approaching the moment so longed for by all the friends of order and public tranquility: the reign of the men of blood has been destroyed; the war of the Vendée is over; public documents and private information assure us that peace has been signed and that the rule of the Republic is recognized; soon the union of hearts and minds and social peace will be restored in these rich regions . . . But citizens, we have seen with sorrow the latest notes that you have sent us, the slowness with which the payment of contributions of all kinds is being carried out . . . The forced loan and the extraordinary war contribution deserve your attention all the more because they only affect those individuals in the best position to make this slight sacrifice for the nation. All true Republicans express the greatest gratitude to the National Convention for its decree of 12 frimaire and to its virtuous members who have not ceased, in the course of their glorious mission to the departments of the West, to plead for the cause of humanity.[39]

The municipal administrations were similarly pressured:

> You are the magistrates in direct contact with the people, placed between their interests and those of the nation, both of which must be equally dear to you, and if the distress and the misfortunes of the tax-payer require from your justice a favorable decision on the reduction or elimination of his tax, on the other hand the situation of the national treasury makes it your imperative duty to take great care that lack of concern, half-heartedness, or ill will on the part of the taxpayer not be a pretext for avoiding the most sacred duty: to pay what is owed to the State . . .[40]

As a result, a detachment of soldiers and/or a commissioner, whose pay of as much as 10 livres was charged to the taxpayers, was sent to every commune that was late in paying. No delay was possible; it would be a "terrible forfeiture."[41] Some cantons, such as that of Vertou, nevertheless declared that they were determined to pay "taxes only at gunpoint."[42] In the name of justice, the canton of Le Loroux-Bottereau in 1795 owed 57,000 francs for previous years and 11,000 for the current year. The inspector in charge, because of the "scarcity" that required him to have his provisions sent from Nantes, proposed a compromise: the region would pay an annual contribution of 50,000 francs but assignats would not be accepted: "the peasant cries out against repeated taxation and the harshness with which payment is demanded."[43]

To these legal taxes were added arbitrary contributions. The inhabitants of Le Pellerin were required to pay 2,000 livres extra for office expenses and the salaries of municipal employees, clerks, rural police, and the like.[44] In Brion[45] and Saint-Julien-de-Vouvantes,[46] taxes were coupled with abuses: after paying the amount owed "in paper," the taxpayers were required to pay again in coin. The "cupidity" of tax collectors as well as the disappearance of records was responsible. Various measures were taken to remedy the situation; for instance, the department of Deux-Sèvres demanded, in vain, two copies of the names and addresses of taxpayers.[47]

Official requisitions crushed the Vendée. A law of 15 pluviôse of the year IV (February 3, 1796) ordered a collection of horses and mules for the army.[48] The people's response was immediate: the soldiers had already seized the best ones and only old and defective animals were left. Various threatening demands were then sent out. It was not until the third that the

canton of Arthon decided to appoint in each of its communes commissioners charged with drawing up inventories. The mayor probably anticipated
difficulties since, on 20 prairial (June 6, 1796), he requested assistance from
twenty-five men from the post at Port-Saint-Père. Confronted with this situation, the departments, including Deux-Sèvres, protested:

> It is not only, citizen minister, the north of our department but
> almost the entire region that is groaning under the burden of these
> requisitions. In one place there is a canton from which wagons are req-
> uisitioned by an officer of military transport; in another place, a war
> commissioner asks for cattle to transport provisions to a camp; still else-
> where, the coach is halted, horses are seized from a farmer sowing his
> crops, they are attached to the carriage and he is obliged to drive them;
> in yet another place, fodder has to be provided immediately, or cattle
> have to be removed from the plow to be butchered.[49]

The writer thought it better to begin by requisitioning the cattle of the
Republic to provide for the needs of the troops garrisoned in large towns
and "to allow the small communes to supply their respective garrisons." The
abuses of the soldiers made these official decisions even more hateful: in-
cursions of all kinds, plundering, hostage taking, and continual seizures
of cattle, even with their equipment, without vouchers for an unlikely reimbursement. All cantons suffered the same evils, and, as the municipal authorities of Sainte-Pazanne declared, the pretexts offered, "subsistence for
the troops," "services of the Republic," often served only to "conceal a theft."[50]

For three years, armies had been traversing the region, putting everything to fire and the sword, and the soldiers had adopted the habit of indulging in gratuitous violence and horrible crimes. It was not unusual for
them to kill Vendeans, decapitate them, and parade their heads on the end
of a pike. General Gauvillier, commander-in-chief of the army, expressed
his indignation on 30 prairial of the year III: "For me, it is a crime against
man, humanity, and French generosity."[51] In Le Louroux-Béconnais, Rossignol gave "several sword blows to the head of an unfortunate man who
refused to house him and threatened to tie all the municipal authorities to
horses if a horse was not given to a woman."

The directory also needed soldiers, and conscription proliferated. The
mayors, who had very few men, submitted reluctantly, as in Champdenier
(Deux-Sèvres):

There is no canton under our authority in which we do not see old men and widows almost reduced to indigence and the prey of despair at the departure of their children; we would like to dry the tears of all those families by leaving among them young men more suited for agriculture than for the handling of weapons; but the orders of the military and superior authorities no longer make it possible for us to provide for any exemptions.[52]

The situation was all the more dramatic because the conscripts were called on to advance the money necessary to clothe them—that is, "in the absence of a uniform, trousers lined with skin between the legs and a Marseille jacket of wool, a double vest, a police cap, two pairs of shoes, two pairs of stockings, three shirts, three collars, three brushes, two combs, a leather sack, a sword, and a belt."[53]

Daily humiliations were also the rule. "Exhortations" were addressed to peasants to habituate them to working on the days "called Sundays and holidays";[54] the "external signs of worship"[55] and of the monarchy were destroyed with fury. In Aigrefeuille, feudal deeds were burned "to the repeated cries of 'Down with the tyrants and their deeds! Long live the Republic.'"[56] Freedom of movement was interfered with and sometimes challenged altogether. Some districts even required women, children, and old men, accused of espionage and having rendered all kinds of services to the rebels, to return to live in their burned-out villages.[57]

Finally, the directory, following the coup d'état of 17 and 18 fructidor of the year V (September 3 and 4, 1797), completely called into question the freedom of worship granted by the Convention and guaranteed by Hoche. It adopted the idea of the police captain of Le Loroux-Bottereau; he agreed "that we should allow priests to preach peace, good order, and even obedience to the law," but opposed any form of public worship: "I repeat, if we tolerate public worship, it's all over; the region will never be habitable for anyone who is attached to Republican government." Freedom of conscience was thus not at all recognized by the "Second Directory." For the Vendée, instability remained, while the Republicans were intent on achieving respect for the anticlerical spirit blowing from Paris with "argumentative fervor."[58] This practice was all the more resented because the condition of the region was disastrous.

The Living Conditions
of the Vendeans

CONTRARY TO A PRECONCEIVED IDEA, BEFORE 1793 THE MILITARY Vendée was characterized by its great wealth. All official and unofficial reports confirm it:

> Before the civil war, the entire region on this side of the Loire, long known by the name Vendée, comprised nine hundred square miles. Two hundred thousand horned animals nourished by its soil supported agriculture and France; the inhabitant of the Alpes-Maritimes and the Pyrénées came to exchange his gold for the superb mules he could get in our region; two million wool-bearing sheep supported French industries; our cloth and our yarns covered Europe and India . . ."[1]

Southern Loire-Inférieure and southwestern Anjou lived comfortably, particularly because of vineyards and stock raising. Northwestern Deux-Sèvres went through a veritable agricultural revolution.[2] Prefect Dupin explained this by the fact that Choiseul had instituted free circulation of wheat in 1766:

> The peasant then came out of his stagnation; he cultivated fields that had long lain fallow. He cleared even the most arid hillsides; woods and vines disappeared. Wheat was worth a lot of money, and they wanted to plant wheat everywhere; the plow furrowed all the fields high enough to be out of the reach of floods. Six years were enough to change the face

of the whole country; prodigious quantities of wheat were harvested; it was the most brilliant period of prosperity in the region.

The Gâtine, rich in woodlands, turned out to be a source of profit, producing tannin, beams, rafters, and planks, most of which were shipped on the Sèvre Niortaise to the department of Charente-Maritime. It also contained many varied fruit trees, which made it possible to export every year "a large quantity of fruits of all kinds." For example, Thouars was famous for its almonds, which were sold in Angers and Saumur; but the almond trees were cut down during the war.

Vendée drew its principal income from cattle raising, supplemented, despite rather infertile soil, by substantial production of grain, cabbages, and turnips.[3] Vendée alone fed at least three departments and supplied the markets of Paris.[4] Following the uprising, a number of towns, such as Brest, went through an extremely difficult period, even approaching famine. According to Dupin, the peasant of the Vendée was fairly enlightened about his own interests and much less a creature of habit than was commonly believed.[5]

It is obviously difficult to determine with precision the economic situation of insurgent communes during the crisis. The only sources that we have are particular descriptions by Vendeans or Republicans which generally complement one another despite their lack of precision.

The troubles of 1792 had little effect on agriculture; only commerce suffered. According to official reports, harvests were even good, generally one-fourth higher than in preceding years.[6]

In 1793, with the majority of able-bodied men engaged in warfare, and despite the efforts of the people who had remained behind, the harvest, at least in the canton of Le Loroux-Bottereau, was estimated at one-fourth of normal, and exchanges at one-third.

In 1794, the terrible year decreed by the Convention, the ruin of the region was complete. Fighting prevented peasants from working the land, and the infernal columns devastated everything: "They have burned," lamented an observer,

all the villages and cottages, massacred some of the remaining peasants, burned wheat and grasses in the barns and on the threshing fields; killed or devoured a countless number of ewes, sheep, and cattle; carried off or destroyed all the horses and mules; consumed in flames all the wool, linen, and flax, and all the furniture.[7]

The production of the communes of the West was reduced to one-fourth; this included the departments of Morbihan, Finistère, and Côtes-du-Nord.[8] The remaining herds were ravaged by a frightful epizootic disease; those animals that survived perished for lack of feed.[9] The little wine harvested was lost because the barrels had been requisitioned for saltpeter.[10]

In 1795 peace seemed to restore courage to the peasants, and there were hopes for a better harvest.[11] "But poverty is so great that it is insurmountable," even for rich farmers. Tenant farmers were reduced to begging their landlords to postpone the payment of debts and rents. Some were sometimes forced to feed themselves with purchased cattle or seeds in reserve; others were driven to begging.

The year 1796 was just as unfavorable: "Either the laborer was unable to provide the land with the necessary work, or else the year is naturally sterile." The small quantity of grain sown did not germinate. For his personal consumption, the farmer was forced to buy grain at "an exorbitant price" because of scarcity, giving in exchange, "with bitter tears," half his "personal cattle" and the hay to feed them. In Deux-Sèvres, the harvest was lost "for want of men, cattle, fertilizer, and plowing."[12]

The situation improved temporarily in 1797, but since the peasants had been able to sow only one-third of their fields, the harvest "merely kept them from dying of hunger."[13] The two following years were catastrophic: frozen hard enough "to split stones," the ground was impossible to work. The end of the decade was thus very precarious. In ten years production costs had been multiplied by five:

> The great majority of landowners were unable to take care of reconstruction. To find tenant farmers, they were obliged to offer reductions or even advances. The interest on money is in such disproportion to agricultural profits that many prefer to use it in commerce. Still more are obliged to abandon the cultivation of their lands, hence the need to allow farmers to plow under the feeble product of this harvest if we do not want to devour in advance the harvests of later years and afflict the country with an almost irremediable sterility.

Taxes did not help to improve the situation; to pay them, "they have to sell the furniture and hurry to get rid of the harvest at very low prices ... the result is a decline pernicious for agriculture." Various reports from administrators on tour and from mayors, such as the mayor of Machecoul, reveal the state of extreme poverty in the Vendée. "Our citizens," wrote the latter,

> are living in distress, to say no more. There is nothing exaggerated either in the picture of the devastations we have endured, or in that of depopulation, or in the idea that may have been given of the decline in income from the land. We can assure you that there are many properties that have produced no net income since the war and on which taxes must be paid. There are particularly the houses of Machecoul, which, not having been totally destroyed, have been made habitable by repairs that absorbed the revenues of several years. Several owners, who had received no income during the insurrection and who lacked the resources to make repairs, have leased these houses for a number of years, on condition that the tenants use the price of rent for all those years for repairs and restoration.
>
> The lands of the upper and lower marshes of the commune of Machecoul are still producing nothing this year. These lands have been under water for several months. The wheat will be rotten as it was last year. However, when these lands are not submerged or are only temporarily so, they are the most productive. But there is every reason to fear that tenant farmers will again be unable to pay their rent this year and that they will harvest almost nothing.

To complete the misfortune, an earthquake made things even more tragic. "Fortunately," the representative went on,

> no one perished despite the fact that we have reason to believe that the shocks were more violent in Machecoul and nearby than in other neighboring cantons. The buildings, both in Machecoul and in the surrounding countryside, have been severely damaged. Many walls have crumbled, and others are weakened to the degree that it is indispensable to knock them down.[14]

The overall situation, as the ministry itself admitted, was catastrophic:

> All the rural areas have been devastated. They have lost in fires their villages, their farm buildings, and all their plowing equipment, and in

the fighting a large part of their cattle and one-third of their population. The vines covering the hills of the Sèvre and the two upper banks
of the Loire perished for lack of care and have burdened the land with
useless wood, for lack of men to clear it away. The fields, deprived of
plowing for three years, are uncultivated or very inadequately cleared.
The farmers of this department, forced to buy absolutely necessary provisions in the markets of Nantes, console themselves only with the
always receding hope of receiving compensation and help . . .[15]

Towns were similarly affected, perhaps Nantes especially:

Besieged for three years, stricken with the most atrocious acts of
tyranny, subjected to all the military burdens, it [Nantes] has seen its
merchants imprisoned or forced to go elsewhere in search of the peace
and freedom suitable for industry, its goods carried off in great quantities, its vessels requisitioned, its capital lost through the insurrection of
the colonies, its commerce annihilated by the war at sea.[16]

In an attempt to provide a remedy, merchants were charged with buy-
ing grain abroad.[17] J.-B. Thoinet received 1 million francs for this purpose
in 1794.

Poverty was so great that it degenerated into famine.[18] Consequently, all
sorts of new malefactors wandered through the region: hungry laborers and
former soldiers took to robbery and became veritable brigands, murderers,
and highway robbers. The country faced the classic problem of reintegrating soldiers into society after a long campaign. The disarmament of the
troops, such as that of the territorial guards in 1796, had often been carried
out without fixed rules, varying according to location, with no instructions
having been issued: "Some took advantage of this to keep their weapons,
which made those who had surrendered them grumble."[19] Excesses increased, and, depending on political choices, crimes were attributed to one
side or the other. For example, in the canton of Le Loroux-Bottereau, in
pluviôse of the year VII (January and February 1799), "twenty to twenty-
five armed and masked men invaded the home of Sauvestre de La Por-
cherie, a peaceful and inoffensive man. His only crime was that he was
faithful to his God and his king." For the writer, the brigands in question
could only be Republicans:

They broke down the door with the shaft from a cart, seized their victim and demanded his money. At the answer that he had none, they lit a bundle of large wood in the fireplace and stretched him out on top of it. Sauvestre then gave him the coins he had in his closet. A second time, the brigands demanded his gold, and stretched him out again on the fire. Sauvestre then gave them the few pieces of gold he had left.[20]

The same gang then besieged Moreau's house in La Blanchetière and burned his feet. On the other hand, they were unable to break down doors in La Basse-Pouèze and Le Houx. Again in messidor (June and July 1799), several thefts of money and weapons were committed involving threats and injuries. In thermidor (July and August), a gang of fifty-seven Chouans cut down the liberty trees in several communes of the canton of Le Loroux-Bottereau.[21] Confronted with general indifference, the brigade of gendarmes, which had fled, complained in a report of the "weakness" and "lethargy" they encountered: "The attitude of the brigands, it seems, has satisfied the wishes of the people." Similar scenes took place almost everywhere.[22]

In the canton of Frossay, the municipal authorities complained that it was impossible for them to carry out any policing. "Outside the villages, the brigands rob, pillage, and murder every night and often during the day"; it was all the harder to capture them because some were disguised as national guards.[23] According to a central commissioner, this situation was widespread throughout northern Deux-Sèvres: "The systematic pillaging and murder is taking on an alarming character."[24] The brigands ravaged a few houses in Cerisay and Saint-Porchaire, burned the home of citizen Fournie in Bouillé-Lorets, sacked the police barracks in Argenton-Château, and committed several excesses there, notably against the wife of Brigadier Moreau and his daughter, aged fifteen, who was raped before their eyes. On 8 brumaire of the year VIII, 1,500–2,000 "brigands" appeared in Saint-Loup; they even threatened Parthenay. In La Chapelle-Saint-Laurent, eight to ten brigands on horseback pillaged and tore all the papers of the administration and took 1,267 livres from the tax payments for the year VI from the commune of Chanteloup.[25]

Millers were often targeted.[26] Peasants already heavily taxed by bonds and permits, accused them of "skimming" the flour and "shortweighting" them. Confronted with this crime, the unarmed persons were most frequently left to fend for themselves. To defend themselves, the inhabitants of

Brière made three cannons out of wood bound with iron.[27] Militias were organized and night watches set up, but all these measures were insufficient, as the mayor of Salartenne complained:

> Famine will not be long in making its disastrous effects felt in the region without a better ordering of things . . . The farmer is not left in peace in his cottage; his wife and his daughter are raped in front of him. He is made a witness and sometimes an accomplice of this infamy. Death pursues him from every direction and despair makes him abandon his land. Soon, these fields will be covered with ruins instead of the beautiful harvests they used to produce . . .[28]

A justice of the peace named Brière complained that peasants could no longer leave their cattle in pastures unless they guarded them day and night: "They are even forced to lock them up; it is an immense harm and a considerable loss of time."[29] To protect against these dangers, the administration asked the Vendeans for support, but made the mistake of persisting in failing to distinguish between common criminals and political rebels: "Do you know, citizens, who are the men who violate your shelters and attack your persons and property with criminal hands? They are the émigrés, the priests, who are hiding to plan new outrages, and their satellites." It urged informing: "Arrest and denounce all the individuals in hiding or unknown to you." And it threatened: "If you do not take this firm resolution . . . your blood will flow again, and we will have the sorrow of being unable to stop it."[30]

In addition, because hunting had been suspended since 1792, wolves were proliferating; they were as hungry as the men, whom they attacked, even in houses. To promote hunting, decrees were published[31] and rewards offered for every capture: ten livres for an adult, three for a cub.[32] On 10 messidor of the year VI, the rewards were increased to forty francs for a male and for a female who was not pregnant, sixty francs for one who was, and twenty for a cub.[33] To receive the reward, the hunter had to present a head, the left ear, or both. But in this case as well, the unarmed population was powerless (138 wolves were killed in the year V in Deux-Sèvres, 118 in the year VI, 128 in the year VII, and 98 in the year VIII), and packs caused major damage.[34] Generous soldiers were rare, like those in Thouars who agreed to give out cartridges,[35] as were the generals like Gilibert who allowed a few rifles to be handed out.[36]

However, not all governments were absolutely deaf to the complaints from the Vendée. The Convention even recognized, in its session of September 29, 1794, that

atrocities had been committed in the unfortunate lands of the Vendée. Barbarous leaders, who still dare to call themselves Republicans, have caused to be killed, for the pleasure of killing, old men, women, children. Even patriotic communes have been the victims of these monsters whose execrable crimes we will refrain from describing in detail.[37]

Logically, the Assembly had decided on 30 prairial of the year II to try to reconstitute destroyed tools by sending 4,000 scythes and 20,000 sickles; this was clearly insufficient, as the administration itself admitted.[38] For its part, the commission on subsistence and supplies multiplied initiatives: construction of grain lofts, advice, compensation. The main purpose of the lofts, made obligatory by the law of 3 germinal of the year II (August 9, 1793) and concentrated in canton capitals, was providing for the immediate needs of the army. Later, because of the lack of grain in local markets, these became public depots where all the available wheat was collected; to this end, canvas, for sacks,[39] and carts were requisitioned, along with drivers, who were paid.[40]

Various recommendations were also given to local populations to avoid famine.[41] Attention was drawn to the consumption of potatoes, "which in times of scarcity have provided such invaluable resources for humanity." To feed the cattle, farmers were advised to remove all the new shoots from trees: "the bull likes them as much as hay." On occasion, shoots of ivy and the like could be used.

Compensation provided invaluable help.[42] Depending on circumstances, it was distributed by communes, districts, or arrondissements. In Vendée, the finest ram was bought for fifty livres; a cow for four hundred; a filly for two hundred, and so on. For the year 1796 alone, the department granted almost 60,000 francs as the price of "encouragement."[43] In Loire-Inférieure, on the day of the agricultural celebration, the names of the best peasants were "proclaimed" and "citizens who carried out plantings" were encouraged.[44]

On occasion, experiments might be attempted. An engineer proposed that a rich patch of ground in a suitable location be selected and managed for the benefit of and at the expense of the nation: "The first expenses of the establishment would be for twelve steers chosen from among those belonging to the nation, twenty fine ewes, the two finest bulls, two fine stallions, some fine mares, four or six rams with fine ewes from Mortagne, and the largest type of pig . . ."[45] This livestock would increase and be improved through breeding. "Starting from this kernel, there would gradually spread good methods of farming, fine types of animals, and the grains whose usefulness had been demonstrated by experience. Novelty would no longer inspire mistrust because people would be reassured by success." This experiment, supplemented by distributions of animals, would foster emulation among farmers. The project was not unique; there were even proposals to nationalize the land and to set up a kind of collective farm.

However, for lack of resources, the commission was essentially a failure, as the mayor of Salartennes explained: "Everything is lacking for agriculture: wagons, plows, iron, steel, straps to tie steers, steers themselves, cows, horses, animals of all kinds, day workers and laborers conscripted by the army."[46] According to him, those principally responsible were the brigands and the volunteers who were completing the methodical work of the civil commission of Nantes.[47]

Bourasseau, former member of the superior council of Châtillon, summarized the situation in very bitter terms in an address to the minister:

> The amnesty, general pacification . . . The implementation of the new constitution had given rise in the heart of the Vendeans to the consoling thought that the mistakes and the fury of the revolutionary government had died out and that its iron scepter was definitively broken; they deluded themselves with the glittering hope that this immortal code was going to become something to be enjoyed by all of the French . . . Stofflet, Charrette, and Sapinaud again wished to draw the sword and resume their ambitious and guilty plans; alas, for the Vendée all hope immediately vanished like a dream. Pillage, the seizure of cattle and grain, corvées, searches, arbitrary imprisonment, murder, and rape reappeared with a fury equal to that of Robespierre.
>
> The armed forces compel the communes to make payments in kind, although the constitution provides that only the legislature has the right to do so . . . they remove peasants from their work in the fields by forcing them to transport materials and provisions without compensation and sometimes over great distances. What advantage have they gained

from the law of August 4, 1789, that abolished corvées? . . . The armed forces punish a commune with huge fines and imprisonment . . . Pillage is forbidden, we are told; yes, but it goes unpunished. If we propose ways of preventing it, they do not want to use them . . .[48]

The situation could not fail to traumatize the people and make the local authorities take stock.

ELEVEN

Local Authorities Confront
Their Consciences

THE NEW CONSTITUTION ADOPTED ON AUGUST 22, 1795, TRANSFORMED
the administrative tradition. It stated that now only towns of more than
five thousand inhabitants would have a municipal government. From then
on, one town hall for each canton in the countryside would be enough,
along with one municipal agent to represent each commune. It was therefore necessary to carry out new elections and appointments, a source of serious difficulty.

The Establishment of the New Administrative Structures

The stirring zeal of the early days had soon cooled among the patriots.
Honors were less flattering in the context of the problems that had been
created. There was thus a nearly universal rejection.

Various pretexts were offered for avoiding government service: illness,
lack of time, lack of interest, and so on. Some pointed out the bad working conditions. In Le Pellerin, for example, the agents had not been reimbursed for their expenses in purchasing paper, ink, wood, and candles.[1]
They did not even have a secretary, although "none of them was familiar
with writing." Arthon lacked the bare minimum of furniture: for a desk,
the clerk had to use a barrel. On many occasions, Paimbœuf voiced its distress: "We have been without money for a long time; we owe a great deal and
no one wants to give us credit . . ."[2] In Bressuire on 11 floréal of the year V,

the mayor asked for 250 livres for office expenses, or else he would be "up to my neck in filth, cold, without window glass or fire, and all the papers in disorder . . ."[3]

The abandonment of municipal offices paralyzed the administration: "The result is general confusion that threatens to take over the machine and block all its cogs."[4] The provisional commissioners reacted by issuing futile threats. In the absence of any other solution, former municipal authorities were reappointed, to the great anger of municipal agents: "Devotion has its limits, even when it comes to serving the Republic," protested the representatives of Le Pellerin.[5] "Saint, commissioner to the cantonal administration, attributes the general lack of interest not only to lack of concern, disgust, and the refusal to act, but also to the fatherly care required by every family." Deux-Sèvres, particularly the canton of Les Aubiers, was deeply affected by this reaction: "The agents are so unconcerned and apathetic that they have never had a quorum at a meeting of the municipal administration, and sometimes they do not even bother to come to sign letters, copies, certificates, and other documents."[6]

Every new election produced another failure. On February 7, 1796, only thirty-one electors came to vote in Le Pellerin. The next attempt had no greater success. The municipal authority then held an extraordinary session on April 11 (17 germinal),

> during which it declared it could no longer fulfill its functions and de-
> cided that notice would be posted calling for a third assembly on 28 ger-
> minal (April 17) . . . If no one were to accept, the municipal agent
> threatened, the department would be asked to appoint commissioners
> with the duty of administering the commune, which would be an extra
> expense for the citizens.[7]

People elected refused to accept office or exercised it very sporadically. In Sainte-Pazanne and Port-Saint-Père in the Retz region, there was not a single meeting of the municipal authorities for six months, and the president himself refused to attend. In Saint-Hilaire-de-Chaléons, Chemeré, and Chauvé, no one would accept the most minor office. Confronted with this kind of opposition, departmental authorities proposed to appoint municipal agents themselves and to force them to accept office. In the event of a refusal, "a garrison would be sent at the expense of the communes . . ." The persons concerned would thus have the excuse that they had been forced and would no longer fear "the reproaches and threats of their fellow citizens."[8]

In fact, all these initiatives, as in La Chapelle-Bassemère, were without effect.[9] Four of the members elected on 3 vendémiaire of the year VI (September 25, 1798) refused to attend the meeting on various ingenious pretexts: the first, Laurent Bertin, cited his business; the second, Jacques Vivant, a notary, the fact that his home was too far away; the third, Louis Herbelin, a barrelmaker, his age (seventy-two); the last, Pierre Bahaud, the fact that he was related to one of the members of the commission.

Accepting office was not free of danger. There are many examples: Boutin, the mayor of Le Loroux-Bottereau, was shot by the Vendeans on 16 ventôse of the year II (March 6, 1794).[10] A year later, Aubin L'Homme du Paty, first assistant to the president of La Chapelle-Bassemère, recognized as a "good patriot," was carried off by four unknown men and found drowned three weeks later.[11] On December 25, 1795, Brillaud, president of the canton of Secondigny, suffered the same fate.[12] Similar actions were carried out against Republican collaborators and informers. For example, the mother-in-law of Mauget, a municipal agent of Le Loroux-Bottereau, was assassinated along with her two servants. Rault, the commissioner of the cantonal directory, prepared a detailed report:

> Marie Ollivier, widow of Mathurin Chon, aged about sixty, was found . . . at around eight in the morning, her two feet suspended by two ropes, one held her and the other strangled her. A handkerchief was in her mouth, tied behind and very tight, and her arms tied behind her back. Perrine Viaud, her personal maid, aged thirty, was found lying on the floor, wearing a skirt and a light bodice, her head toward the widow Chon and her feet toward the door, her two arms behind her back. A handkerchief had been used to strangle her and another was over her mouth and went behind her head. Jean Bonnaud, a manservant, aged twenty-five, was found in a separate room, lying on his bed, his feet on the floor, his face on the mattress. Nothing had been stolen.[13]

In addition to murders, there were daily harassments, doors broken down, windows broken, physical assaults, and so on. In Port-Saint-Père, the municipal agents declared that it was impossible for them to visit several villages without exposing themselves to violence: they were insulted, assaulted, and chased back to their houses, which they no longer dared to inhabit.[14]

They were also the target of organized gangs. In Clisson, for instance, the military commanders, Constantin and Belorde, had their furniture stolen;[15] in Les Herbiers, the commander of the guard was wounded.[16]

In view of the weakness of the public authorities, some elected patriots chose to explain themselves to the people: "To secure bread for our families and restore our ruined and devastated property is a sacred duty . . ."[17] Others took refuge in the departments or even emigrated: Vivant, brother of the notary of La Chapelle-Bassemère, chose to go to the United States.[18] These attitudes troubled the administration. "In fact," explained the municipal officers of Savenay, "the administration will be paralyzed until the wheels of the carriage to which it is hitched have been completely replaced."[19]

Various solutions were adopted to remedy the situation. The first was the establishment of a list making possible "continuous surveillance of individuals, whether emigrants or not." Some communes were asked not to omit children as young as twelve:[20] "The aim is to draw a sharp line of demarcation between good and bad citizens in order to protect the former and to pursue the others" (3 floréal, year IV).[21] The second solution consisted in reprimanding the established authorities "who wish only to make themselves popular and to secure the indulgence of the people."[22] Prosecutorial authorities were fully aware of this and publicly proclaimed it on 6 floréal of the year IV: "Chouannerie can exist only through the weakness, cowardice, or malice of the citizens. A precise, active, and well-coordinated relationship must be established step-by-step among the national guards of each canton, and frequent and continuing patrols be carried out to provide mutual assistance."[23]

In accordance with the law of 17 floréal of the year IV,[24] mobile columns of the stationary national guard were set up in every canton despite almost insurmountable difficulties: "The municipal agents were reluctant to designate one person rather than another . . ."[25] On 19 vendémiaire of the year IV, the ministry of the interior went even further in a circular on security: every individual who was traveling had to carry a passport signed by the municipal officers of the commune or the canton (title III).[26] The department of Deux-Sèvres was put in a state of siege,[27] and there was even talk of hostages.[28]

In order to pursue "the scoundrels," some districts, such as Vihiers, decided to set up commissions made up of "citizens known for public spirit and honesty."[29] On 21 nivôse of the year IV, Hoche established emergency regulations for the entire region.[30] Although freedom of commerce was restored and guaranteed, the people were obliged not to come to the aid of the rebels on pain of punishment: communes were condemned to pay one-fourth of their grain if found to have supplied provisions; they would have to pay ten thousand livres or the equivalent in grain for a murder if the criminal was not found, and young men would be held for at least six months; in case of insurrection, those guilty would be given a military trial, punished in accordance with law, their families held for six months, and their grain and cattle confiscated; whoever hid an émigré, a deserter, or a rebel, or was found in possession of a rifle, would pay a fine in grain equivalent to one-third of his income.

Following these decisions, Vendeans and patriots refused to be involved with the State. According to the administration's own admission, the failure was apparent: "A scandalous agitation is demoralizing the nation and drying up all the sources of public happiness." Although obstacles were countless they could be overcome: "Only one thing is needed, a sincere, strong, and single will." It was a matter of instilling this will in the heart of the citizen, which would happen when "the hearts of all the French . . . beat with a sincere love of the liberty that sanctified the dawn of the revolution . . ." It needed to be proclaimed "to the feckless egoists who hold public affairs in contempt that their peace, their fortunes, and their lives are in danger as long as they remain in their dismal apathy; to the irresolute that it is time to declare themselves, to tear themselves away from the gnawing anxiety eating away at them . . ." The task was not easy; it would require patriotism, enlightenment, unlimited devotion, feverish activity, a spirit of helpfulness, and a sense of method. Even everyday duties required effort: "Mayors and other agents must walk between two pitfalls: unjust suspicion and partiality; weakness and rigor; haughtiness and familiarity; liberticidal tyranny and alarming credulity . . ." Above all, it was important "to avoid excesses, to practice justice, firmness, and decency. This salutary continual surveillance deprives the administrator of his sleep only so that the citizen may peacefully enjoy his own . . ."[31]

REALIZATIONS BY THE LOCAL AUTHORITIES

In ventôse of the year V (February and March 1797), the directory intended to enforce the law of July 5, 1793.[32] According to Article III, "The leaders, commanders, and captains, the originators and instigators of armed gatherings without the authorization of the proper authorities, either known as

Chouans or by any other name, will be punished by death." Military commissions were established, and their sentences were immediately executed
and published. Special rewards ranging from 300 to 2,400 livres were given
to whoever "facilitates the arrest of a priest subject to deportation or a leader
of the assassins."[33] Further, all inhabitants who had played a role in the war
of the Vendée lost their civil rights. The departmental decree of Nantes
even declared their exclusion from any assembly.

Following this promulgation, some local administrations came to the
defense of their citizens. Commissioner Rault, witness to all the earlier trage-
dies, pointed out in an address to the executive directory of the department
of Loire-Inférieure that the strict application of the law and its accompanying decree would amount to the suppression of municipal assemblies;
all the notables present had, willingly or under duress, played a role in help-
ing the insurgents. Since day laborers were not present, only well-off and
intelligent people attended the primary and communal assemblies in the
countryside. If kept away, they would feel nothing but disgust and aversion
for the regime. "Barely stifled discontent will be reborn in the hearts and
minds of good people otherwise inclined toward union and peace." Rault,
relying on the principles of the Declaration of the Rights of Man and
Citizen, explained that following the directory's decree to the letter would
have serious consequences, such as the abandonment of the very idea of municipal meetings and of all kinds of public functions. Several officials had already decided to resign. The commissioner raised several sensible questions:
How could administrations be imposed? How was it possible to demand taxes
from people who had had all their rights taken away? "If they are good enough
to pay, they should be good enough to govern."[34]

The government overrode these objections. There ensued some serious
troubles, which the military leaders, by their own admission, could not control
for lack of manpower. Deux-Sèvres, for instance, had only eleven hundred
soldiers in a precarious position, suffering, among other things, from cold and
hunger.[35] Misery was even greater in Le Loroux-Bottereau: "Bread that the
dogs don't want, no shoes, or clothes, or meat, or vegetables, or pay, or wine;
what do you expect them to do? They are men, after all."[36] The battalion in
Thouars even signed a petition to "solicit an increase in rations because it was
receiving only two pounds of bread and a half pound of meat per day."[37]

In addition, the men were not always available because of their many
tasks where they were stationed: watching traffic, carrying letters, ensuring
the cleanliness of public places, and so on.[38] Often, they were not called out

because they frequently indulged in pillaging, as in Aubiers in 1799. "The joy
that we felt at the defeat of our enemies," explained the mayor of Bressuire,
"was severely tempered by the pillage to which the troops gave themselves
over. We can only describe it to you by the expression of some of the soldiers who said that they had made a raid. This conduct unworthy of Republicans caused consternation for all our fellow citizens."[39]

The directory of Le Loroux-Bottereau was just as explicit:

> It is no longer possible to keep this troop for another week, for the
> countryside will show nothing but vine leaves, trees cut down, and
> streets full of chicken feathers. The most revolting plundering is driving
> the people to despair. They have cut down the trees to make clogs, they
> stole a maple trunk from the village clogmakers, and they threatened to
> shoot us.[40]

The district of Paimbœuf was also very unhappy with the conduct of
the volunteers, "who have no more respect for the property of Republicans
than for that of the brigands."[41] In Frossay (Loire-Inférieure), they were
always in search of food "and devastated houses by walking every day on the
roofs";[42] the village "will soon be nothing but a pile of stones and dust," the
procurator complained.[43] For heat, the garrison of Machecoul took planks
and beams from ruined houses.[44] And in Saint-Philbert-de-Grand-Lieu,
the troops forced the inhabitants to keep their houses open so the troops
could cook.[45]

Troops in camp still behaved as though in conquered territory, with no
concern for popular distress. Even the agents of the government, whom it
was their mission to guard and protect, complained and declared themselves
"embittered by this terrorism."[46] The government authorities became aware
of a complete reversal among their mayors, who, disgusted by the state of
affairs, showed themselves indifferent if not hostile to the government, to
which they explained themselves openly:

> We are not afraid to tell you that every resource has been taken
> from us by lack of confidence in the promises of the government. How
> many times have we not made the most solemn commitments without
> being able to fulfill them? How many times has the hope of citizens
> that our appeals and promises had managed to win over not been dis-

appointed? The result is that not one individual wants to cooperate under any conditions whatever . . .[47]

As a result, a large number of municipal authorities contravened administrative decisions, refrained from playing patriotic songs at the beginnings of plays or from carrying out new conscription (leading to the failure of the Jourdan law), and blocked the collection of taxes or at least refused to assist in doing so.[48] They even, as in La Chapelle-Thireuil, made "frankly insulting remarks" and demanded that a line of demarcation be set between civil and military authorities.[49]

The reaction was immediate and sharp: all municipal authorities were immediately reprimanded and ordered to set a good example on pain of dismissal and "even greater punishments (*sic*)."[50]

Two anonymous reports (signed "X") of 23 and 26 ventôse of the year VI (March 10 and 13, 1798), sent to the ministry from Nantes, indicated the state of mind of the population on the eve of elections.[51] The first pointed out the reappearance of criticisms of the government, even from people apparently rallied to the Republic: passions were flaring; agents were being threatened; the discontented were raising their voices. Since the region lacked troops, the danger was all the more acute. The guilty parties were unquestionably the priests who "are agitating and abusing more than ever their treacherous influence in order to indoctrinate the weak at the time of the former Easter holidays." Popular gatherings to say the rosary were taking place every evening: "The inhabitants are summoned by a horn" or by bagpipes.[52] The second report spoke of "subversive activities" showing up almost everywhere: in Saint-Sauveur and Landemont, the peasants had even fired their rifles to test their weapons. It also complained of priests "who preach rebellion" and proclaim the coming end of the government. In fact, this period, far from restoring the authority of the administration, consecrated the legitimacy of the clergy.

The Legitimacy of the Clergy
and Its Activity

THE VENDEAN CLERGY WAS DECIMATED DURING THE WAR. OF THE SIX
priests in charge and the nine native priests in La Chapelle-Bassemère on
the eve of the Revolution, eight died in the "storm" and two in exile.[1] The
survivors, aged and worn out, nevertheless managed to comfort their flocks
and lead them to peace.

A Decimated Clergy

The revolutionaries always considered the clergy the principal enemy. The
law of August 26, 1792, condemned to deportation all nonjuring clergy as
well as those whose actions had caused disturbances or whose removal was
requested by six persons domiciled in the same department. Infirm priests or
those over sixty were not affected but were to be interned in the department
capital: any contravention was punished with a prison term of ten years. The
decree of March 18, 1793, went further and condemned to death any priest
subject to deportation who was arrested. This early persecution was followed
by the killings during the war by guillotine or drowning: in Nantes, for example, 84 priests were killed on November 16, 1793.[2]

Some were despicably treated, such as Abbé Joseph Cosneau, who held
the living of the *chevallerie* at Maumusson.[3] Arrested by the Blues toward
the end of 1794, he was tied to the tail of a horse and dragged to Ancenis,
passing through Saint-Herblon. There he was mutilated with sword blows,

then tied to a plank and put in the Loire. Soldiers on the banks made a game of shooting their rifles at him. Abbé Louis Jousset, hidden in Le Cellier, his native parish, was caught saying mass in the neighboring forest; he suffered an even more horrible fate. After frightful torture, he was killed and his remains were fed to the dogs.[4]

Priests, perhaps more than any other group, were subject to "public" persecution. As J.-R. Colle wrote in his *Petite histoire de La Rochelle,* because ideologues had filled the people with antireligious propaganda, whenever the situation worsened, those who wished to preserve their faith were held responsible, and hatred was naturally turned against the priests.[5]

For example, after the defeat of General Marcé at Le Pont-Charron on March 19, 1793, the troops that arrived in disorder in La Rochelle demanded, with the support of the people, the head of their leader. In order to create a diversion, the district commissioner, Crassous, ordered the commune prosecutor to liberate four priests on the pretext of sending them to the île d'Oléron. Hardly were they in the street when the crowd, stirred up by the wigmaker Darbelet, rushed at them, struck them with sticks, and forced them to return to prison. Excitement reached its peak; the populace, drunk for blood, slaughtered the four priests horribly:

> The men struck renewed blows, the women seized the heads to bang them on the ground, another took pleasure in passing a bloody ear in front of the women, a sailor opened a stomach with a razor . . . A woman cried out: "This is better than holy water." The bodies were then dragged to the dock, still being subjected to many blows. "A man named Lionet sneered and flourished scraps of flesh and a crucifix." All the priests had their heads cut off, stuck on pitchforks, and paraded through the town. The death certificate includes the incredible indication: "priests dead as victims of popular emotion." The next day, March 22, other priests suffered the same fate; their remains were cut into pieces and disputed by their killers, saying things like "You've got a bigger one than mine . . ."

Scenes like this were repeated everywhere, sometimes with cynical cries from the crowds: "Let them be immediately canonized so they can carry the bullets to the eternal father . . ."[6]

Although it is difficult to determine an exact figure for the victims of such treatment, it is at least possible to provide the minimum numbers of those who died natural or violent deaths (see table 12.1).[7]

Table 12.1.   Priests who died violent or natural deaths

Department	Priests recorded in 1789	Priests in hiding		Priests who remained and died during the war		
		Number	% of priests recorded	Number	% of priests recorded	% of priests in hiding
Anjou (49)	333	192	57.65	116	34.83	60.41
Loire-Inférieure (44)	445	141	31.68	41	9.2	29.01
Vendée (85)	760	247	32.5	123	16.18	49.79

Anjou was heavily affected by repression, for four reasons: the heavy concentration of priests in a small territory; the proximity to centers of persecution; the great efficacy of the infernal columns; and perhaps also the significant number of those who had crossed the river during Galerne's expedition. The figures for the Vendée must be qualified because they reflect the whole department; clearly, most of the priests who remained in hiding were in the northern part. Insurgent Loire-Inférieure suffered only 29 percent of the deaths, which is little in comparison to the neighboring departments. There are various reasons for this: a large area in relation to the 141 priests in hiding; well-developed means of protection; and substantial popular complicity.

To the loss of refractory priests must be added that of the constitutionals: 66 for the Vendée of the 209 registered (33.5 percent) and 18 out of 44 for Anjou (44.26 percent). In fact, if the defrocked priests are eliminated from these total figures (81 for the Vendée and 8 for Anjou), Vendée lost 54.68 percent of its constitutional priests and Anjou, 50 percent. These substantial numbers can be explained: once captured by the insurgents, these priests were immediately shot or placed in front of the troops in battle. Some were even driven to suicide. Very few of the refractory priests incarcerated in Republican prisons survived. At the tribunal, which was conducted by national guards, the presentation itself contained the sentence "This is a priest." The judges then inexorably touched a little ax, saying nothing, or replied, "Death."[8]

A CLERGY SUBJECT TO REAL PERSECUTION UNTIL 1799

Some émigré priests took advantage of apparent periods of reconciliation to return. Their conditions as exiles were often difficult, particularly in Spain. Many had even had to work at nonclerical jobs in order to survive. Some demonstrated particularly notable talents, such as Abbé Mouilleron, the curé of Sainte-Marie, who learned to make chocolate; he made his fortune in London, where there is still a street bearing his name.[9] Many of these priests were arrested as soon as they landed; this happened to at least twelve in Quiberon.[10] They were shot at La Garenne in Vannes, along with Monseigneur de Hérie, the bishop of Dol.

Although latent and sporadic, the persecution of the clergy was nonetheless real. In one of its first instructions to the national commissioners of each department, the Directory pointed out the refractory priests: "Frustrate their treacherous plans, block their maneuvers, surround them with active, continual, tireless surveillance; give them no quarter; let them, without seeing you, feel you everywhere and at every moment . . ."[11] Individual testimony about this tyranny is eloquent. On August 23, 1797, Abbé Jacques Gobineau, the curé of Gené, closed his parish register with a marginal note: "The little curé of Gené was absent from his parish and obliged to go into hiding for the following two years."[12] Abbé Chevalier, the curé of Saint-Lumine-de-Coutais (Loire-Inférieure), was more precise:

> During the month of August 1798, persecution having again been decreed and orders having been given throughout France to make the most careful search for priests, and home visits having begun and been ordered for the entire month, we were forced to keep ourselves more carefully concealed and to withdraw into the forest, unable to carry out any of the work of our ministry, until the end of the month, when the said visits ended according to the terms of the decree.[13]

In 1797 this priest had already been forced to flee and to go into hiding because of a fresh outbreak of local violence. The narrative of Abbé Mathurin Billot, the vicar of Frossay, is just as painful:

> From that unhappy time ('94) we have been wandering here and there, without ever leaving our diocese, throughout which the lord bishop of Nantes had given us his powers as soon as he learned of our refusal to

acquiesce to the infamous oath. We have rendered the greatest services wherever the terrible persecution forced us to retreat. In the month of August 1796, conforming to the orders of Monsieur de Chévigné de Boischollet, vicar-general of Monseigneur de La Laurencie, we traveled to Frossay in order to serve mass as a successor to Monsieur Jean-Baptiste Picard, who died in the Bouffay prison in Nantes. We stayed there a year and a few days. During all that time, the ministry was extremely difficult. We were the only Catholic priest in the entire area. The last Thursday of the month of August 1797, we were again driven out by the Republicans. We wandered once more until this day, December 30, 1799, not knowing when the evils desolating our unfortunate nation will come to an end . . .[14]

As for Abbé Michel Gillier, the vicar of Legé, he made revealing observations about the kind of life to which he was condemned:

The reader will probably be surprised to see no witness signature on most of the certificates that are contained in this register. It was impossible for me in those times of trouble and confusion, which will be difficult to imagine in the future, to inscribe each one in its proper place. It sometimes took me more than six weeks to find a few people to give me a precise idea, which I immediately wrote down on loose sheets of paper, and later recorded them in better order. It would further have been very troublesome for me to carry this register with me, being forced to change hiding places at every moment by the almost continual searches that the enemy constantly made in the woods and the different pieces of land scattered throughout the parish. I often was even obliged to flee after beginning a ceremony of baptism or burial, although I always took the precaution beforehand of informing myself of the position of the enemy, undertaking nothing when I saw any danger.[15]

The administration granted very few periods of respite to the clergy, particularly under the "second directory." The department of Deux-Sèvres even asked its agents to arrest temporarily "all the priests who ought to be reminded of the government's severity."[16] Persecution was no doubt less violent than it had been, but harassment continued. Evidence can be found in the report of a tour by the captain-commander of the gendarmerie of the department of Loire-Inférieure, dated 20 prairial of the year VII (June 7,

1799). After observing that the peasants were suffering from taxes, the officer, named Cuny, complained that the priests had seized the opportunity to rouse the "torch of fanaticism," and that two crosses had been restored. He went on, "The priests, particularly in La Chapelle-Bassemère and Haute-Goulaine, say mass in public. Two weeks ago the priest Robin gave communion to children."[17] Cuny considered arresting Robin and conferred with the authorities of Le Loroux-Bottereau. After consideration, they determined that such an arrest would be untimely, even though the time and place of the mass were known. They also recognized that the general complicity of the people and "that of his family" made the arrest very problematic.

Hunted down and worn out, several priests died. The curé of Carquefou, Abbé Gabriel Héry, died on April 13, 1798, on a farm; he "was buried in a cellar" in the village of La Baumerée.[18] Abbé Yves Marchais, the curé of La-Chapelle-du-Genêt, "having taken refuge in a house in the village," was "buried, without a priest but with the attendance of the whole parish, who recited the rosary aloud."[19]

On 17 brumaire of the year VI (November 9, 1798), the administration again made use of disguised gendarmes, as it had in the past. However, any abuses were sharply condemned:

> What purpose is served by this misplaced harshness that has been allowed in some places against those who, it has been thought, should be punished according to law? It serves as a pretext for your enemies to slander the government. When the government tells you to arrest and deport the rebellious priests, it does not tell you to subject them to humiliation, to heap insults on them, to be, in a word, more severe than the law.[20]

There were many arrests, such as that of Abbé Charles Paizot, vicar of Iré, on June 9, 1799; he had hidden in a cellar under two cords of wood.[21] In Maumusson, fourteen priests were arrested by gendarmes disguised as hunters.[22] Death sentences were infrequent: the authorities wanted to avoid creating martyrs and transforming places of execution into pilgrimage sites like Auray and Vannes.[23] In addition to imprisonment in departmental prisons and various fortresses, among them that of Ré, the priests were deported to Guyana. "It was abandonment and exile in all their bitterness," explained Abbé de Beauregard, vicar-general of Luçon.[24] However, despite the dangers, the nonjuring clergy were extremely active.

AN ACTIVE CLERGY

Not only did the priests ensure the continuity of worship in the parishes under their care, they might also be led to take care of other communities, sometimes very distant. Evidence of this can be found in various certificates in clandestine parish registers. For instance, in addition to his own parish, Abbé Robin, curé of La Chapelle-Bassemère, took care of about a dozen others: Saint-Sébastien, Saint-Main, Mauves, Le Loroux-Bottereau, Carquefou, Saint-Sauveur, Landemont, Le Cellier, La Varenne, Saint-Julien-de-Concelles, Thouaré, and even Nantes.[25]

Parishes were thus regularly served by one or more priests, whether or not they were incumbents. Carquefou was privileged; between 1791 and 1801 it enjoyed the simultaneous or successive services of close to thirty priests.[26] Aware of their mission, these clergy attempted through the administration of sacraments to maintain the rhythm of the Gregorian calendar, with its respect for Sundays, feast days, and ritual practices.

Some priests were even bold enough, in the midst of repression, to conduct processions. On Sunday, June 18, 1797, to celebrate Corpus Christi, Jacques Galpin, the curé of Melay, followed by the great majority of his commune, came "out of the building in which he held his ceremonies."[27] Abbé René Ayrault, vicar of Coron, even had bells rung to announce services and appeared in public wearing his vestments.[28] He replied to the reprimands of the cantonal commissioner by saying that he was ready to respect the law provided "it in no way affected his religion." Abbé Robin, curé of La Chapelle-Bassemère, after restoring a procession in honor of Saint John on July 8, 1797, was questioned by Rault, commissioner of the directory. An explanation was then communicated to the departmental authorities. "I was more than a little surprised myself," wrote Rault,

> at the procession on Saint John's Day this month in the village. That day I was in Le Loroux and did not learn of it until the evening. I immediately went to see the priest Robin, to whom I read the provisions of the law concerning regulation of public worship. This is what he answered: "I am very distressed, citizen, to have given reason for the civil authorities to censure me and to have stimulated their particular concern. The action I took today contains nothing that should alarm you or any of the authorities. I can only reproach myself for it and I swear on my faith as a priest that I will not repeat it. I was led into error,

and this is how: several people came this morning to assure me that a decree had come from Nantes relating to the restoration of public worship and particularly of processions. As a result, they urgently requested that I conduct one. I did not think that I ought to refuse on the basis of the affirmation they had made about the law that had been passed. I was all the less afraid because, in Landemont and Saint-Sauveur, which are only a mile and a half away, they have processions every Sunday. In truth, I know that they have them in Maine-et-Loire. So, it was only this evening, when I read *La Gazette*, that I saw the error into which those individuals had led me. I promise you that I will hereafter wait for your orders and will allow myself no innovation of this kind. I will only point out to you that I did not go beyond the walls of the cemetery adjacent to the church."[29]

In spite of the administration, these processions proliferated throughout the region, some at night by torchlight, as in Clissé.[30] Whenever there was a slight lull, priests catechized and baptized children "who could not be baptized because of the insurrection" or who had had emergency baptisms. Weddings were also performed, under cover of darkness. Even formal solemn services were celebrated. In 1797 François Chevalier, the curé of Saint-Lumine-de-Coutais, was assisted by six priests: Abbé Massonnet, rector of Saint-Même; Abbé Guilbaud, rector of Paulx; Abbé Rohard, rector of Issé; Abbé Leauté, vicar of Saint-Aignan; Abbé Pelletier, vicar of Saint-Colombin; and Abbé Esnault-Vignardière, the priest in charge of Saint-Mars.[31]

In addition to these ceremonies, there were exhumations of bodies that had been hastily buried "at the place of their martyrdom," in order to "give them a more fitting grave."[32] A municipal agent of Montravers, for example was surprised to encounter at a small distance from the commune a refractory priest wearing a crucifix and walking at the head of a funeral procession.[33] The priestly fervor that was put into action can be observed simply by reading the surviving clandestine parish registers.

The religious education of young seminarians was not forgotten. Once they had been educated, the seminarians went abroad to be ordained by the legitimate bishops and then returned to insurgent territory. This was the case for two priests named Peuriot and Durand, taken care of by Abbé Souffrand, vicar of Maumusson. Ordained priests in London in 1796 by Bishop de La Laurencie of Nantes, they were immediately sent back to the military Vendée, one as vicar of Anetz, the other as assistant to Abbé Souffrand.[34]

As early as 1794, some priests, such as Abbé Boisselier in Boussay, reopened schools, with a girl taking care of "children of her sex."[35]

Republicans were not always insensitive to the priests' courage, which sometimes provoked admiration or even esteem. Abbé Souffrand of Maumusson was even on very good terms with the commander of gendarmerie in Ancenis, whom he once invited to dinner. During the meal, they heard someone shouting, "Long live the king." The gendarme thought he had been betrayed and went pale. The priest immediately reassured him and, laughing, took him to see a trained crow in a cage which he had taught a few words, in particular the compromising exclamation that had caused such alarm.[36]

Events of this kind were not isolated, as demonstrated by Abbé Agaisse, vicar of Trans. "How many times," he writes in his *Mémoires*, "not knowing what would become of me, surrounded by enemies, ill, have I not wandered day and night, often without food." Despite his precautions and his agility, he was captured in the parish of Château-Thébaud, where circumstances had made him the priest in charge. "It was a Saturday. 'You will have no trouble, I promise you,'" he was told by the staff officer to whom he was presented, "'if you want to celebrate high mass in the presence of the army, in that church still standing at the edge of the village.'" The abbé, strangely surprised, agreed to everything, suspecting some trick. The next morning at eight the church was filled with soldiers who sang the mass themselves. The sermon followed, and the curé did not mince words: "Soldiers," he exclaimed,

> you are Christians, since you are attending mass today. You believe in God, and you must therefore follow His commandments. But God prohibits murder and injustice. And you have come to ravage our fields and burn our houses. One day, I saw the roads covered with the bodies of women, children and old men that you had unjustly massacred; could they have possibly done you harm?

He then exhorted them in the name of religion and humanity to behave with more gentleness, and explained to them what the life of a Christian soldier should be like.

> These fierce men listened to me with extraordinary attention and seemed to be touched. After mass, several of them came to shake my

hand: "Thank you," they said, "thank you for your good teaching. Thank you for having said mass for us; we have not had that happiness for a long time . . ." They then put a patrol of twenty soldiers at my door to protect me from any harm.

It did not take long for Abbé Agaisse to realize the plans that were hidden by this consideration. "'Citizen,' the commander said to me, 'you are beloved in this parish; all the inhabitants and those nearby have great confidence in you; everywhere we have gone people have spoken well of you; you must surrender arms.'" The reply was sharp:

> I have never been involved in political matters; I have preached my religion and that is all; as minister of a God of peace, I have never stirred up civil war which I regard as the worst of evils. I know that priests have been accused of being the cause and the authors of war; but that is a calumny. The only cause should be sought in the humiliations, the injustices, and especially the violence done to young men to force large numbers of them to leave; I have seen it with my own eyes. That is the true cause of the war and not the Catholic priests. However, I will do my best to see that my parish is calm and free of troubles.

Emissaries were sent throughout the commune to try to bring the inhabitants together; several hundred men agreed to meet. After exhorting them to give their opinion, the priest engaged them in dialogue:

> My friends, they are asking for weapons. You want peace, and I want it as much as you do; but can we trust the Republicans after what has just happened, after everything you have seen? As minister of a God of peace, I strongly urge you to peace; but what is to be done to save the parish, which is threatened with pillage? This is my advice to you, you are free to follow it or not. Besides, you should talk; everyone should give his opinion . . . your land has not been planted; you have no communication with Charrette; you run the risk of dying from hunger, fire, or the sword. Well, let's not attack but stay on the defensive. Everyone should be armed; whoever has two weapons should give one to those who have none, to protect us from further oppression, especially after being taken in so many times by hypocrisy and fine words.

The advice was followed. Once weapons had been redistributed, twenty-six poor rifles and pikes were given to the Blues. Peace was sealed, the parish avoided being pillaged, and the priest even received a certificate of security from Hoche.[37]

Heroic actions were countless, with the love of the priesthood mixed with foolhardiness. Abbé Clair Massonnet, curé of Ligné, refused throughout the period of persecution to remove his ecclesiastical habit. "A disguise would be completely useless," he explained to his worried parishioners, "because I would always be recognized by my white hair."[38] To someone who pitied him for continually being obliged to flee and to hide, Abbé Souffrand, curé of Maumusson, replied, "If the Republicans knew how happy I am to be persecuted for the good cause, I imagine they would tear their hair out in fury."[39] The priests consequently became extremely popular and inspired admiration in their parishioners through their courage, as an inhabitant of Frossay wrote of his curé, Abbé Mathurin Billot:

> Toward the end of 1796, Monsieur Billot, provided with confirmed powers, returned to Frossay to resume his apostolic labors; but he could still celebrate mass only in hiding, in the greatest silence, and in this critical situation he performed several first communions . . . Intrepid, energetic, and always keeping his head, he covered the district of Paimbœuf, all of whose parishes he is said to have visited, especially at night and in disguise, spreading the graces of his ministry everywhere.
>   . . . He was an indefatigable man, and I, who saw him at work, cannot understand how he could withstand so much travail and escape from so many dangers . . .[40]

Their intrepid zeal made it possible for these men of the Church to count on the absolute protection of all the faithful, the members of their family they had never abandoned; they lived with them through all the events of the war, sometimes risking their lives to follow them into battle or exile or to welcome them on their return.

REACTIONS OF THE POPULATION TO THE REFRACTORY CLERGY

The population provided the clergy with the means of survival and, when necessary, protected them. Without their normal salaries, the clergy were obliged to live from day to day, from offerings from the faithful and from their families. Since the priests had a burdensome ministry and many duties, their economic situation was even more difficult because they were ruined by the crisis. Some lacked even the bare minimum to carry on their ministry, as Abbé Chevallier, curé of Saint-Lumine-de-Coutais complained on April 13, 1795: "Until now, we have been unable to perform baptisms or draw up certificates; almost always in hiding, we dared do nothing in public; and since the peace proposals made toward the end of last year, during which persecution was not overt, I have had neither official paper, nor holy oils, nor baptismal water."[41]

Some lacked even the bare necessities. There ensued a reaction in some parishes that favored a return to the situation of the Old Regime. On January 30, 1796, the inhabitants of La Chapelle-Bassemère made an agreement with their curé recorded in the parish register. The tithe, abolished by the law of January 1, 1791, was restored:

> All the parishioners assembled in response to the call of last Sunday and on this day to provide a stipend for the priest who has remained here. With one voice, all have decided that he would be given a tithe of one thirty-sixth, immediately established, and that a list would be made of landowners and artisans who do not pay the tithe, who will provide for repairs to the church.[42]

The representatives of the *fabrique,* an illegal institution that had nonetheless been put in place at the uprising of March 10, signed the document. The same year, Abbé François Garaud, curé of La Bruffière, was given 1,200 francs and his vicar 900; each sum paid in two halves, the first in March, the second six months later.[43] On January 15 of the following year, the municipal council appointed two men to collect the tax that had been imposed: "They are to give it to the municipal officers who will settle with the priests." Exceptionally, this commune decided on April 12, 1795, to make immediate necessary repairs to the church, which had been burned.

As the occasion arose, inhabitants of the region defended their clergy, assisted them, or gave them refuge. They devised many subterfuges and hiding places to conceal them from the Blues. Abbé Chevallier, curé of Saint-Lumine-de-Coutais lived in an undiscoverable hiding place in a private house. "It was in the back, in the darkest part of the second bedroom," explained the widow of the owner, that the hiding place was located, to the left coming in from the family bedroom. The setup was very ingenious, because the room was both very deep and very dark. If someone suspected something and took a few steps, he would come up against a wall which naturally appeared to be the back wall. But, in fact, this wall was only a thick partition made of bricks set flat, and was therefore very solid and made no sound if it was struck. The hiding place was three meters long and one and a half meter wide. You entered through the attic. To get there, you climbed up through the part of the room opposite the hiding place; there was a ladder out in the open. Once in the attic, you had to cross its entire length, feeling your way or with a lantern. In the far corner, old man Guitteny [her husband] had constructed a trapdoor. Beneath that, a short ladder allowed you to go down into the hiding place. On the bottom of the trapdoor were two grips of solid leather that Monsieur Chevallier could hang on to in case someone thought of testing the planks to see if they could be lifted. In order to conceal the joints, the cautious man had piled up all kinds of imaginable stuff, straw, hay, flax, and junk of all kinds.[44]

Foreseeing the course of events, old man Guitteny had built the wall himself with the help of one of his workers, "a trustworthy man." "That is why," the widow went on, "during the night, in order to be seen by no one, he carried the bricks from his oven and silently built the little hiding place."

Abbé Courtais, curé of Maisdon-sur-Sèvre, even lived in his presbytery: "A hiding place, cleverly concealed, had been set up behind the kitchen fireplace, between a staircase wall and a bedroom wall. A trapdoor opened under a bed in the room above. At the slightest alert, devoted friends came to warn him and he slipped into it. The trapdoor was closed and the tiles replaced."[45] Cuny, a gendarme lieutenant who carried out inspections, was distressed.[46] The administration admitted that it was powerless "to neutralize this clergy that does so much evil."

The authorities suspected the refractory priests, "those incorrigible enemies of the Republic,"[47] of being at the source of troubling gatherings, even though these never turned into real demonstrations. Some mayors, like that of Saint-Lumine-de-Coutais, claimed the contrary.[48] In their opinion, the clergy played a moderating role. In this context, any religious act provoked a systematic reaction from the authorities which was ineffective because of the obvious complicity of the people. In order to limit this complicity, several solutions were proposed, including sending fifteen missionaries to "spread through the countryside a light that would dissipate this lie."[49]

Seven years after the beginning of the war of the Vendée, the ideological and political situation of the region was extremely difficult and even desperate. The directory had turned out to be incapable of remedying all the excesses, as a report evaluating a mission sent to the minister on 29 messidor of the year VII (July 16, 1799) indicates.[50] Its author, Marnou, observes that the crisis remains "terrible" and that minds are not yet well "settled." "This state of affairs" is caused by the different classes confronting one another locally, "on one side the Republicans, on the other the royalists." The former "exaggerate" and are "turbulent." The refugees, as he calls them, are devoted men, to be sure, but made mistrustful and of a particularly difficult character because of their misfortunes. Among the latter are the former rebels, "rather conquered than submissive," and a certain number of influential partisans, on the watch for a favorable opportunity to revolt. These two opposing classes are always ready for a confrontation, and it would be opportune to put an end to this situation. Without causing discontent on either side, the government should try to rally all hearts, to bring one side back to fraternal moderation without seeming, by doing so, to protect the others, the victims of denunciation and harassment. The important thing is to inspire in the people confidence in the government, to appear to believe that they are sincere, to maintain them in their "duty without violence" — in short, to maintain order and "gain time," which, alone, can settle everything. The author goes on to note that violence always provokes violence. "And foreign powers ask only to stir the West to revolt to embarrass the government." Since few able-bodied men "were killed during the war (*sic*)," a resumption of the insurrection is to be feared "at the first opportunity that presents itself."

In fact, this period of instability consolidated the legitimacy of the clergy and its institutions. The *fabrique*, with no legal existence, survived despite harassment from the administration and even channeled various popular reactions. At the end of the Revolution, it challenged the legal order. It was all the stronger because it was persecuted and independent of any higher authority. Not only had it not disappeared, despite the wishes and the actions of the established authorities, but also it attained during this period an authority greater than any it had ever had under the Old Regime.

For example, the assembly of the parish of Saint-Pierre-des-Echaubrognes sent a petition to the mayor calling for his resignation.[51]

At the same time, the legality represented locally by the municipal administration was rejected and marginalized by society. As Marnou judiciously noted, the administration should have taken advantage of this period to heal wounds. In fact, it kept them constantly open and even, on occasion, made them bleed.

PART FOUR

Consequences

THIRTEEN

The Problem

MANY CONTEMPORARIES AND HISTORIANS HAVE SUGGESTED FIGURES
for the number of victims of the wars of the Vendée and for the percentage
of property destroyed. Depending on the positions adopted, differences in
magnitude range from twelve to one.

Some writers, for obvious ideological reasons or from fear, have minimized events. Others, conversely, seem to exaggerate them, particularly the
witnesses, horrified by the piles of corpses and the ruins. In a letter sent to
the minister of the interior on February 12, 1796, General Hoche estimated
that "six hundred thousand French people perished in the Vendée," and he
asserts that at the time "the total population of rebel territory had been reduced to one-fifth of its male inhabitants."[1] For André Sarazin, conservator
of the municipal archives of Angers, this estimate appears reasonable, taking
into account the victims on both sides.[2] Evidence rediscovered, surveys carried out, and lists established by some curés, who had remained in or returned
to their parishes, support these impressions. The Bignon Commission, set up
after the battle of Le Mans, had a tally in three days (December 22–24, 1793)
of 661 victims.[3] On orders of Carrier and Bignon, 100 prisoners were shot in
Nantes on December 29; 96 on December 30; 115 on December 31; 120 on Janu-
ary 1, 1794; 290 on January 2; 101 on January 3; 210 on January 4; 252 on Janu-
ary 5; 200 on January 6; 59 (women) on January 7; 52 (women) on January 8;
97 on January 17; 56 on January 18; 207 on January 19; and 26 on January 25;
the total was 1,971 victims. And these are only a few examples among many
others. Clearly such massacres filled those who reported them with horror.

Associations and individuals, impassioned or curious, have tried and
are still actively attempting to establish complete lists of the dead. Despite

some clear results, the difficulties are often insurmountable, precisely because of the specificities of this war. Aside from deaths on the battlefield,
with bodies almost always buried on site and unregistered, entire groups of
captured inhabitants were executed without trial. Priests and civilian officials both recognized that it was difficult if not impossible to provide exact
local estimates: either they were unable to keep a record, or they did it im-
perfectly for lack of paper or because of circumstances, or else original documents, most of which were clandestine, have disappeared. The documents
of La Chapelle-Bassemère, explained Abbé Robin, "were torn up and seized
by the heretical arsonists or burned with our clothes because we were pursued too closely . . ."[4]

Some registers were reconstructed in the succeeding months, or even
years, from memory and with the help of contemporary witnesses. This is
the case for those of Abbé Barbedette, curé of Le Luc, who concludes his
document by explaining:

> These names above, to the number of 569, of the persons massa-
> cred in various places in the parish of Le Grand-Luc have been referred
> to me by relatives who escaped from the massacre to be inscribed in this
> register, insofar as it was possible to gather them in a time of the most
> atrocious persecution, the dead bodies having lain unburied for more
> than a month in the fields of each village of Le Luc; which I can attest
> to be only too true, after being an eyewitness to these horrors and sev-
> eral times exposed to being a victim of them.[5]

Abbé Massonnet, curé of Ligné, who had taken refuge in Le Loroux-
Bottereau, apologized for probable mistakes: "There will perhaps be mistakes in the names, the witnesses, the months, and the days; considering
that the people who have come to record them here are not very well educated. There is no order for the dates, people did not come at the times indicated."[6] Even these documents are not intact because of the tenacious persecution by the military. For example, only four "massacres" are noted on the
second register of La Chapelle-Bassemère (February 1, 1796, to March 1,
1797), which has suffered a good deal from tearing and bad weather. The
compiler explained: "A sheet covering ten weeks is missing, torn up by the
Republican troops when I was obliged to hide in a cellar and my servant was
captured." Moreover, "we were always harassed by the Republicans, and we
had to carry it in a pocket and often hide it in the hedges."[7]

Relatively reliable registers are rare. There is only one known to us, that of La Remaudière and La Boissière, communes on the border between Anjou and Loire-Atlantique.[8] There are three reasons for this: the small number of inhabitants (around 1,500 under the Old Regime); the fact that the rector, Abbé Charles Billaud, in charge from 1790 on, knew his flock well; and the fact that the rector stayed in residence during the events. Although the list of victims is complete, with sex, age, condition of the victim, and place, the abbé asks the reader not to be surprised to find no order in it: "The registers having been burned or lost," he was "obliged to gather the inhabitants together to make new ones." As a result, "it is totally impossible to establish a sequence of dates."

Although probative, these details are nevertheless limited, and any extrapolation should be avoided. War and repression did not have the same consequences everywhere, even in two neighboring communes, for various reasons: local conditions, proximity to centers of repression, excesses or, conversely, magnanimity, internal rivalries, and the like. Does this mean, on the basis of such observations, that any evaluation, even approximate, is impossible? I do not think so, with respect either to human or to property losses.

AN ATTEMPT AT AN ESTIMATE OF INHABITANTS WHO DIED

The solution to the problem of making an estimate can only be both local and general. It must take into account two figures: the population under the Old Regime and that under the Empire; the difference, with a few reservations, would correspond to the number of inhabitants who died.

The idea is not new in itself. Various attempts along these lines have been made, starting with pre- and postwar censuses. The failure has been obvious, because the figures registered by administrators were, for the most part, erroneous, under- or overstated. With a few exceptions, these mistakes were deliberate, as Baron Dupin, prefect of Deux-Sèvres, explained while preparing the statistical report for the department:

> In 1790 . . . everything contributed to exaggerate the size of the population: municipal officers wanted to favor their curés, whose stipend was established on that basis; each commune wanted to be a capital or to have official establishments, or to have a larger number of electors; there was not a census carried out at the time which was not more or

less influenced by these petty interests; the fear of taxes never ceased; it was a time when people were being persuaded that they would no longer pay anything . . .

The census of the year IX left the prefect just as skeptical:

> I have trouble believing that the result obtained is not a little below the truth, especially with respect to the number of individuals. In the eyes of the peasant, a census is always the harbinger of a new tax, and he tries to hide the number of his children as well as the number of his cattle and the quantity of grain he has harvested; besides, the communes that suffered from the war have a tendency to exaggerate their losses; this is a sentiment common to all these unfortunates . . .[9]

Dupin's curious mind led him to use a different kind of reasoning. The idea came to him of comparing birth certificates of 1789 and 1801, multiplied by a coefficient, variable depending on populations, corresponding to the average rate of procreation for 1,000 inhabitants. However, with respect to the data from 1801, he came up against some difficulties: the lack of precision in the civil records of several communes, "the peasants being convinced that they had fulfilled all their duties when they baptized their children"; and, more seriously, some missing registers, "seeing that they were sent blank." The suggestion, which was a good one, needed to be followed up and worked on.

Population estimates on the basis of a single year are subject to criticism, notably because of fluctuations. As a consequence, an annual average over ten years has been established for each period: 1781–90 for the Old Regime (registers were well kept, which was no longer the case beginning in 1791); 1803–12 for the Empire. Before the Concordat, civilian registers are questionable for the reasons mentioned. From that date on, with peace restored, local administrations were strong enough to overcome possible resistance and to enforce respect for obligatory registration. To be convinced of this, the records merely need to be compared to parish registers. I have, however, carefully refrained from counting the insertion of certificates concerning the period of troubles and transcribed after court judgments.

The question remains of the absolute reliability of the results. Some inhabitants, for various reasons, fled from the insurgent region. At first, these refugees were concentrated in the local metropolises: Angers, Nantes, Niort,

Ancenis, Saumur, Cholet, and Tours. In a second stage, by a decree of the representatives of the French people to the army of the West on 2 ventôse of the year II, the refugees were ordered to "bury themselves" in the interior of the region; this decision was made by the authorities, who were not unaware

> that these refugees . . . are not all patriots and that on the contrary it is known that several are in correspondence with the leaders of the rebels and secretly send them help of all kinds, that the very great majority of these alleged patriots are tenant farmers who, to conciliate both sides, live with the Republicans while they provide clandestine services to the rebels.[10]

In order to assuage the "just concerns of the nation on such a suspect proximity" and "to remove all true or false patriots from the theater of war . . . all the refugees in the communes six miles or more from the banks of the Loire and in the space included between the Loire and the sea, from Nantes to Tours, have three days to declare their names, professions and domiciles." By the next day, they were required to go to department capitals where the administration assigned obligatory residences. The influx was so great, five to six thousand individuals in Nantes in three years (March 1793 to early 1796), that their living conditions quickly became very difficult and most of them were "in the most frightful poverty."[11] This transfer was so sudden that reception centers were overwhelmed. Some towns, such as Angers, for lack of financial resources, tried to provide temporary remedies, by assigning these men and women to perform public works, or to act as a watch, and the like.[12]

On 26 brumaire of the year II, the National Convention granted a certain amount of assistance, supplemented by the decree of 27 vendémiaire, published on 6 nivôse,[13] in theory amounting to a total of 20 million francs for 1794. As an example, Vendée was supposed to receive 300,000 livres.[14] In fact, temporary assistance amounted to 167,217 livres; 85,550 livres for the canton of Fontenay-le-Comte; 2,635 for the canton of Foussay; 1,085 for L'Hermenault; 20,185 for Sainte-Hermine; 340 for Lagnon; 7,799 for La Châtaigneraie; 5,820 for Fougereux; 3,228 for Mouilleron; 6,040 for Pouzauges; 520 for Floulière; 4,240 for Chantonnay; 2,490 for La Jaudonnière; 600 for Caillère; 5,363 for La Roche-sur-Yon; 5,285 for Challans; 5,907 for Montaigu; and 5,130 for Les Sables-d'Olonne. The remainder was absorbed by the war effort.

On September 3, 1793, every "single man" received 100 livres; each woman, 80 livres; each couple, 160; each child, 50; and each orphan eighteen or younger, 70.[15] On September 9, 1794, with overt war over or almost over, the representatives of the people delegated by the National Convention "authorized the inhabitants known as refugees of the Vendée to return to their families."[16] Three days later, in order to encourage people to return home, the indemnities granted were substantially reduced: single men and women head of households were given only 25 sous; couples and childless widows, 15; and children younger than twelve, 10.[17] Despite this measure, it seems that at first returns were limited, with the single purpose of attempting to salvage what had escaped the flames. Various surveys, in Bressuire[18] and in La Chapelle-Bassemère,[19] reveal that genuine reintegration began only at a later stage, beginning in 1796. Between 1800 and 1802, most of those who had fled had returned home.

Some artisans from surrounding areas had also settled in the region, for example in Beaurepaire.[20] However, this movement was not as widespread and significant as some writers have claimed, precisely because of the distressed state of the military Vendée and distrust of outsiders. In any event, the failure of some natives to return and the arrival of migrants roughly balanced, so that the effect of these two phenomena, limited in scope as they were, was relatively slight. The coefficient selected, twenty-seven, appears to be an accurate average.

All departments affected have been treated in the same way, except for Deux-Sèvres, whose depository containing Old Regime parish registers was destroyed on December 20, 1805. The loss would have been irreparable if Baron Dupin had not already enumerated the births of 1789, although we must recognize the limitations in using the figures for a single year.[21] The average annual population during the Empire has been calculated on the basis of the years 1803–12, the only ones for which records are available. The attempt at an estimate of housing destroyed has been subject to the same methodological constraints.

An Attempt at an Estimate of Housing Destroyed

To the best of our knowledge, no serious work has been done to try to estimate the housing destroyed. Some writers have carefully avoided approaching this subject, while others have systematized it. Reading the latter would lead one to believe that the totality of cities, towns, villages, and hamlets caught up in the repression were razed—that there was total ruin. In this, they are merely echoing some witnesses, reports like one from Bonsergent, tax officer for public buildings in Bressuire, sent to the departmental director on 17 nivôse of the year VI: "They are in a state of devastation that must be seen in order to get a clear idea of it; it would be difficult to provide an estimated rental value for rubble."[22] Montaigu, Le Loroux-Bottereau, Vallet, Clisson, and others were said to be no more than heaps of stone. Tradition maintains that only three houses were left in Châtillon, two in La Chapelle-Bassemère.

In the face of these descriptions, any hope of evaluation or counting seemed vain before the discovery of an impressive file entitled "Allowances for Reconstruction Granted to the Vendeans," concerning Deux-Sèvres, Loire-Inférieure, and one-third of Vendée.[23] The lists are administrative in origin and therefore official. On the occasion of his visit to Vendée in 1808 Napoleon I was astounded and distressed at the desolate condition of the region. In a solemn declaration on August 8 in Napoléon-Vendée, the emperor decided to stimulate reconstruction by indemnifying the affected populations. A decree followed immediately providing for exemption from taxes for fifteen years and for various subsidies. All houses that had been destroyed by the war and were rebuilt would benefit from these advantages under two conditions: the subsidies would not go beyond January 1, 1812, and they could not exceed one-fourth of the value of the house, with an upper limit of 800 francs per house. Provision was made for payment in two stages, the first when one-third of the reconstruction was done, the second when the work was completed.

In 1808 only Vendée was affected. In 1811 Napoleon extended the measure to Deux-Sèvres and Loire-Inférieure. In the year XIII, Prefect Dupin had already obtained for the inhabitants of Bressuire and Châtillon, who were rebuilding their houses, exemption from the land tax for ten years.[24] Beginning on August 15, 1811, subsidies were reserved for various builders. In case of a change, the subsidies were given to the last contractor involved.

Since the distribution of these sums required a certain equity, and in accordance with article IV, individual files were established:

Any owner claiming the subsidy is required to submit a petition to us containing his name, profession, and domicile; the location and condition of the habitation destroyed during the civil war, the time of the reconstruction work, detailed expenses for that reconstruction; petitioners will attach accounts, notes, notarized documents, and certificates from the authorities in support of their declarations.[25]

The application of this regulation was a veritable disaster, because some residents categorically refused to fill out the required forms, and others were unable to do so. Prefects then asked mayors to serve as intermediaries. They were to go to the "locations with two members of the municipal council," to draw up "a report of their visit and an estimate"; they were then to send the petition to the subprefect who would verify it and send it to the prefecture. Here, too, the administration came up against the same problems: "some owners are still hesitant to prepare a declaration," some "mayors, despite all the explanations that have been given, have not clearly understood what was asked of them." This was true of Mayor Jean Plessis of La Bernadière, in Vendée, who mixed up value of the house and income. "Clearly," the official in charge of verification explained, "he has not understood the purpose of the operation. As his signature indicates, he is illiterate." Philosophically, the official observed that "this document presents the enormous advantage of showing the consequences of the destruction on incomes, since all of them, without exception, have fallen by one-third or one-fourth." Mailloux and Brains were two other examples of this kind.

More seriously, three mayors neglected to provide the values of destruction and reconstruction: two in Deux-Sèvres (Saint-Jouin-de-Milly and Saint-André-sur-Sèvre) and one in Loire-Inférieure (Bouguenais). In order to avoid possible mistakes, prefects asked mayors to rely on the services of engineers charged with making sure that operations were properly carried out. Faced with a task of such magnitude, on January 9, 1812, the prefect of Deux-Sèvres asked the minister of the interior to authorize him in addition "to hire intelligent people who would be compensated."[26]

The lists that were established all had the same format (see table 13.1).

Table 13.1.

Names of owners	Date of destruction of house	Value of house before destruction	Was it rebuilt and when?	Value of rebuilt house	Comment

Preparation of the lists was generally careful, even meticulous, particularly because the lists were verified by competent authorities. The chief engineer,

Duvivier, frequently expressed his pleasure on the point.[27] Some mayors, such as Boishuguet of La Limouzinière, even provided detailed lists of expenses, including purchase of materials, transport, and the like, "which means that estimates come in at a rather high figure."

The reliability of these documents is undeniable, even if, according to the engineer Duvivier, "this account cannot be considered anything more than a very inaccurate image with reference to a very large number of communes," because it sharply understates the reality. "The number of houses destroyed," this high official went on, "far exceeds what the mayors have indicated," particularly in the southern part of Loire-Inférieure. He estimated that the number should be doubled, "and it is very likely that that estimate would still understate the reality . . ." Some mayors, including those of Vellet and Vertou, agreed and expressed their regret.

Since houses that were not rebuilt were registered, it is easy (on the basis of systematic use of survey records prepared at the same time or in the immediately succeeding years) to establish relationships between the houses destroyed, whether or not they were rebuilt, and existing houses. Combined geographical data make it possible to determine the average number of inhabitants per house. Values recorded were as a general rule based on the same fiscal sources. The total real value of housing destroyed and recorded, whether or not the housing was rebuilt, is thus known, as are losses and gains.

In La Chapelle-Bassemère, evaluations adopted refer to the survey carried out the year before. On the basis of the master lists and the description and valuation under the Old Regime and the Empire of the 362 houses declared destroyed, it is possible to determine the unit value and total value of the 1,014 houses in the commune, the average value, the percentage in terms of value of the housing destroyed and of housing rebuilt or not rebuilt, the number of principal residences, geographical and sociological distributions, and thus the social strata most affected, types of housing, numbers of doors and windows, the locations of these openings, and the like, invaluable data that call into question many received ideas.

The idea of indemnifying the populations that had been victims of the disaster had already been expressed in Nantes on 5 brumaire of the year V.[28] But because of bias, the turbulent context, and the lack of resources, the idea had to be abandoned. The will of the emperor, joined with that of the administration, was able to overcome these difficulties, and a substantial number of projects were completed, as we can determine from reading records of payment.

FOURTEEN

The Human Aspect

THE TOTAL POPULATION UNDER THE OLD REGIME OF THE 773 communes affected by the war was 815,629: 288,580 Vendeans (16,240 fewer inhabitants than in the 1792 census, down 5.68 percent); 219,314 for the southern part of Maine-et-Loire, including the towns of Angers and Saumur; 208,807 for the southern part of Loire-Inférieure, including Nantes; and 98,928 for Deux-Sèvres, the arrondissements of Thouars and Parthenay taken together.

At least 117,257 people disappeared between 1792 and 1802, or 14.38 percent of the population. In absolute numbers, Maine-et-Loire was the department most affected, with 44,107 fewer inhabitants; then Vendée, with 30,711; then Loire-Inférieure, with 26,897; and finally Deux-Sèvres, with 15,542. In percentages, Maine-et-Loire lost 20.11 percent of its population, Deux-Sèvres 15.71 percent, Loire-Inférieure 12.91 percent, and Vendée 10.64 percent. In fact, the last figure needs to be qualified, since it refers to the department as a whole. If we confine ourselves to the 158 really insurgent communes, the proportion of the lost is on the order of 14.86 percent, higher than for Loire-Inférieure and fairly close to the figure for Deux-Sèvres.

All of the 79 cantons that made up the military Vendée were affected by this hemorrhage, except for Luçon (more than 280 out of a population of 8,463 in 1790, or 3.4 percent). The zone most affected forms a large ellipse, with the longer horizontal axis extending 175 kilometers from Saint-Jean-de-Monts to Saumur, and the vertical axis from Saint-Florent-le-Vieil to La Châtaigneraie, reaching a maximum length of 94 kilometers. The cantons making up its epicenter were located geographically at points where departments intersect. These were principally Cholet (−4,025, or 37.86 percent of

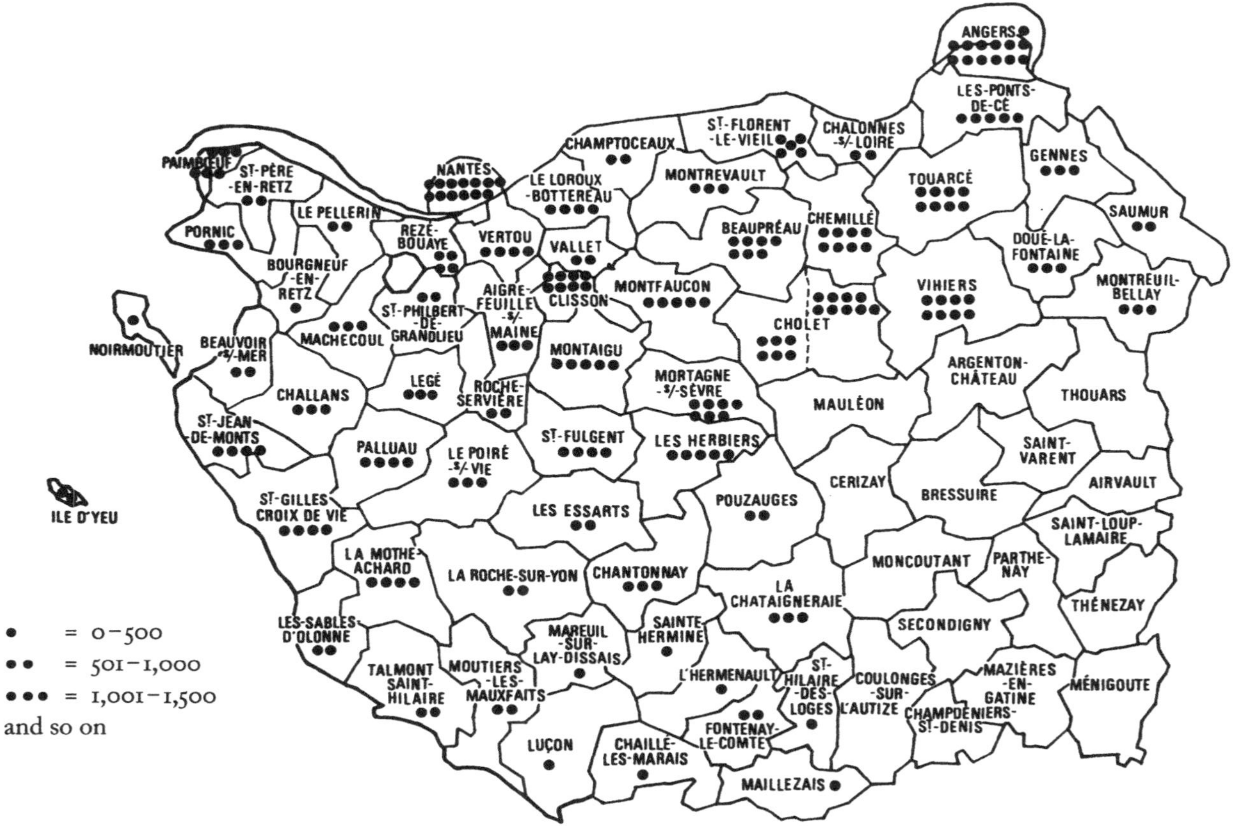

Map 14.1. Loss of population in number

• = 0–500
•• = 501–1,000
••• = 1,001–1,500
and so on

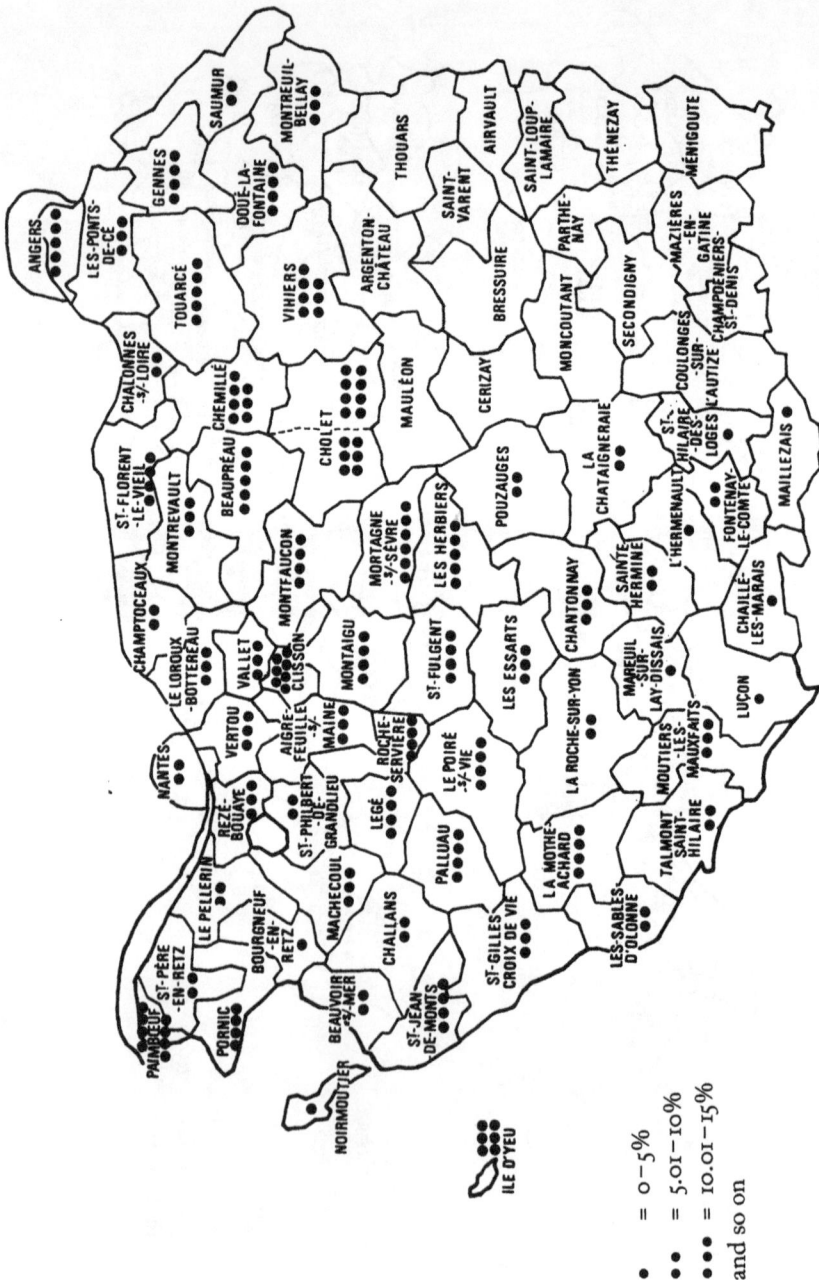

Map 14.2.   Loss of population in percent

• = 0–5%

•• = 5.01–10%

••• = 10.01–15%

and so on

the population); Vihiers (-3,980, 30.55 percent), with an appendix in the north in the commune of Thouarcé (-3,682, 22 percent); Chemillé (-3,617, 30.3 percent); Mortagne (-3,017, 27.16 percent); Les Herbiers (-2,367, 20.16 percent); Clisson (-3,523, 30.5 percent); and the whole of the arrondissement of Thouars (-3,770, 26.51 percent). Out of a population of 130,662, this corona lost 36,907 or 28.24 percent. Outside this area, circumferences can be drawn around the towns of Nantes, Angers, Saumur, Les Sables-d'Olonne, and to a lesser extent La Roche-sur-Yon.

These variations have various explanations. The primary ones are obviously connected to the war. A town such as Cholet, although preserved from destruction by a special decree of the Convention, was the scene of many battles, the first victims of which were the inhabitants of the nearby countryside and the inhabitants of the town, whether or not they were combatants. To this should be added the ravages of local conflicts, often very costly in human lives, and Galerne's expedition—that is, the march on the other side of the Loire.

The second set of reasons was the direct result of systematic repression. The strategy of the infernal columns was decisive. In the first stage, they moved rapidly through the countryside, killing and destroying what they found on their passage. The objectives adopted were particularly cantonal capitals, towns, villages, and large hamlets, concentrated targets that were easily accessible and sources of plunder. In the second stage, the columns took up positions and spread out, relying on the "revolutionary cavalry" when it was available.[1] It might be thought that conditions had changed and that, barring surprises, the population was prepared and had hidden in the depths of the woods. In fact, this was generally not the case, as indicated by the table of the dead listed according to size of towns (see table 14.1).

In Loire-Inférieure and Maine-et-Loire, the percentage of the dead was proportional to the size of communes, whereas in Vendée it was inversely proportional. Drawing any conclusions from this would, in my opinion, be hazardous.

In this evaluation, then, two principal factors played a role, the first tied to the activity of the infernal columns, whose trajectory is easy to follow, the second tied to the proximity of large towns and of the Loire, more, it seems, than to demographic density (Maine-et-Loire, 54.07 inhabitants/square kilometer; Loire-Inférieure, including Nantes, 98.11; northern Vendée, 43.53; southern Vendée, 43.48; Deux-Sèvres, arrondissement of Thouars, 39.79, and of Parthenay, 29.63, for an average of 31.2) and urban concentration.

Table 14.1. Population loss according to size of town (by department)

Department	Towns and number of inhabitants					
	0–1,000	1,000–2,000	2,000–3,000	3,000–4,000	4,000–5,000	Over 5,000
Maine-et-Loire	72,667	67,122	18,970	3,807	8,357	6,362
	−13,588	−13,083	−3,604	−1,431	−1,685	−2,856
	−18.69%	−19.49%	−19%	−37.58%	−20.16%	−29.17%
Loire-Inférieure	14,375	61,895	14,887	9,453	22,558	5,359
	−1,031	−6,401	−4,322	−1,730	−2,795	−1,150
	−7.17%	−10.34%	−18.30%	−18.30%	−14.39%	−21.46%
Northern Vendée (15 cantons)	63,091	61,079	26,371	13,272		5,022
	−9,513	−9,514	−2,787	−1,349		−108
	−15.07%	−15.57%	−10.51%	−10.16%		−2.15%
Total	150,134	190,098	60,229	26,533	30,915	16,743
	−24,133	−28,998	−10,714	−4,511	−4,480	−3,114
	−16.07%	−15.25%	−17.78%	−17%	−14.95%	−18.60%

Maine-et-Loire and Deux-Sèvres clearly had multiple handicaps. Their territory, although larger than that of Loire-Inférieure and northern Vendée taken together (6,564.18 square kilometers as opposed to 5,791.84 square kilometers), embraced many centers of repression that were nearby, numerous, and extremely virulent. In the north, these centers were Nantes and Angers, not forgetting the sporadic actions of the fleet; in the east, Saumur, Tours, and Châtellerault; and in the south, Niort. Moreover, it seems obvious that the particularly dramatic consequences of Galerne's expedition principally affected Anjou because of the crossing point over the Loire at Saint-Florent-le-Vieil, a hypothesis that it is unfortunately impossible to verify (see table 14.2).

As for Vendée and Loire-Inférieure, bounded on the west by the Atlantic Ocean, in addition to the horrors of the infernal columns which were essentially the same everywhere, they suffered only the reprisals of the towns of Nantes and Niort. The other towns, Les Sables-d'Olonne and Paimbœuf, with small populations and no real resources, were able, to their great regret, to carry out only very limited actions.

All contemporary observers were struck by the monstrous character of the repression that pitilessly exterminated women, children, old men, the infirm, and mature men indiscriminately. Baron Dupin was categorical:

> The census of the year VIII gives rise to observations that are of some interest. In the arrondissements of Thouars and Parthenay, the female population exceeds the male population by about a fourteenth in the first and a twelfth in the second. But it is surprising that this proportion is not larger. In fact, before 1790, the peasants' ambition was to place their sons in cloisters or at least in the priesthood; it is therefore probable that at that time there were a few more women than men; and because men are usually more exposed than women to the hazards of war, it should be expected that the number of women today would greatly exceed that of men in the first arrondissement after a war that devoured more than one-third of its population. There are thus grounds for surprise in finding that the two sexes are still of approximately equal numbers and that, consequently, as many women as men perished. This trait in itself is enough to characterize the war of Vendée.[2]

A sampling carried out in La Remaudière, a commune located in the canton of Le Loroux-Bottereau, whatever its limitations, confirms this idea.[3]

Table 14.2. Number of towns according to size and percent

Department	Communes according to size								
	0–500	500–1,000	1,000–1,500	1,500–2,000	2,000–2,500	2,500–3,000	3,000–3,500	Over 3,500	Total
Maine-et-Loire	43 23.36%	76 41.30%	35 19.02%	16 8.69%	7 3.80%	1 0.54%	1 0.54%	5 2.71%	184 100%
Loire-Inférieure	6 7.60%	15 18.98%	23 29.11%	19 23.05%	3 3.79%	3 3.79%	3 3.79%	7 8.86%	79 100%
Northern Vendée	39 24.68%	62 39.24%	29 18.35%	11 6.96%	11 6.96%	1 0.63%	3 1.89%	2 1.26%	158 100%
Southern Vendée	64 39.50%	67 41.35%	21 12.96%	7 4.32%	1 0.61%	1 0.61%		1 0.61%	162 100%
Total	152 26.07%	220 37.73%	108 18.52%	53 9.09%	22 3.77%	6 1.02%	7 1.20%	15 2.57%	583 100%

In 1790 the population was estimated at 1,494—744 for La Remaudière itself and 750 for its "daughter," La Boissière-du-Doré. One hundred eleven victims were registered (7.42 percent of the population), only 9 of whom were soldiers (8.1 percent of those killed). The 102 others were "massacred" by Cordelier's column on March 10 and 17, 1794. The first, very quick passage of the column accounted for 9 people (1 woman and 6 men, including 5 peasants, 1 tenant farmer, and 1 servant); the second, for 93. Eighty-one people (79.41 percent) without defenses were handed over to the soldiers; 32 were children younger than fifteen, and 24 were fifty or older. In addition, there were 9 mothers and 8 couples who preferred to die with their offspring rather than to flee without them (see table 14.3).

Table 14.3. Table of repression of nine mothers and eight couples killed in La Remaudière

	Mothers					Couples		
1 infant	*2 infants*	*3 infants*	*4 infants*	*5 infants*		*1 infant*	*2 infants*	*3 infants*
5	1	1	1	1		4	2	2

Table 14.4 obviates the need for any comment on the monstrous character of the repression. Fifty-four families were directly affected (see table 14.5). The sociological distribution was as follows: 71 peasants (69.6 percent), 8 tenant farmers (7.84 percent), 4 millers (3.92 percent), 1 servant (0.98 percent), 14 weavers (13.73 percent), 4 clogmakers (3.92 percent)—that is, 79 peasants (77.45 percent) and 23 artisans and merchants (22.55 percent).

The war also had perverse effects in the short, medium, and long term, and aggravated the difficulties of the survivors or inflicted new ones. This was the case, for example, with venereal diseases, unknown in the military Vendée before 1793. On many occasions, Baron Dupin attempted to draw the attention of the political authorities to these illnesses, which seemed to him to be particularly tragic: "They are widespread . . . in all places where

Table 14.4. Table of repression according to age and sex of inhabitants killed in La Remaudière

	Age in years												
	<1	1	2	3	4	5	6	7	8	9	10	15	20
Female		3	1		2	1		1		1	3	2	2
Male	3		1	2	1	1	1	2	1	2	2	2	5
Total	3	3	2	2	3	2	1	3	1	3	5	4	7

	Age in years											
	25	30	35	40	45	50	55	60	65	70	75	Total
Female	5	3	1	7	1	3	1	7	2	1	2	49
Male	1		1	5	2	4	5	4	4	4		53
Total	6	3	2	12	3	7	6	11	6	5	2	102

Table 14.5. Table of repression in relation to fifty-four families affected in La Remaudière

Number of family members						
1	2	3	4	5	6	Total
Number of families						
31	12	2	5	3	1	102

troops have stayed. The location of nurses has become extremely difficult, and this is one more reason for persuading mothers to fulfill this sacred duty themselves."[4] A solution would obviously be for "the government to have all soldiers given leave examined and to have those infected by this frightful disease treated and cured before being sent home to their families."

Many former soldiers also had declining sight and hearing, "which must be attributed to the fatigues and loud noises of the artillery." Blindness appeared more common in the arrondissements at war, such as Parthenay, which was due, according to officials, "to trouble and sorrow." Doctor Delahaye of Parthenay also observed a "frightening" increase in the number of madmen following the terror. In his *Mémorial de Sainte-Hélène*, Las Cases alludes to this: "What struck me in Vendée and surrounding territory was the proliferation of the number of madmen, perhaps more than in other parts of the Empire."[5]

Another problem was that of public education: "Remedy for all evils . . . the only means capable of reintegrating all of the French into their human dignity or instilling in them their rights and their duty, by providing them with the undisturbed enjoyment of liberty that has so gloriously been won . . ." The revolutionaries had wanted to universalize education in order to struggle against

> ignorance that degrades men, brutalizes them, shamefully subjects them to the dual yoke of superstition and despotism; ignorance, blinding the inhabitants of the countryside to their true interests, makes them indifferent to a revolution which has delivered them from the harshest servitude and which is favorable to their interests in every way; finally, only ignorance has made them take up arms for the restoration of tyranny and has fomented the most horrible war. . .[6]

In fact, not only had the Revolution done nothing locally for education, but it had destroyed the entire existing infrastructure, as Baron Dupin explained: "If we consider that the unfortunate war of Vendée was not fed only by the ignorance of the peasants; that there were *collèges* in Parthenay, Thouars, and Bressuire, and schools in all the villages, we cannot help being troubled about the future."[7] The situation was such that "in twenty years, the rural communes will no longer supply a single man who knows how to read and write; hence there will be no more municipal authorities." As usual, the prefect proposed remedies:

> Our system of primary instruction is not bad, but it has been clumsily made unpopular by proscribing any religious books in the schools. Besides, it is absurd to have only one teacher for several communes. In a region in which during the winter, which is the season for study, the roads are impassable and wolves cause great depredations, what mother would want to send her children to a school two miles away? There has to be a school in every commune; and expense should be of no concern when we are considering the foundation of liberty. The schoolmaster should be paid by funds from the commune and all children taught for free. If the slightest charge is imposed, as in the current system, avarice or poverty will depopulate the school . . .

Even the idea of restoring the former *collèges* and endowing them with former church property to supply their needs was proposed:

> These institutions should be given a solid organization so that they may be a brake on the young and train them in the habit of work. And if the department could pay a modest scholarship in each of these *collèges* for a certain number of students from the indigent classes, what a powerful cause for emulation would be introduced into primary education . . .

Insurgent Vendée was not alone in suffering these evils. The Republic had lost many men, and border regions were particularly exposed; heads of families, and even the infirm, had been obliged to march en masse under the orders of Westermann and other generals. "Republican" towns had paid a heavy tribute because of the battles in which they had had to engage for their own defense and because of their active participation in the repression. Angers lost 23.21 percent of its population (7,106 people); Paimbœuf, 39.43 percent (2,881); Fontenay-le-Comte, 6.77 percent (1,018); Nantes, 9.37 percent (7,074 permanent residents); Les Sables-d'Olonne, 6.6 percent (605); and Niort 5.51 percent, (688).

Despite these difficult conditions and the prevailing poverty, to the surprise of the administration the number of abandoned children did not increase. Indeed, in the devastated and depopulated communes, there was a movement among Vendeans for adoption. Las Cases was indeed surprised: a large number "of individuals . . . were taken in when they were children, even though it was not known where they came from. Some had wounds on their bodies, the cause of which they did not know, probably having gotten them in the cradle." At this description, the emperor exclaimed: "That is civil war and its frightful consequences; these are its inevitable results, its certain fruits! While a few leaders make a fortune and survive, the bulk of the population is always trampled; it escapes from none of the evils . . ."[8]

FIFTEEN

Assessment of Property Destruction

FOR THE SOUTHERN PART OF LOIRE-INFÉRIEURE (76 COMMUNES), the northwestern part of Deux-Sèvres (70 communes), and the northeastern part of Vendée (38 communes), a minimum of 10,309 houses burned has been counted out of a total of 56,760, or an 18.16 percent destruction. If the 9 communes of Loire-Inférieure not affected by the repression are excluded (Paimbœuf, 709 houses; Saint-Père-en-Retz, 378; Saint-Brévin, 282; Saint-Michel, 382; Sainte-Marie, 495; Moutiers-Prigny, 202; La Bernerie, 294; and Préfailles and La Plaine-sur-Mer, 508), the housing stock really affected is reduced to 53,276 units and the percentage of destruction increased to 19.35 percent.

Proportionally, the communes of Deux-Sèvres were the most devastated: 3,267 houses out of 9,346, or 34.95 percent. Then come Vendée,[1] with 1,785 houses out of 10,358, or 17.61 percent; and Loire-Inférieure,[2] with 5,257 houses out of 33,572, or 15.65 percent. These figures correlate with the loss of human life, although they are slightly lower for Vendée (17.73 percent loss of population for the communes studied) and higher for Loire-Inférieure (12.94 percent loss of population for the communes considered). The geographical distribution confirms the impression of contemporaries, for whom the repression was the cause of the majority of deaths. Communes were obviously unevenly affected, as table 15.1 indicates.

Fifty percent of the communes lost more than 20 percent of their housing, and 10.29 percent lost more than half. One-fourth of the communes of Deux-Sèvres lost half or more. In percentages, the towns of Argenton-Château (160 houses out of 189, 84.65 percent) and Clazeay (57 out of 66, 86.36 percent) were the most affected. For absolute figures, see table 15.2.

Table 15.1. Distribution of percentages of housing destruction according to number, percentage, and department

Department	Percent									Total
	0–9	10–19	20–29	30–39	40–49	50–59	60–69	70–79	80–89	
Loire-Inférieure:										
Number	27	18	10	8	3		1			67
Percent	40.3	26.87	14.92	11.94	4.48		1.49			100
Deux-Sèvres:										
Number	14	7	13	13	6	4	5	5	3	70
Percent	20	10	18.57	18.57	8.57	5.71	7.14	7.14	4.29	100
Vendée:										
Number	8	12	11	6	1					38
Percent	21.05	31.58	28.95	15.79	2.63					100
Total:										
Number	49	37	34	27	10	4	6	5	3	175
Percent	28	21.14	19.43	15.43	5.71	2.29	3.43	2.86	1.71	100

Table 15.2.   Housing destruction by commune and department according to concentration

	Number of communes by department							
	Loire-Inférieure		Deux-Sèvres		Vendée		Total	
Number of houses	No.	%	No.	%	No.	%	No.	%
500–549			1	1.43			1	0.51
400–449								
350–399	2	2.94					2	1.14
300–349								
250–299	1	1.47					1	0.57
200–249	6	8.82					6	3.4
150–199	3	4.4	2	2.86	1	2.63	6	3.4
100–149	10	14.71	4	5.71	3	7.89	17	9.66
50–99	10	14.71	14	20	11	28.95	35	19.89
0–49	36	52.94	49	70	23	60.53	108	61.36
Total	68	100	70	100	38	100	176	100

The magnitude of the destruction was often related to urban concentration, because of the tactics adopted. Bressuire holds the painful record for houses destroyed: 507 out of 632 (80.22 percent), followed by Clisson (366 out of 874, 41.87 percent), La Chapelle-Bassemère (355 out of 1,014, 35 percent), Vertou (233 out of 1,979, 11.77 percent), Saint-Julien-de-Concelles (232 out of 1,077, 21.66 percent), Moisdon (217 out of 644, 33.69 percent), Le Loroux-Bottereau (211 out of 1,368, 15.42 percent), and Gétigné (204 out of 462, 44.15 percent). All these towns, except for Bressuire, were located in Loire-Inférieure.

The damage inflicted has been evaluated at 18,847,741 francs for 160 communes: 9,937,998 francs for 66 communes of Loire-Inférieure, 6,362,363 francs for 66 communes of Deux-Sèvres, and 2,547,380 francs for 28 communes of Vendée. The total sum was distributed as table 15.3 shows.

Table 15.3. Distribution of damage by commune (according to size) and department

| | Number of Communes by Department | | | | | | | |
| | Loire-Inférieure | | Deux-Sèvres | | Vendée | | Total | |
Value in francs	No.	%	No.	%	No.	%	No.	%
850,000–899,999	1	1.52	1	1.52			2	1.25
800,000–849,999								
750,000–799,999	1	1.52	1	1.52			2	1.25
700,000–749,000								
650,000–699,999								
550,000–599,999	3	4.55					3	1.87
400,000–449,999							2	1.25
350,000–399,999	2	3.03					2	1.25
300,000–349,999	2	3.03						
250,000–299,999	1	1.52	2	3.03	1	3.57	4	2.5
200,000–249,999	5	7.58	1	1.52	5	17.86	11	6.87
150,000–199,999	4	6.06	7	10.61	1	3.57	12	7.5
100,000–149,999	8	12.12	10	15.15	2	7.14	20	12.5
50,000–99,999	13	19.7	18	27.27	6	21.43	37	23.13
0–49,999	26	39.39	26	39.39	13	46.43	65	40.63
Total	66	100	66	100	28	100	160	100

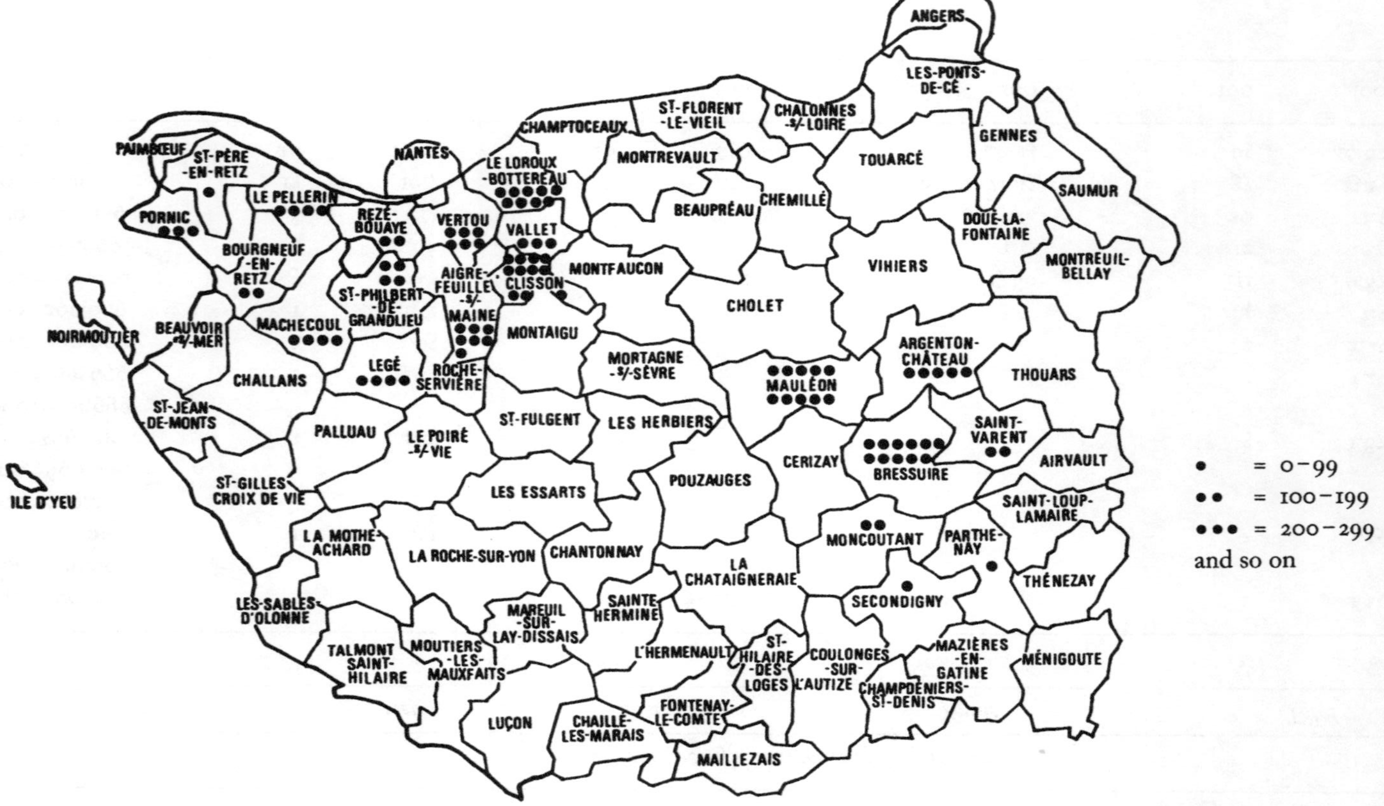

Map 15.1. Number of houses destroyed

Legend:
• = 0-99
•• = 100-199
••• = 200-299
and so on

Map 15.2. Percent of existing houses destroyed

= 0–4.99%
= 5–9.99%
= 10–14.99%
= 15–19.99%

and so on

Ruin was almost universal, as an official explained in an "observation" report on the canton of Palluau in Vendée, done at the request of the sub-prefect of Les Sables-d'Olonne in the year VIII.[3] In order to support his argument, he presented the real situation of the region by estimating losses in the form of a table (see table 15.4).

Table 15.4. Situation of the canton of Palluau presented by an official

| Place | Degree of destruction | | | |
	Housing	Livestock	Agriculture	Trade
Palluau	5/6	all or 5/6	2/3	4/6
Grande-Lande	5/6	1/2, 2/3	2/3	
La Chapelle	3/6	1/3, 2/3	1/3	
Saint-Christophe	4/6	2/3, 3/4	1/2	
Saint-Etienne	3/6	1/2, 1/3	3/6	2/6
Saint-Pail	1/2 or 3/6	2/3, 4/6	1/2	

Confronted with this situation, the people were in a state of complete helplessness. Solidarity among Vendeans then played a major role; people moved together into houses, stables, and barns, intact or partially collapsed; huts were hastily built of branches, and when the situation became extremely difficult, people went into exile, abandoning the little that remained to marauders. Pillage thus completed the work of the flames.[4]

The condition of patriots was hardly better. According to a weekly report from the administration of Nantes in the year IV, they "sleep every night in the hedges and can no longer support the frightful poverty that is crushing them."[5] With the return of peace, even though it was precarious, reconstruction was cautiously begun: two houses in 1793. At first, until 1795, reconstruction was exclusively for the people who had remained in place. The most urgent cases were dealt with first, as the mayors explained. The mayor of Saint-Martin-des-Noyers, for example, made efforts to give a more precise assessment "for roofs and barns that had been burned, with all the more reason because the owners all began by rebuilding them before restoring their houses, correctly determining that they were more useful for agriculture . . ."[6]

The behavior of the inhabitants was basically the same from one department and one commune to the next, although it appears that Loire-Inférieure began large-scale reconstruction in 1796, a year before Vendée and Deux-Sèvres. Until 1801, the rate of reconstruction was chiefly a reflection of political instability. After the Concordat, it depended on the economic situation, which varied from year to year. According to the mayor of Châtillon, repaired houses "were badly done." The mayor of Les Brouzils pointed out that it was extremely infrequent for houses to be restored all at once: "They begin by rebuilding the barn, then two or three years later the house, which they roof months or even years later."

Major work posed three problems: the lack of money, the scarcity of materials, and insufficient manpower, particularly a lack of craftsmen. Different circumstances produced different resolutions of these problems. In order to rebuild their principal residences, some owners sold the rest of their property, houses, lands, and valuables.[7] The inhabitants of Argenton-Château, for example, carried on "a fairly lucrative trade in the soil" around their houses, which "is dark earth spread in the fields to fertilize them."[8] Prefect Dupin was shocked to observe that the damage thus caused was considerable: "Every day, the inhabitants make new ruins, tearing out their floors, ripping up cellars, yards, and gardens to remove this precious soil that is four or five feet thick, sometimes more . . ." "And yet," he concluded, "this is so to speak the only industry in this unfortunate country." (See figures 15.1, 15.2.)

Other inhabitants were obliged to rely on large loans, often at usurious rates. "Heavily indebted, they are then forced to sell their livestock" and even seeds.[9] In the case of nonpayment, they were subject to "eviction proceedings."[10] Tenants, in addition, were given the assurance that they would not have to pay rent for a certain period, determined by agreement depending on the extent of the work already done or planned. More often than not, improvised solutions were devised: reusing old materials that were more or less sound and appropriate; systematic cutting of wood for framing; cutting of heather and straw for roofing, and the like. The whole community or the whole family participated in the work. "Their ignorance is so great," exclaimed Baron Dupin, "that it has the most disastrous effects."[11]

The scarcity of workers, particularly masons and carpenters, was felt everywhere. The prefect of Deux-Sèvres proposed to the government that it

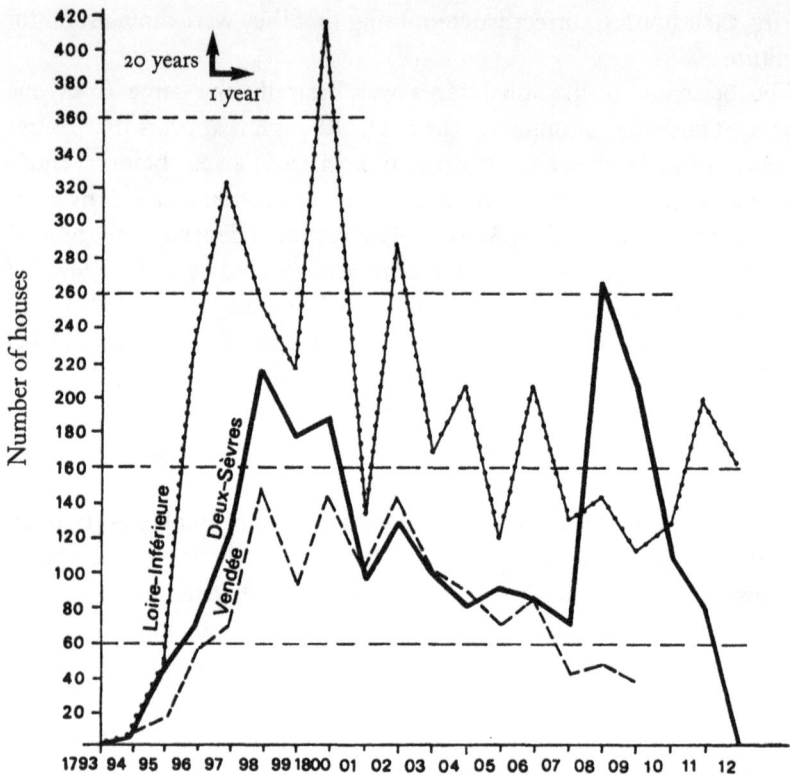

Figure 15.1. Total reconstructions in three departments (on the basis of 6,942 houses)

station in the devastated regions "a few battalions from the old province of Limousin, where all the men are masons, with permission to work."

Two thousand six hundred ninety-eight of the 10,309 houses destroyed were not restored for lack of tenants or resources. The communes concerned thus experienced the definitive loss of 4.75 percent of their housing stock (26.17 percent of the houses destroyed), a percentage with a minimum value of 4,411,799 francs (23.4 percent of the value destroyed). A letter of August 15, 1812, to the prefect of Nantes from Régnard, the chief engineer of roads and bridges, charged with the verification of petitions, confirms this fact: "Kindly find attached hereto the result of my visits to the burned houses in the process of reconstruction in my tour from September 14 to 28 inclusive.

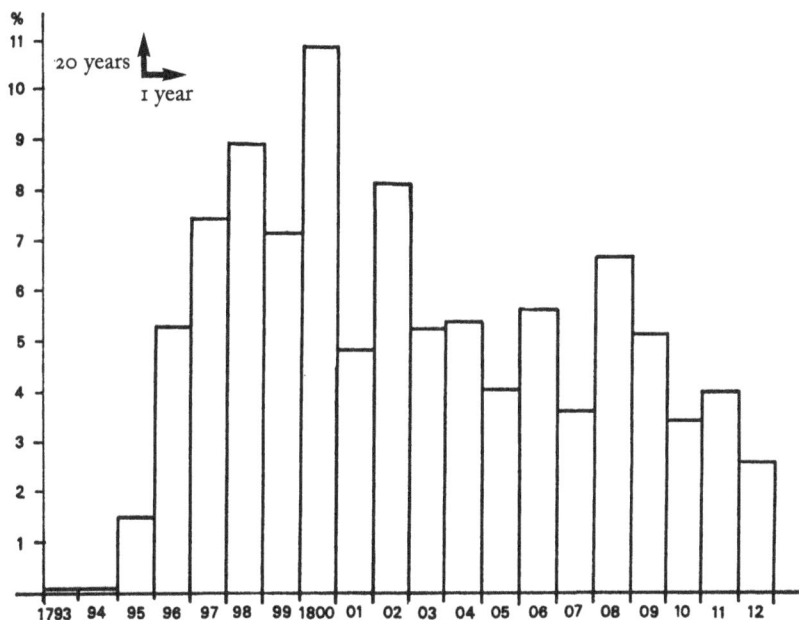

Figure 15.2.   Percentage of total reconstructions in three departments (on the basis of 6,942 houses)

I saw many abandoned ruins, especially in Machecoul."[12] Euphemistically, the official survey classified them as "hovels."

Only twenty communes rebuilt at prices higher than those before destruction (nine in Loire-Inférieure, ten in Deux-Sèvres, and one in Vendée) and one at equal prices.[13] The value of restored housing is estimated at 10,373,365 francs, or a total loss of 8,474,376 francs (44.96 percent). Three communes did not rebuild their burned housing: Glenay in Deux-Sèvres, with 1 of 167 houses destroyed; Poiré in Vendée, with 15 of 149; and Bazoges in Vendée, with 28 of 184. Forty-four communes lost at least half the value of destroyed housing.

In addition, on April 22, 1813, a report from the second office of buildings to the minister of the interior estimated the destruction of personal property, "furniture, linen, cattle, and tools," for the department of Deux-Sèvres alone at 3 million francs. However, it "considers this value restored today, not that all property has been reconstituted but because the new is

Map 15.3. Percent of destroyed houses not rebuilt

• = 0–4.99%
•• = 5–9.99%
••• = 10–14.99%
•••• = 15–19.99%
and so on

Map 15.4. Number of houses not rebuilt

• = 0–49
•• = 50–99
••• = 100–149

and so on

Map 15.5. Percent of houses not rebuilt in relation to property before the Revolution

more valuable than the old, which was not very plentiful even in castles."[14] (See table 15.5.)

Table 15.5.   Housing not rebuilt by number of communes, department

Percentage housing not rebuilt in relation to housing destroyed	Department							
	Deux-Sèvres		Vendée		Loire-Inférieure		Total	
	No.	%	No.	%	No.	%	No.	%
100	1	1.96	2	6.25			3	2.17
90–99								
80–89	3	5.88	2	6.25			5	3.63
70–79	2	3.92	1	3.13	6	10.91	9	6.52
60–69	6	11.76	2	6.25	7	12.73	15	10.87
50–59	5	9.8	4	12.5	3	5.45	12	8.7
40–49	6	11.76	2	6.25	7	12.73	15	10.87
30–39	6	11.76	6	18.75	10	18.18	22	15.94
20–29	10	19.61	5	15.63	6	10.91	21	15.22
10–19	9	17.65	6	18.74	10	18.18	25	18.12
0–9	3	5.88	2	6.25	6	10.91	11	7.97
Total	51	100	32	100	55	100	128	100

Unfortunately we have no precise document on this subject.

Obviously, fiscal concessions and the provision of indemnities stimulated owners, particularly in Deux-Sèvres and Loire-Inférieure. Oddly, it seems that these factors had no direct influence in Vendée. Two million francs in the fiscal years 1810 and 1811 were placed at the disposal of the ministry of finance and the ministry of the interior. At the outset, the sum was to be distributed equitably among the three departments, with Maine-et-Loire excluded. Following various reports noting the "good restoration" of Loire-Inférieure, partial transfers were decided, particularly in favor

Map 15.6.   Value of reconstruction in relation to property before the Revolution (percent)

• = 40–49%
•• = 50–59%
••• = 60–69%
•••• = 70–79%

and so on

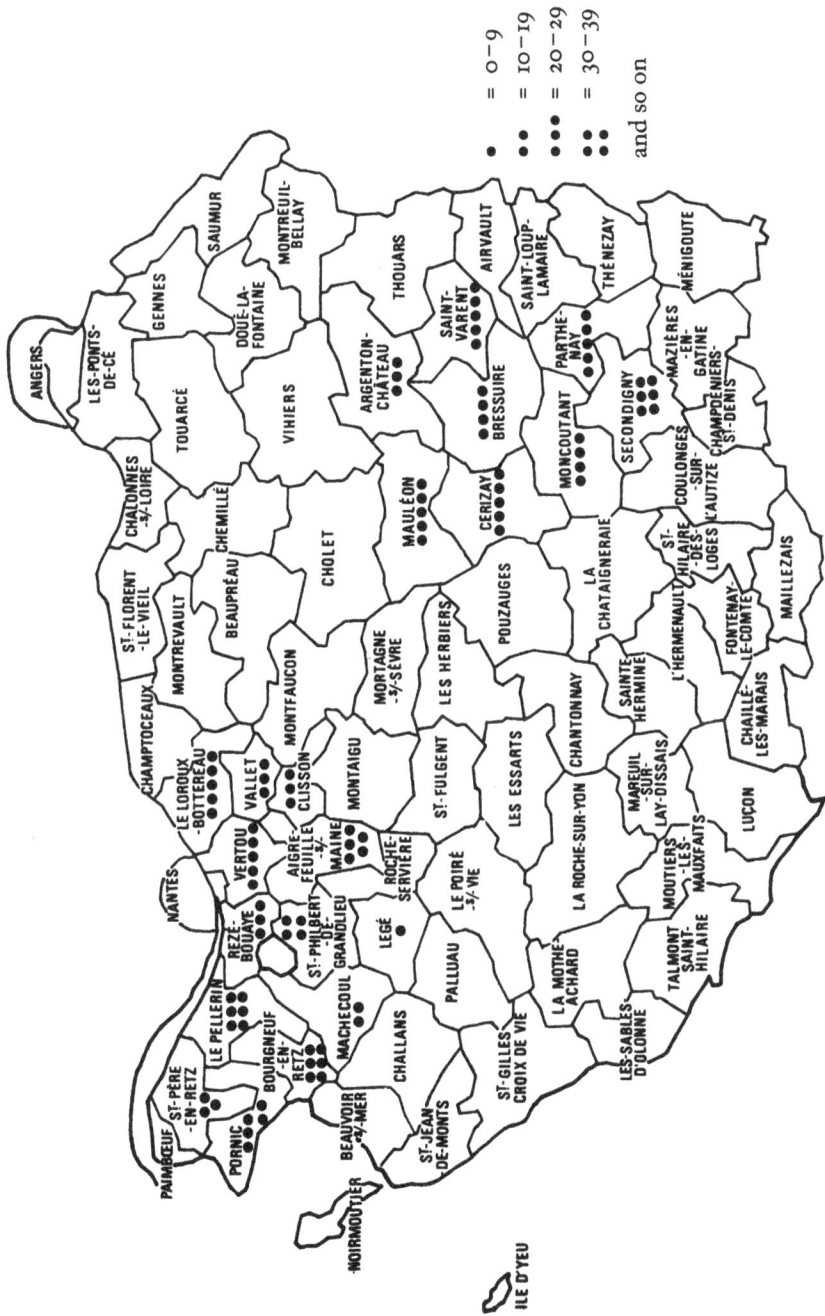

Map 15.7.   Loss of value of rebuilt housing in relation to value before the Revolution (percent)

Legend:

● = 0–9
●● = 10–19
●●● = 20–29
●●●●● = 30–39

and so on

of Deux-Sèvres. As a result, Vendée received 700,000 francs (35 percent),[15] Loire-Inférieure 210,000 (10.5 percent),[16] and Deux-Sèvres 971,188.45 (48.56 percent).[17] The grants awarded were substantial, as the carefully kept accounts confirm. For Vendée alone, 2,398 vouchers were paid, and the department as a whole was involved.[18]

To grasp the real situation as a whole is difficult, if only because of the data. It thus seems to me necessary to study a specific case in order to provide a clearer sense of local trauma. For reasons already stated, I have chosen the example of La Chapelle-Bassemère.

In 1792 the housing stock of the commune was made up of 1,014 houses, 83 percent of which were "street-level" houses, 12 percent "built-up" or "high-ceilinged" houses with external connections between floors, and 5 percent multistory houses with internal connections between floors.

The "street-level" houses were in accordance with French tradition, particularly south of the Loire. Generally they were longer than they were wide, of the type called *bloc à terre* by geographers. They contained only one inhabited room, its size depending on the financial resources of the owner. The fireplace was in the center, and the floor was of packed earth or lime ash. This simple construction was found in villages and hamlets. Houses lined the long streets that ran out from the central square. In the countryside, two stables, one on either side of the house, with a stable and various outbuildings to the rear, formed a rectangular arrangement. The inhabited part was thereby protected. An oven, if there was one, heated it in the winter.

The "built-up" houses were rare. They were located chiefly in the valley, occasionally on the plateaus. They were especially used as a means of defense against flooding, with the ground floor as living space and the second floor as storage for the most precious objects: crops and seeds. The external staircase was designed to permit livestock to take refuge above in case of need. The purchase price of one house might be double that of another, because most of them were provided with more resistant cement "spaces." Lime was used sparingly until 1825, date of the construction of the kilns of Montru and La Chapelle-Heulin.[19] But when the kilns of Liré and Bouzillé were the only ones in the region, the cost of transport was high. Lime carried on barges or in special tipcarts was delivered in blocks of varying sizes. It then had to be slaked with water in holes 60 centimeters deep. The richer houses were adorned with pieces of limestone that had been cut in half; they had been diverted from cargoes transported by sailors. Both stories were some-times covered by squares of fired clay.

The multistory houses were extremely rare, amounting to no more than thirty, located in the centers of villages and featuring limestone jambs.

Finally, there were the castles or "noble" houses, residences for the bour-geois of Nantes. About fifteen were former domains of the sixteenth cen-tury, distinguished from multistory houses by their size. Modeled on royal or noble castles, they were based on a classic building style for the Loire val-ley. One entered through a courtyard, in the form of an H or an inverted U, in proportion to the size of the whole. The principal room was the reception hall. Symbolically, in La Petite-Charaudière, it contained the guillotine.[20] Beyond the park was found an orchard and sometimes, outside, a vineyard.

These residences were constructed of schist from the region. The roof-ing was of "boot shank" tiles, also called channel tiles, without rims, and therefore more primitive than the classic Roman *tegula*. The round tile was a simple clay slab, thin, curved lengthwise, and flat. It was set flat on the roof, with a very slight slope to prevent sliding. At the edges, the tiles were fixed with mortar. These heavy roofs easily collapsed when they were not main-tained. Solid and sophisticated frames were required. The principal woods used were from "pruned" trees, "high wind" oaks, and especially "planta-tion" trees.

When Doctor Lecerf arrived in Saint-Julien-de-Concelles in 1865, he was surprised at the general condition of the housing, which had not changed since the eighteenth century. He set this out in a demographic study given an award by the Academy of Medicine in 1895: "The squalid hovels of the past where some of today's landowners still park three-fourths of their farmers and tenants are often houses . . . that have for a floor only a square of packed earth."[21] They were usually sited below ground level and were therefore humid, and the tiles protected from neither heat nor cold. Vivant and Glébeau supplement this description: in winter, wind and snow came through the tiles and the split wood boards. An old resident, Louis Joyer (1863–1967), adds that in heavy rains a veritable stream ran through the house. Mere "shovelfuls" of earth were used to divert it.

But what most surprised Doctor Lecerf was the absence of openings: "These houses are without windows, the doors having to serve simultane-ously for exit, airing, and lighting." A detailed study of the official survey con-firms this assertion. In 1812, of the 951 remaining houses, 687 (72.2 percent) had no windows. The number of doors varied from one to four, as indicated in table 15.6.

Table 15.6. Distribution of doors in houses in La Chapelle-Bassemère

| | Number of doors | | | | |
	1	*3*	*4*	*5*	*Total*
Number of units	147	524	1	15	687
Percentage in relation to 687 houses	21.4	76.25	0.15	2.18	100
Percentage in relation to 951 houses	15.46	55.1	0.11	1.57	72.24

The remaining houses were distributed as shown in table 15.7.

Table 15.7. Distribution of doors and windows in houses in La Chapelle-Bassemère

| | Average number of doors and windows | | | | | |
	1 door, 2 windows	*2 doors, 1.5 windows*	*3 doors, 6 windows*	*4 doors, 6 windows*	*5 doors, 12 windows*	*Total*
Number of units	73	129	27	27	8	264
Percentage in relation to 264 houses	27.65	48.86	10.23	10.23	3.03	100
Percentage in relation to 951 houses	7.68	13.56	2.84	2.84	0.84	27.75

"And in these dwellings," according to Lecerf, "what a heap of chests, beds, and closets." The single room, bustling with the whole family, was used for everything: kitchen, dining room, bedroom, and sometimes attic. It was in fact not infrequent to see four or five beds, two or three closets, a table, and various other objects in a room that averaged 40 square meters in size. Aside from the fact that the inhabitants wanted to protect themselves from bad weather, this accumulation diminished available space. The small number of openings was thus not the consequence of the taxes on doors and windows created in 1797.[22] The significant dimensions of the courtyard were the result of the fact that in summer people infrequently lived inside these dark rooms. In winter, they left the door open or lit a candle, which, along with the hearth, provided weak light. These candles, made out of rolled resin, called *rousine,* set in the fireplaces, gave off an intolerable odor and choking smoke.[23]

On the eve of the Revolution, most of these houses belonged to the peasantry, the others to artisans, merchants, *rentiers,* working bourgeoisie, and miscellaneous persons (see table 15.8).

Table 15.8.   Ownership of houses in La Chapelle-Bassemère before the Revolution according to socio-professional categories

	Peasantry	Artisans and merchants	Rentiers	Working bourgeoisie	Others	Total
Number of units	538	195	204	14	63	1,014
Percentage	53.06	19.23	20.12	1.38	6.21	100

Ten percent of these houses were owned by nonresidents, outsiders in the community. The value of the housing can be estimated at 1,142,162 francs; 839 houses (83 percent) had a value of between 50 and 1,000 francs, for a total value of 436,000 francs. A detailed analysis shows the proportions that appear in table 15.9.

In reality, the average was different, in the range of 600 francs, with 443 houses, or 44 percent of the total number. This was the typical house in La Chapelle-Bassemère: one door and no window. The remainder, smaller in number, had distinctly higher value, as table 15.10 indicates.

The distribution of housing value according to social categories can be seen in table 15.11.

Table 15.9. Value of La Chapelle-Bassemère houses before the Revolution according to number of units

	Value in francs		
	0–500	500–1,000	Total
Number of units	223	616	839
Percentage in relation to 839 houses	26.58	74.42	100
Percentage in relation to 1,014 houses	21.84	60.33	100

Table 15.10. Number and value of bourgeois houses and castles in La Chapelle-Bassemère before the Revolution and relation to total

Type of unit	Number of units	% in relation to 1,014 houses	Value in francs	% in relation to total value
Bourgeois houses	161	15.76	442,000	38.77
Castles	14	1.37	252,000	22.1
Total	175	17.13	694,000	60.87

Table 15.11. Distribution of housing value before the Revolution according to socio-professional categories

	Peasants and seamen	Artisans and merchants	Rentiers	Working bourgeoisie	Others	Total
Value in francs	304,387	291,405	444,440	32,300	69,630	1,142,162
Percentage	26.65	25.51	38.91	2.83	6.1	100
Average value of house in francs	565.77	1,494.38	2,178.62	2,307.14	1,105.23	
Number of owners	328	118	37	7	25	515

The *rentiers,* particularly the nobles (with 22.72 percent of the value of the town's wealth) were the richest owners; they still owned the castles and the large farms. In absolute terms, the peasants came next. Although a large number of them had become landowners, relatively they were the least wealthy. The working bourgeois (notaries, lawyers, tax collectors), not very numerous, owned large properties within villages such as La Petite-Charaudière and La Guérivière. The artisans and merchants, in addition to the walls of their shops, individually owned some village houses.

Geographically, these houses were grouped chiefly in the villages of La Chapelle (136 houses, 13.4 percent of the total) and Barbechat (51 houses, 5 percent), in large hamlets of 10 houses (Bois-Viau, Beau-Chêne, and Norestier) and of 23 houses (L'Epine) (366 houses, 36 percent), and little villages of 5–9 houses (183 houses, 18.4 percent). The remaining 278 houses (27.4 percent) were either isolated (59), or grouped in units of 2 (48), 3 (69), 4 (52), or 5 (50). The housing was thus relatively grouped together, but unevenly, depending on the canton (see table 15.12).

Table 15.12. Geographic distribution of housing before the Revolution

Cantons	Number of houses	% of total (951)	% 1–5 units	% 6–10 units	% 11–137 units
Chapelle	502	52.80	35.25	17.15	47.60
Vallée	244	25.65	23.81	23.47	52.71
Barbechat	205	21.55	30.30	33	36.70

La Chapelle, except for the town (137 houses), was a "canton" of hamlets. La Vallée was primarily a zone of villages, most often situated on the banks of the Loire. The situation was mixed in Barbechat. In fact, the largest and most burdensome houses, except for the castles, were located in towns or large villages, the places of residence for artisans, merchants, and *rentiers.*

The infernal columns ravaged the region, killing en masse and systematically destroying houses, 357 of which were burned, or 35.2 percent of the total (see table 15.13).

The principal targets chosen by the military were the town of La Chapelle, a few large villages or hamlets on the plateaus (Beauchêne and Le Prau,

Table 15.13.   Distribution of housing destruction according to socio-professional categories

	Peasants and seamen	Artisans and merchants	Rentiers	Working bourgeoisie	Others	Total
Number of houses destroyed	170	116	49	5	17	357
Percentage of total houses destroyed	47.62	32.49	13.73	1.4	4.76	100
Percentage in relation to property before the Revolution	31.6	59.49	24.02	35.71	26.98	

for example), the castles, symbols of the Old Regime, and, on occasion, iso-lated houses or little villages. On the other hand, the gunboats concentrated their attacks on the large villages of La Vallée. Numerically, the peasants were the most affected by the repression, followed by the artisans and mer-chants, the *rentiers*, the "other," and the working bourgeoisie.

Relatively, the artisans and merchants suffered most from the crisis. More than 60 percent of their wealth disappeared. The peasants and the working bourgeoisie lost only a third, and the *rentiers* and the "others" a fourth. Although the number of principal residences destroyed was very high among the peasants, they came in at fourth place in relation to the number of owners. They were preceded by the artisans and merchants, the working bourgeoisie, and the *rentiers* (see table 15.14).

This demonstrates a paradox of the repression, because the inhabitants most favorable to the Revolution were the most affected. This paradox is explained by the choice of targets, the places of residence of artisans and merchants and the working bourgeoisie. As a result, the value of houses de-stroyed was significant: 580,160 francs, nearly 51 percent of the housing stock. Table 15.15 demonstrates this destruction according to socio-professional categories.

The *rentiers* were the most affected: half the value destroyed belonged to them. They were followed by the artisans and merchants, the peasants, the working bourgeoisie, and the "others." In absolute terms, the working

Table 15.14.   Principal residences destroyed according to socio-professional categories

	Peasants and seamen	Artisans and merchants	Rentiers	Working bourgeoisie	Others	Total
Number of principal residences	86	55	12	3	4	160
Percentage in relation to number of houses owned	50.59	47.41	24.49	60	23.53	15.78
Percentage in relation to number of owners	26.22	46.61	32.43	42.86	16	

Table 15.15.   Value of housing destroyed according to socio-professional categories

	Peasants and seamen	Artisans and merchants	Rentiers	Working bourgeoisie	Others	Total
Value of housing destroyed in francs	100,380	136,830	301,300	24,100	17,550	580,160
Percentage in relation to total value of property owned	32.98	46.96	67.79	74.61	25.2	
Percentage in relation to total value destroyed	17.3	23.58	51.93	4.15	3.01	100

bourgeoisie was the most affected: more than 75 percent of the value of its housing had disappeared. The *rentiers* had especially to lament the loss of their castles and other principal houses; farmhouses were generally saved. The same was true for the artisans and merchants. The peasants, principal agents of the revolt, lost nearly a third of the value of their housing.

By 1795 the population had begun rebuilding according to circumstances. In the first year, cautiously, one house was built; the next year, a period of peace, thirty-six. That quantity was not again reached until 1802.

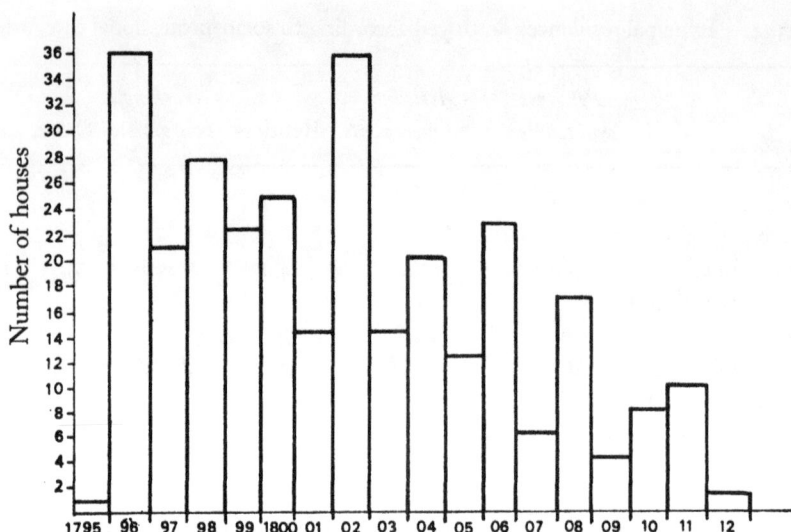

Figure 15.3.   Rate of reconstruction in La Chapelle-Bassemère

In the intervening years, the average number of houses rebuilt was twenty-two. Thereafter, the number declined (see figure 15.3).

In 1812 the housing stock was practically reconstituted, except for 63 houses. They belonged to 62 owners: 44 peasants, 2 seamen, 12 artisans, and 4 *rentiers*, who had disappeared during the crisis, died, or emigrated. The value of the stock not rebuilt amounted to 55,320 francs: 25,870 for the peasants, 2,050 for the seamen, 18,400 for the artisans, and 9,000 for the *rentiers*.

The 294 remaining houses were rebuilt principally through mutual aid of the inhabitants, who reused old materials.[24] Bourgeoisie, artisans, merchants, peasants, and *rentiers* financed themselves and profited from the economic recovery. Others were on occasion obliged to sell some of their burned property in order to finance the reconstruction of their principal residence. Between 1796 and 1810, 45 houses thus changed owners: 27 were sold by peasants, 10 by merchants and artisans, 7 by *rentiers*, and 1 by a nonresident bourgeois. These houses were bought by 41 peasants and 4 artisans, who alone had the necessary funds. The destroyed housing was rebuilt at distinctly lower cost, since it lost 155,502 francs in value, or 13.61 percent of its total value before the events (see tables 15.16 and 15.17).

The *rentiers*, noble or bourgeois, were the owners who rebuilt at the lowest prices. Without available funds, unless they sold possessions, it was

Table 15.16. Value of rebuilt housing according to socio-professional categories

	Peasants and seamen	*Artisans and merchants*	Rentiers	*Working bourgeoisie*	*Others*	*Total*
Difference in cost of reconstruction	−32,783	−20,909	−102,960	6,800	−5,650	−155,502
Percentage in relation to total cost difference	−21.08	−13.45	−66.21	4.37	−3.63	100
Percentage in relation to total value of property owned	−10.77	−7.18	−23.17	21.05	−8.11	

Table 15.17. Rebuilding costs according to socio-professional categories

Costs	*Peasants and seamen*	*Artisans and merchants*	*Rentiers*	*Working bourgeoisie*	*Others*	*Total*
Lower:						
No.	72	33	13	2	8	128
Percent	65.45	55.93	72.22	50	88.89	64
Equal:						
No.	33	9	2			44
Percent	30	15.25	11.11			22
Higher:						
No.	5	17	3	2	1	28
Percent	4.55	28.81	16.67	50	11.11	14
Total:						
No.	110	59	18	4	9	200
Percent	55	29.5	9	2	4.5	100

impossible for them to restore their property completely. Farmers contributed largely to rebuilding and restoring housing, freely or in return for payment in kind. They were followed by peasants, artisans and merchants, and "others." Only the working bourgeoisie followed a different policy: notaries and lawyers experienced a particularly profitable period, and thereby had large financial advantages. Except for those bourgeois, the majority of members of all socio-professional categories were affected.

In addition to its immediate consequences, the destruction had three other medium- and long-term effects. Heavily damaged, 113 houses were abandoned between 1812 and 1850.[25] In addition, the rebuilt housing was of a different character because, particularly in towns, it was of an urban type, with two floors connected internally and many windows. These constructions were monotonous. They all had the same pattern: a central door framed by an average of three to five openings. The difference between the center of the burned town and the untouched periphery is still visible today; the farther one goes from the central square, the more houses have maintained the Old Regime structure, and they are now badly deteriorated. The work was too hasty, and the materials used unreliable and badly handled.

The Vendée-Vengé

AFTER THE FALL OF ROBESPIERRE, IN ACCORDANCE WITH THE LAW of 22 vendémiaire, the Thermidor Convention undertook a series of long trials against "the revolutionary committee, its troublemakers, and its accomplices."[1] "The assassins of the Vendean people," such as Carrier, were not spared.[2] In the midst of popular outbursts, the judges assumed an air of incredulity, wished to understand, demanded explanations, dissected testimony, and analyzed arguments. The evidence came together to indicate that the war of the Vendée should not be understood a priori exclusively through religious reflexes or royalist sentiment, but through a convergence of reasons that were more ordinary and more concrete, supplementing one another and evolving in time.

One of the most important arguments emphasized the divisions among the local social strata, whose actions were motivated by the general wealth of the region. In addition to reports from Old Regime officials, generals and commissioners confirmed this phenomenon. On 18 pluviôse of the year II, Choudieu complained to the Convention that Ronsin and Rossignol had abandoned "to the brigands the harvest of the plains of Doué, Thouars, Loudun, and the île Saint-Aubin, so abundant this year that it would have been enough to feed the entire Army of the West for a year."[3] Barère and Legendre agreed on 3 ventôse (February 21), declaring that before the war, the insurgent departments "supplied six hundred head of cattle a week from what was called Easter to the time that was called Saint John's Day."[4]

The people had thus been specialists, implying classic differences in location: artisans, merchants, and bourgeois lived in towns and villages, while wine growers, cattle breeders, peasants, and woodsmen lived in the countryside.

One group was chiefly criticized for their mercantile spirit, the other for their narrow-mindedness, lack of dynamism, and systematic hostility to any form of cooperation, as exemplified by their resistance to the construction of new roads in order to facilitate the free circulation of merchandise.

In addition were the disappointments engendered by the revolutionary policies that had at first been welcomed: continuation and even increase of taxes; more extensive conscription; abusive requisitions; and increased political dependency. The countryside felt itself a victim of these painful measures, all the more because they were transmitted through the towns by a group of privileged and enthusiastically activist "functionaries." In September 1788 Arthur Young was struck by this attitude:

> Nantes is as *enflammé* in the cause of liberty, as any town in France can be; the conversations I witnessed here prove how great a change is effected in the minds of the French, nor do I believe it will be possible for the present government to last more than half a century longer, unless the clearest and most decided talents are at the helm. The American Revolution has laid the foundation of another in France, if government does not take care of itself.[5]

Locally, and perhaps more radically than in Paris, power relations were very soon openly expressed, either based on the new national will, the source of law, and the theoretical values promulgated and orchestrated by the Constituent Assembly, or based on individual will, local independence, the source of ancient custom guaranteed by the *fabrique* and its representatives. Logically, the established authorities approached the problem in religious terms and, in the name of reason and unification, dealt with it in human terms by marginalizing the clergy, who were seen as the organizing force behind the opposition.

Because of the context, as early as 1790 this rejection of dialogue and compromise degenerated into a number of humiliating, harassing, arbitrary, and sometimes even violent measures, with the deliberate intention of exceeding government decisions. Threatened both physically and in their beliefs, many priests chose to escape from repression and, rejecting exile, hid in safe places among their families and friends, whose interest in their plight they stirred while awakening or stimulating popular faith and simultaneously adopting an offensive posture toward events. These populations, accused of complicity and antirevolutionary sentiments, then had the same arguments unleashed against them, and the same methods applied, with the difference that these were more visible, more tangible, because they were more systematic. The situation quickly became explosive, which was demonstrated daily by isolated local disturbances in which anything became a pretext for resistance.

Widespread understanding of the situation occurred on the occasion of the conscription lottery of March 1793. The explosion is understandable in human terms, for the departure of able-bodied men would leave the oppressed population even more helpless against the state, the administrations, and the clubs. Even worse, the conscripts would perhaps even be required to apply the terror to their own relatives, friends, and compatriots, and so they felt forced into revolt. As for the "patriot" conscripts, their reaction was the exact opposite. All of them, faced with the rising tension, feared the consequences of the inevitable explosion for their own families.

The characteristics of the war of the Vendée can thus be explained: it was a popular war in origin and in its participants; it was a rural war because of the environment in which it took place; it was a clerical and then a religious war because of the impulses that armed the Vendeans; it was a political war through the democratic choice of its leadership.[6] In fact, the war was above all a crusade for individual liberty, the security of persons, and the preservation of possessions. In the face of the "tyrant of oppression," the Declaration of the Rights of Man and Citizen joined with Saint Thomas Aquinas to provide moral justification for rebellion. The text of the Declaration is unambiguous: "When the government violates the rights of the people, insurrection is, for the people and every portion of the people, the most sacred right and the most indispensable duty" (article 35). Could the Constituent Assembly have anticipated the boomerang effect of the old affirmation of the rejection of arbitrary rule, whatever its origin? In the Vendeans' view, their revolt was both legitimate and legal. The Vendée thus became a considerable moral force; it could be defeated only by disproportionate strength, the weight of numbers, time, and massacres. The repression was in proportion to the danger faced by the new regime: confronted with a popular revolt, its entire "popular" legitimacy was called into question. And it was a war. Killing was thus done in the name of national unity, an argument identical to that of 1685—the indivisibility of the Republic, fraternity, liberty, and patriotism.[7] As Napoleon asserted, only ideological frenzy could explain this murderous folly;[8] was the Committee of Public Safety not the "sanctuary of truth"?[9]

A sense of cold and logical purpose imposed itself on the leaders as well as on the participants. Robespierre boasted of it before the Committee:

"We must crush the internal enemies of the Republic or perish along with it; in this situation the first maxim of your policy must be that we lead the people by reason and the enemies of the people by terror . . . This terror is nothing but prompt, severe, and inflexible justice."[10] The genocide occurred in the context of this unchallenged logic. As early as October 1, 1793, the Convention solemnly proclaimed it to the army of the West: "Soldiers of liberty, the brigands of the Vendée must be exterminated; the soldier of the nation demands it, the impatience of the French people commands it, its courage must accomplish it . . ."[11] From then on, the terrorist mission took precedence over military operations: "depopulate the Vendée" (Francastel, January 4, 1794);[12] "entirely purge the soil of freedom of that cursed race" (General Beaufort, January 30, 1794);[13] and "execrable" was the term used by Minier.[14]

Carrier denied having any magnanimous feelings: "Stop talking to us about humanity toward these fierce Vendeans; they will all be exterminated; the measures adopted ensure us a prompt return to calm in the region; but we must not leave a single rebel, for their repentance will never be sincere . . ."[15] It was a futile calculation and a singular political illusion, for those measures led precisely to a delay in the return to calm.

With the principle accepted at every level, the application followed with no compromise possible: "No mercy to the conspirators . . . guilty of treachery against the Republic."[16] Women and children were condemned, with aggravating circumstances: the former, as source of reproduction, were "all monsters,"[17] the latter were just as dangerous, because they were or were in the process of becoming brigands. Carrier explained: "Children of thirteen and fourteen bear arms against us, and even younger children are spies for the brigands. Many of these little scoundrels have been tried and condemned by the military commission . . ."[18]

Hallucinatory witness reports have come down to us, such as this one from Le Bouvier des Mortiers taken down in Le Luc (Vendée), in the village of La Nouette:

> A woman suffering from the pains of childbirth was hidden in a hovel near the village; soldiers found her, cut out her tongue, split her belly, and took out the child on the point of their bayonets. A quarter mile away, you could hear the howls of this unfortunate woman, who was on the point of death when help arrived.[19]

Lequinio even asked to be allowed to take no more prisoners. "If I may say so," he proclaimed to the Convention, "I would like to have the same measures adopted in all our armies; with our enemies then reciprocating, it would be impossible for us to have any more cowards . . . This is indispensable in the Vendée if you want to bring it to an end."[20] He was heard: Westermann,[21] as Francastel attests,[22] boasted after the battle of Savenay, "Kléber and Marceau are no longer here, we no longer take prisoners." The directory in Angers was unambiguous on the subject: "To restore public opinion, we will destroy the greatest number of them possible . . . Prisoners such as leaders, armed men, or men found wounded, surgeons, doctors, and so-called royalist officers will be tried on the spot, in accordance with the decree of the directory and existing laws . . ."[23] Nor were patriots spared—besides, there were no more patriots, explained Carrier: "I can assure you that not a single patriot remains in the Vendée. All the inhabitants of this region have taken a more or less active part in this war . . ."[24] When Gaudin protested, he was interrupted and threatened with sanctions by the members of the Convention. Representatives Hantz, Garreau, and Francastel were just as categorical:

> All the inhabitants now in the Vendée are rebels, all relentless . . .
> On this footing, the war will be completely terminated only when there
> is not a single inhabitant left in the Vendée . . . If we can reach the
> rebels, it is all over for them; once the centers have been thoroughly dis
> solved, we will conduct cavalry charges in the region that will kill every
> one they encounter . . .[25]

Maignen called for "striking without distinction: stop using small measures that suggest lack of resolution."[26] The holocaust was coupled with the total ruin of the region. For Barère, "it is a matter of sweeping the soil of the Vendée with cannon and purifying it with fire."[27] "Patriotic" fire, was Lequinio's ironic comment.[28] The reprisals were thus not frightful but inevitable acts that occur in the heat of battle in a long and atrocious war, but indeed premeditated, organized, planned massacres, which were committed in cold blood, and were massive and systematic, with the conscious and explicit intention of destroying a well-defined region and exterminating an entire people, women and children first, in order to eradicate a "cursed race" considered ideologically beyond redemption.[29] "The war," Hantz and

Francastel repeatedly said, "will end only when there are no more inhabitants in that unfortunate land."[30]

With pride and unconcealed joy, Bourbotte and Turreau themselves prepared a report on operations: "You would have to travel far in these regions before encountering a man or a cottage. We have left behind us only corpses and ruins."[31] It was a matter "of sacrificing everything to the national vengeance."

In April and May 1794, the Convention declared itself "reassured": "the hideous hydra" of the Vendée "can no longer speak counterrevolution, since it is all it can do to survive."[32] On 18 brumaire of the year I, Merlin had even proposed to the Convention removing "the name of Vendée from the table of departments," in order to replace it with the more evocative name of "department Vengé";[33] the measure was applied a few months later. Thereafter, certain place names, "soiled by the presence of brigands," were changed: the île Bouin became the île Marat, Noirmoutier became the île de la Montagne, and so on.[34] Even the idea of colonization was proposed in order to redevelop the land now devoid of people: "Few citizens remain in those regions that are so beautiful and so fertile; one of the finest regions of the Republic is almost totally abandoned, without agriculture, and offers to the eyes of the traveler who trembles as he goes through it only ashes and corpses"; it is a "vast desert, a monument to the revenge of liberty." Consequently, Merlin proposed a decree, the four final paragraphs of which set forth concrete suggestions for carrying it out:

> 3. Two representatives of the people will travel to Nantes and to all the towns of the Vendée, and will prepare an inventory of the legacies formerly possessed by the rebels and all those who took part in the war of Vendée and have not abjured their error.
>
> 4. These legacies will be distributed to farmers who have remained loyal in the region and who have the right to indemnities.
>
> 5. To the refugees from Germany who have abandoned their property because of their patriotism.
>
> 6. The departments will send to the representatives of the people in the Vendée one family of impoverished farmers per canton, to receive a piece of land to farm as their property. The departments will supply them with the means to travel to the region and the expenses advanced by them will be reimbursed by the national treasury.[35]

The Convention sent this "fine proposal, although simple and easy to carry out," to the Committee of Public Safety, because it seemed too precipitous, as Fayau explained:

> If the brigands of the Vendée no longer existed, as people have long been inclined to say, I would vote to adopt the articles presented by Merlin. But we must not hide from ourselves the fact that the brigands still exist . . . Merlin's plan is fine; but to carry it out, the representatives of the people will have to be accompanied by armies. Not enough has been burned in the Vendée . . . it is necessary that for a year no man or animal be able to find sustenance on its soil. The colonies that you would send would perhaps be new sacrifices that you would be making.

In a decree of August 31, 1793, the general council of Vendée had already ordered its chief procurator-syndic and, through him, the procurator-syndics of the districts, "to sequester all the possessions of the rebels of this department," a measure carried out by September 4.[36]

If, despite intentions, the genocide was not carried to its conclusion, this was solely because "of the insufficiency of resources."[37] Turreau said that he was "desperate," because he found it dreadful to have his "zeal" and his "opinion" "suspected." Moreover, the troops, a majority of whom were volunteers known as "death's heads" from the name of their insignia, were slow, undisciplined, and obsessed with plunder.[38] Lequinio complained about it because it was "often carried to extremes. Many simple soldiers have amassed fifty thousand francs and more. We have seen them covered with jewels and indulging in all kinds of spending of monstrous prodigality."[39] Doctor Thomas, a patriot from Nantes, was astounded: "A soldier had taken twenty-four gold louis from a brigand whom he had killed. Another soldier killed his comrade to get this gold, and twenty or thirty killed each other in this way." The troops, including officers, overloaded with plunder of all kinds, consequently became less and less effective as they penetrated into the interior of the region and came up against some resistance, even slight or subjective. This was true in Le Luc. Cordelier's two columns, after "scrupulous searches"[40] made it possible for them "at little expense to take the top off a whole nest of pious frauds brandishing their insignia of fanaticism" (564 persons),[41] were seized with "panic fear" at the sight of three Vendean horsemen: "The [Martincourt] column brought along with it the [Crouzat] column that had not yet fired a rifle . . . so that instead of crushing the enemy," Cordelier admitted, "I was forced to take up position only in Léger," nine kilometers distant.

The assessment cannot be evaded: the military Vendée lost at a minimum nearly 15 percent of its total population (117,257 out of 815,029), a large proportion because of the organized repression, and nearly 20 percent of listed housing (10,309 houses out of 53,273); but, relying on the sampling carried out at La Chapelle-Bassemère, more than half the value of housing disappeared in the flames.

The sectarianism of the directory, its blunders, and the resumption of religious persecution after 18 fructidor (September 1797) were the source of a new crisis in 1799, which locally degenerated into armed conflict. The pacification of the region and its reconstruction were exclusively the work of Bonaparte. Everything played out between mid-October and the end of the year 1799, and concluded with a "proclamation of the consuls of the Republic to the inhabitants of the departments of the West" on 7 nivôse of the year VIII (December 28, 1799).⁴² This was the turning point in relations between Vendeans and the government, the purpose of which was to prevent "an unholy war from setting aflame a second time the departments of the West." After condemning the actions of the "Vendeans who went over to the English . . . men to whom the government owes neither consideration nor a declaration of principles," the consuls specified that they were addressing "citizens dear to the nation, who were seduced by their artifices and to whom are owed enlightenment and truth."

The arbitrary actions of preceding governments were recalled in a few words:

> Unjust laws were promulgated and carried out, arbitrary acts threatened the safety of citizens and freedom of conscience; everywhere conjectural inscriptions on lists of émigrés affected citizens who had never abandoned their country or even their homes; finally, great principles of social order were violated.

"The government will forgive, will show mercy to those who repent"; it "is constantly working to prepare the reform of bad laws and for a more equitable arrangement of public contributions. Each day is and will be marked by acts of justice . . ." There was a challenge to the past and an amnesty, to be sure, but also and above all total freedom of worship: "The Consuls declare as well that total freedom of worship is guaranteed by the constitution, that no magistrate can call it into question; that no man can say to another man: you will practice only one religion, you will practice it on only one day." This sentence, printed in special type, was decisive.

This very cleverly worded proclamation for the first time established a congruence between the legitimacy of the refractory priests and a form of legality. It even gave these priests a role as intermediaries:

> Everyone will henceforth have only one feeling, love of country. The ministers of a God of peace will be the prime movers for reconciliation and concord; let them speak to the hearts of the people the language learned in the school of their teacher; let them go into the churches that have been reopened for them to offer with their fellow citizens the sacrifice that will expiate the crimes of war and bloodshed.

The word *sacrifice* was not chosen at random, referring as it did to a fundamental theological concept.[43] The Mediterranean Bonaparte was in close touch with Catholic sensibilities, and the clergy was correct in perceiving this. The proclamation was followed by four decrees abolishing the previous restrictions and vexations and granting the right to appointment to public office to "the former nobles or relatives of émigrés deemed worthy of confidence"; a promise to respect the consular constitution, which did not interfere in the spiritual realm, replaced the constitutional oath. The declaration, of which 2,000 copies were distributed, was strictly adhered to and was considered a victory by the Vendeans: their identity had been recognized and their fight justified. The Concordat of 1801 merely extended it.

The future emperor became even more popular when he implemented a series of practical measures: the foot burners were tracked down and arrested; wolf hunts were organized in which the court participated;[44] back taxes were reduced; plants, seedlings, and agricultural materials were distributed; and homeless inhabitants were rehoused.[45] The consequences of this policy were immediate, particularly in the economic realm; agricultural production notably increased and by 1801 was providing basic necessities to the population.

Exiled priests returned in triumph, and popular feeling was deeply stirred, as in Le Loroux-Bottereau. According to an eyewitness,

> The entire population in Sunday dress had come out on the old Nantes road, at the entry to the rue des Forges, where a bonfire had been

prepared. A few moments earlier, all of them had wanted to gather around the man whose absence had been so bitterly lamented.

At the sight of these familiar faces, of this multitude whose cries of joy reached the heavens, of the little children kneeling to ask for blessing, the saintly old man [Abbé Peccot, who had been a refugee in Spain][46] forgot the sufferings of exile. The immense joy that flooded his heart could not be expressed in words. He took his faithful peasants in his arms, alternately wept and smiled, and let out only these words *inin tenesupas:* "Hello, my children, hello, my dear children, I will come to see you." . . .

The pastor could not master his emotion in the face of the disasters and disappearances brought about by the terror; on his arrival at the rue des Forges, his face was suddenly bathed in tears. A single glance at the ruins had just revealed to him the extent of the misfortunes that had overcome his parish. He looked in vain around him for the crowd of young people whom he had blessed at birth or whose marriages he had celebrated and whom he had left full of strength and health at the beginning of their lives. He hardly dared speak their names or ask for news from their families. For a large number, alas, the answer would have been the same.

The sight of his burned church drew deep sighs from him; the blackened walls and houses without roofs told him that the hearth fire had long been extinguished and that in its place were only ashes and tears . . .[47]

As a general rule, the priests abundantly praised the role that Bonaparte and the return to peace played in these reunions. The union of the Vendean people with Napoleon, emperor "by the grace of God and by the will of the French people," lasted until 1812, and helps to explain the failure of attempted insurrections organized by the royalists. Following repeated military disasters, and especially the catastrophic Russian campaign, Napoleon questioned the privileges that had been granted and became demanding; a series of indirect taxes was levied on the principal products of the region, notably on wine;[48] church property not distributed following the insurrection was again put up for sale. Also, conscription increased in substantial proportions, despite warnings like this one from the mayor of Mortagne: "The moment at which you are setting the number of conscripts for each canton is also the moment to remind you that those under our jurisdiction are and ought to be a very small number; the general massacre of 1793 in the Vendée of women and children as well as men is the cause of the depopulation that has burdened conscription in the clearest way." This depopulation was obviously reflected in the phenomenon of "empty cohorts," which is difficult to evaluate.[49]

The decree calling up those who had been exempt from previous cohorts left married men at home. There was thus a frenetic race to get married, as described by a witness in the canton of Le Loroux-Bottereau:

> Young men were running around day and night in search of a girl, an old maid, or a widow willing to marry them. It was said that a young man from Saint-Julien-de-Concelles asked six girls on the same day who all refused him, and he only succeeded with the seventh. A young man from La Brosse had an even harder time, not reaching his goal until the ninth.[50]

Then the young man would get a certificate of compliance from the mayor, and that was it. As for the conscripts for the year, a substantial number refused to attend the drawing or deserted. Exasperated, the government called out the army at the expense of the communes. This led to general discontent, which the royalists took advantage of for propaganda purposes, making many promises, particularly an end to conscription.[51] Memories of the period recorded by a family of doctors named Renoul are eloquent:

> The drawing for the draft had arrived [for the eldest, Aymé]; there was no exemption and no good number; everyone had to go, but very few returned. I remember the fatal day of the drawing. During that miserable morning, my mother was locked in her room weeping copious tears thinking of the sad fate awaiting her son. He drew number sixty-nine, but because the poor child was still weak from typhus, he managed to get a postponement. Time went by. My parents were extremely anxious; their eldest son might have to leave from one day to the next; and as drawings were pushed forward because they had to replace the soldiers who were killed, the second son could expect to go in a few months. The days went by very sadly in the midst of these mortal anxieties. But what happiness it was when on Easter, at eight in the morning as we were eating breakfast,

Monsieur de Mauvillain came running to the house, shouting: "Long live the king! The emperor is dethroned and Louis XVIII proclaimed king of France."

How can I express the surprise, the joy, the happiness of our parents, who had no expectation of anything of the kind. France was delivered from its tyrant! Their sons, their beloved children were saved! The enthusiasm of the population knew no bounds. I have never forgotten the outburst of joy with which the "Domine, salvum fac Regen" was sung in the church for the first time . . .[52]

All these events taken together were highly significant, and it is thus easy to understand the trauma suffered by the people. For several decades, these events affected the history, the political and ideological sentiments, and the social behavior of the region; the military Vendée was primarily antirepublican until the Fifth Republic, and alternately plebiscitary or legitimist, depending on circumstances and individuals.[53]

The wars of the Vendée thus constitute a particularly dramatic page of French history, which successive governments, with the paradoxical exception of Napoleon I, have marginalized if not reduced to silence.[54] Contemporaries willingly minimized events; only the principally guilty were condemned to death; the others, although convicted of complicity, were released, "not having done it with criminal intent."[55] The Restoration, troubled by the question of subversive challenge and by the violence of the war, chose, in the name of the principles proclaimed in the charter of 1814, to forget. Republicans found it extremely embarrassing to accept that the government had, in the midst of the Revolution, been obliged to sign treaties with insurrectional powers, thereby conferring on them a certain recognition. As for the military, too often defeated in open battle, the Vendean guerrilla war posed for them a technical and intellectual problem that they handled badly.[56] Moreover, many accomplished generals withdrew, like Bonaparte and d'Augereau, or resigned, like Dumas, Bard, who refused to "carry out organized massacres," and Kléber, who "left his command in the face of the savage demands of the Committee of Public Safety." Some historians, such as Michelet, have justified the terror,[57] considered the repressors "heroes" and "martyrs" to whom a monument should be built,[58] characterized the methods adopted as "admirable inventions,"[59] and scorned the Vendeans, "those cowardly barbarians."

Logic itself says that the crueler of the two sides was the one that believed it was avenging God, that sought to match unlimited suffering with unlimited crime. In shedding blood, the republicans did not have such an exalted vision. They wanted to suppress the enemy, nothing more; their firing squads and their drownings were means of shortening death and not human sacrifices.[60]

There are more glorious pages in Michelet, and the argument was adopted too frequently by others in the nineteenth century in order to justify the unjustifiable. Fear is probably at the source of any organized terror, as Marx clearly understood, but can fear justify the openly declared intent to exterminate? And have the ends ever justified the means for anybody? In ancient Asian civilizations, the murder of a man, "bearer of the flying seed," is of course a crime, but not a sacrilege, even if carried out in a temple; the murder of a woman, by breaking the chain of life, is an irremediable stain that must be expiated; the holy place itself becomes for a time profaned. It is the desire to remove every trace of a rebel people from the surface of the earth which defines genocide. The Vendeans were not saints, and they too committed massacres: there is nothing more logical in the inexorable chain of reprisals and counter-reprisals. Nothing, however, can justify the delirium of hatred and its perverse fruits. For the seed of hatred has flowered in the twentieth century in waves of blood. It was to the honor of a few generals that they refused to shed the blood of noncombatants; the generosity of Beauchamp was answered by the generosity of Hoche, for the honor of mankind. Nevertheless, with Sainte-Beuve one may "deem that evil, violent, iniquitous, and inhuman means, even supposing that they had an appearance of immediate utility at the moment of crisis, leave behind, if only on the imaginations affected, . . . long and disastrous traces, contagious in the form of either exaggerated theoretical imitations, or narrow and cowardly fears."[61]

APPENDIX

Appendix. Assessment of human and housing losses by canton (1980 canton limits) in the wars of the Vendée

	Loire-Inférieure					
	Saint-Père-en-Retz	Bouaye[a]	Bourgneuf-en-Retz	Vertou	Machecoul	Vallet[c]
Number of houses in 1792	1,604	3,791	1,767	4,713	2,424	1,403
Number of houses destroyed	59	173	131	514	341	204
Percent of houses destroyed/1792	3.68	4.57	7.41	10.9	14.06	14.54
Value of houses destroyed	48,670	348,170	837,960	1,286,496	432,772	223,909
Number of houses not rebuilt	15	53	27	151	116	59
Value of houses not rebuilt	13,020	82,976	102,560	249,460	209,972	40,350
Percent of destroyed houses not rebuilt	25.42	30.64	20.61	29.37	34.01	28.92
Percent of 1792 houses not rebuilt	0.94	1.34	1.52	3.2	4.78	4.2
Number of houses rebuilt	44	120	104	363	225	145
Percent of destroyed houses rebuilt	71.19	69.36	79.38	70.62	65.98	71.07
Percent of 1792 houses rebuilt	2.74	3.16	5.88	7.7	9.28	10.33
Value of houses rebuilt	38,762	220,767[b]	355,380	756,531	379,593	175,975
Loss or gain in value	−9,908	−90,753[b]	−482,580	−529,965	−53,179	−47,934
Percent value of rebuilt houses compared with 1792 value	79.65	73.22[b]	42.41	58.8	87.71	78.59
Percent loss or gain	−20.35	−26.78[b]	−57.59	−41.2	−12.29	−21.41
Population in 1792	7,214.19	12,145.16	6,291.72	12,012.38	9,352.89	8,613.81
Population in 1802–1812	6,586.50	10,400.69	6,276.85	10,419.25	8,026.32	7,739
Increase or decrease in population	−627.9	−1,744.49	−15.02	−1,593.13	−1,323.84	−875.11
Percent of increase or decrease compared to 1792	−8.7	−14.36	−0.23	−13.26	−14.5	−10.15
Number of residents per house in 1792	4.49	3.2	3.5	2.54	3.85	2.31
Number of residents per house in 1802–1812	4.14	2.78	3.6	2.28	3.47	2.62

a Brain excluded, because only rental values are available.
b Brain and Bouguenais excluded.
c Vallet is missing.
d Two communes with rental values only.
e Two communes with no value.

			Loire-Inférieure				
Paimbœuf	Saint-Philbert-de-Grandlieu	Aigrefeuille-sur-Maine	Clisson	Pornic	Le Loroux-Bottereau	Le Pellerin	Legé
1,225	2,219	3,116	3,233	3,145	3,920	3,210	1,780
none	367	637	1,060	210	856	357	348
none	16.53	20.44	32.78	6.67	21.83	11.12	19.52
none	976,163	1,007,544	1,333,197	186,010	1,589,023	775,170	892,314
none	101	149	282	60	168	97	35
none	284,350	285,320	330,325	52,950	2,119,112	178,940	48,510
none	27.52	23.39	26.6	28.57	19.62	27.17	10.05
none	4.55	4.78	8.72	1.9	4.28	3.02	1.96
none	266	488	778	150	688	260	313
none	72.48	76.6	73.39	71.42	80.37	72.82	89.94
none	11.98	15.66	24.06	4.76	17.55	8.09	17.58
none	624,510	567,090	1,027,342	108,220	838,524	482,820	859,656
none	−352,253	−440,454	−305,855	−77,790	−750,499	−292,350	−32,658
none	63.94	56.28	77.05	58.17	52.76	62.28	96.34
none	−38.07	−43.72	−22.95	−41.83	−47.24	−57.71	−3.66
7,306.45	8,637.12	12,964.70	11,550.43	7,952.05	12,554.60	10,426.05	6,811.97
4,424.62	7,904.44	11,655.70	8,026.79	6,549.31	10,879.46	9,588.29	5,504.62
−2,881.23	−732.18	−1,309	−3,523.64	−1,403.61	−1,675.14	−836.98	−1,307.35
−39.43	−8.47	−10	−30.5	−17.65	−13.34	−8.02	−19.19
5.96	3.89	4.16	3.57	2.52	3.2	3.24	3.82
3.61	3.73	3.92	2.72	2.12	2.89	3.08	3.15

	Deux-Sèvres				
	Moncoutant	Parthenay	Secondigny	Argenton-Château	Bressuire
Number of houses in 1792	1,157	237	130	1,239	2,105
Number of houses destroyed	111	25	3	495	1,158
Percent of houses destroyed/1792	9.59	10.54	2.3	39.95	55.01
Value of houses destroyed	238,416[d]	4,300	3,400	830,946	1,872,596
Number of houses not rebuilt	9	2	1	115	386
Value of houses not rebuilt	3,107[d]	1,000	200	208,670	529,514
Percent of destroyed houses not rebuilt	8.1	8	33.3	23.23	33.33
Percent of 1792 houses not rebuilt	0.77	0.84	0.7	9.28	18.33
Number of houses rebuilt	102	23	2	380	772
Percent of destroyed houses rebuilt	91.89	92	66.66	76.76	66.66
Percent of 1792 houses rebuilt	8.81	9.7	1.53	30.66	36.67
Value of houses rebuilt	160,929[d]	2,500	1,400	583,729	1,218,907
Loss or gain in value	77,487[d]	1,800	2,000	247,217	653,689
Percent value of rebuilt houses compared with 1792 value	67.49[d]	5.8	41.17	70.24	65.09
Percent loss or gain	−32.51[d]	−42	−58.83	−29.76	−34.91
Population in 1792					
Population in 1802–1812					
Increase or decrease in population					
Percent of increase or decrease compared to 1792					
Number of residents per house in 1792					
Number of residents per house in 1802–1812					

[a] Brain excluded, because only rental values are available.
[b] Brain and Bouguenais excluded.
[c] Vallet is missing.
[d] Two communes with rental values only.
[e] Two communes with no value.

	Deux-Sèvres				Maine-et-Loire			
Cerizay	Mauléon	Saint-Varent	Angers	Chalonnes sur-Loire	Les-Ponts-de-Cé	Thouarcé	Beaupréau
1,640	2,252	586					
392	980	103					
23.9	43.51	17.57					
744,724ᵉ	241,893	249,047					
94	203	28					
182,700ᵉ	905,662	38,480					
23.97	20.71	27.18					
5.73	9.01	4.77					
298	777	75					
76.02	79.28	79.28					
18.17	34.5	12.79					
415,130ᵉ	2,298,137	131,597					
329,594ᵉ	120,797	117,450					
55.74	52.12	52.84					
−44.26	−47.88	−47.16					
			30,605.10	9,860.58	15,676.19	16,534.91	15,021.19
			23,498.65	8,962.40	13,510.16	12,852.53	11,981.35
			−7,106.45	−898.18	−2,168.13	−3,682.38	−3,039.43
				−23.21	−9.1	−13.83	−22.27	−20.23

Appendix. Assessment of human and housing losses by canton (1980 canton limits) in the wars of the Vendée (*cont.*)

	Maine-et-Loire				
	Champtoceaux	Chemillé	Cholet-Est	Cholet-Ouest	Montfaucon
Number of houses in 1792					
Number of houses destroyed					
Percent of houses destroyed/1792					
Value of houses destroyed					
Number of houses not rebuilt					
Value of houses not rebuilt					
Percent of destroyed houses not rebuilt					
Percent of 1792 houses not rebuilt					
Number of houses rebuilt					
Percent of destroyed houses rebuilt					
Percent of 1792 houses rebuilt					
Value of houses rebuilt					
Loss or gain in value					
Percent value of rebuilt houses compared with 1792 value					
Percent loss or gain					
Population in 1792	8,925.34	11,938.90	10,632.90	8,721.73	12,284.16
Population in 1802–1812	8,288.71	8,320.93	6,603.90	6,117.89	9,933.17
Increase or decrease in population	637.03	−3,617.97	−4,028.40	−2,603.84	−2,350.63
Percent of increase or decrease compared to 1792	7.14	−30.3	−37.86	−29.85	−19.13
Number of residents per house in 1792					
Number of residents per house in 1802–1812					

a Brain excluded, because only rental values are available.
b Brain and Bouguenais excluded.
c Vallet is missing.
d Two communes with rental values only.
e Two communes with no value.

Montrevault	Saint-Florent-le-Vieil	Doué-la-Fontaine	Gennes	Montreuil-Bellay	Vihiers	Saumur
		Maine-et-Loire				
10,470.49	13,676.37	10,191.38	7,270.03	7,919.47	13,022.65	9,085.50
9,288.14	11,392.52	8,749.20	6,097.68	6,814.06	9,042.89	8,244
−1,181.59	−2,283.94	−1,442.38	−1,172.35	−1,105.44	−3,979.56	−841.5
−11.28	−16.69	−14.13	−16.12	−13.95	−30.55	−9.26

	Vendée				
	La-Roche-sur-Yon	Fontenay-le-Comte	L'Hermenault	Saint-Jean de-Monts	La Chataigneraie
Number of houses in 1792					
Number of houses destroyed					
Percent of houses destroyed/1792					
Value of houses destroyed					
Number of houses not rebuilt					
Value of houses not rebuilt					
Percent of destroyed houses not rebuilt					
Percent of 1792 houses not rebuilt					
Number of houses rebuilt					
Percent of destroyed houses rebuilt					
Percent of 1792 houses rebuilt					
Value of houses rebuilt					
Loss or gain in value					
Percent value of rebuilt houses compared with 1792 value					
Percent loss or gain					
Population in 1792	14,139.82	15,158.16	9,089.85	9,947.51	14,826.80
Population in 1802–1812	13,199.48	14,140.51	8,692.19	8,438.31	13,395.27
Increase or decrease in population	−940.34	−1,017.65	−397.66	−1,509.20	−1,431.51
Percent of increase or decrease compared to 1792	−6.65	−6.77	−4.37	−15.17	−9.65
Number of residents per house in 1792					
Number of residents per house in 1802–1812					

a Brain excluded, because only rental values are available.
b Brain and Bouguenais excluded.
c Vallet is missing.
d Two communes with rental values only.
e Two communes with no value.

			Vendée				
Pouzauges	Chaillé-les-Moutiers	Les Herbiers	Marillezais	Charzais	Les-Moutiers-les-Mauxfaits	La Mothe-Achard

10,377	7,362.30	11,739.86	11,152.95	2,702.78	8,221.10	9,049.24
9,355.60	7,246.47	9,372.86	10,898.86	2,522.98	7,377.98	7,412.14
-1,021.40	-115.83	-2,367.29	-254.69	-179.8	-843.12	-1,637.10
-9.83	-1.5	-20.16	-2.27	-6.62	-10.25	-18.09

Appendix. Assessment of human and housing losses by canton (1980 canton limits) in the wars of the Vendée (*cont.*)

	Vendée				
	Palluau	Noirmoutier	Saint-Fulgent	Ile d'Yeu	Les Sables-d'Olonne
Number of houses in 1792					
Number of houses destroyed					
Percent of houses destroyed/1792					
Value of houses destroyed					
Number of houses not rebuilt					
Value of houses not rebuilt					
Percent of destroyed houses not rebuilt					
Percent of 1792 houses not rebuilt					
Number of houses rebuilt					
Percent of destroyed houses rebuilt					
Percent of 1792 houses rebuilt					
Value of houses rebuilt					
Loss or gain in value					
Percent value of rebuilt houses compared with 1792 value					
Percent loss or gain					
Population in 1792	10,754.42	5,022	8,799.19	1,863	9,174.61
Population in 1802–1812	9,091.51	4,914	7,228.24	1,359.89	8,569.34
Increase or decrease in population	−1,662.91	−108	−1,570.95	−503.11	−605.6
Percent of increase or decrease compared to 1792	−15.42	−2.15	−17.85	−27.01	−6.6
Number of residents per house in 1792					
Number of residents per house in 1802–1812					

[a] Brain excluded, because only rental values are available.
[b] Brain and Bouguenais excluded.
[c] Vallet is missing.
[d] Two communes with rental values only.
[e] Two communes with no value.

| | Vendée | | | | | |
Saint-Gilles-Croix-de-Vie	Saint-Urbain	Mortagne-sur-Sèvre	Sainte-Hermine	Challans	Roche-servière	Montaigu
11,993.38	7,587	11,108.05	8,612.05	11,418.99	5,097.60	13,692.51
10,435.13	6,923.64	8,091.01	8,034.55	10,412.55	4,217.40	11,038.33
−1,558.25	−663.36	−3,017.04	−577.5	−1,006.44	−880.2	−2,654.18
−12.6	−8.74	−27.16	−5.87	−8.81	−17.26	−19.37

	Vendée			
	Luçon	*Chantonnay*	*Saint-Hilaire-des-Loges*	*Les Essarts*
Number of houses in 1792				
Number of houses destroyed				
Percent of houses destroyed/1792				
Value of houses destroyed				
Number of houses not rebuilt				
Value of houses not rebuilt				
Percent of destroyed houses not rebuilt				
Percent of 1792 houses not rebuilt				
Number of houses rebuilt				
Percent of destroyed houses rebuilt				
Percent of 1792 houses rebuilt				
Value of houses rebuilt				
Loss or gain in value				
Percent value of rebuilt houses compared with 1792 value				
Percent loss or gain				
Population in 1792	8,463.49	9,845.28	8,232.39	8,566.82
Population in 1802–1812	8,760.83	8,807.98	7,951.43	7,696.29
Increase or decrease in population	297.34	−1,037.30	−280.96	−870.53
Percent of increase or decrease compared to 1792	3.4	−10.53	−3.43	−10.15
Number of residents per house in 1792				
Number of residents per house in 1802–1812				

a Brain excluded, because only rental values are available.
b Brain and Bouguenais excluded.
c Vallet is missing.
d Two communes with rental values only.
e Two communes with no value.

	Vendée	
Mareuil-sur La-Dissais	Saint-Hilaire de-Talmont	Le Poiré-sur-Vie
6,689.09	9,435.02	8,457.65
6,500.33	8,716.75	7,069.46
−188.76	−718.27	−1,388.19
−2.77	−7.6	−16.46

For reasons of economy, the works and documents cited in this book have not been listed in a bibliography. The reader can find these sources by consulting the original document deposited at the University of Paris IV–Sorbonne and the references noted below. For the same reason, abbreviations have been used, the principal ones being the following:

AC   archives communales
ACP   archives communales et paroissiales
AM   archives municipales
AP   archives paroissiales
B   Barbechat
CBM   Chapelle-Basse-Mer
LB   Loroux Bottereau
St J.-C Saint-Julien-de-Concelles

AD   departmental archives
ML   Maine-et-Loire
        LA   Loire-Atlantique
        V   Vendée
        DS   Deux-Sèvres
        IV   Ille-et-Vilaine

AE   archives épiscopales
AHA   historical archives of the army deposited in the fort of Vincennes
AN   national archives
BM   bibliothèque municipale

RP   parish register
SV   journal *Revue du Souvenir Vendéen*

Authors quoted frequently are treated similarly; to find complete information, refer to the first citation.

Preface

1. Reynald Secher, *Anatomie d'un village vendéen: La Chapelle-Basse-Mer (essai sur les notions de légitimité et de légalité)*, doctoral thesis, *troisième cycle*, defended April 14, 1983, University of Paris IV–Sorbonne (jury: Professors Pierre Chaunu and André Corvisier; *rapporteur*: Professor Jean Meyer).
2. AHA, B⁵ 13.
3. Communal archives of La Chapelle-Basse-Mer. Abbé Robin: Introduction to parish register for the year 1796.
4. Reynald Secher, *Anatomie d'un village vendéen*, pp. 41–44, and more particularly my grandmother, Mme. Germaine Guillot.

Introduction

1. Jean Yole, *La Vendée* (Paris: J. de Gigord, 1936), pp. 17–18.
2. P. Doré-Graslin, *Itinéraire de la Vendée militaire, journal de la guerre des géants, 1793–1801* (Paris: Garnier, 1979), p. 7.

ONE. *Hope*

1. Secher, *Anatomie*, vol. 1, esp. pp. 206–34.
2. In La Chapelle-Bassemère, for example, there were 680 taxpayers in 1775 and 620 in 1789 for the poll tax, which had increased by 21 percent.
3. AD IV, C 2429. Two posts indicated the portion reserved for each parish.
4. APB.
5. AD IV, C 2429.
6. AD IV, C 2429.
7. General Doctor Carré, "Des milices de la monarchie à l'insurrection de 1793. Bretons et Vendéens et la défense du royaume," *Revue historique des Armées*, 1977: 4, pp. 35–66.
8. R. P. Pétard, *Histoire de Saint-Julien-de-Concelles* (Nantes: Bourgeois, 1898), pp. 123–30.

9. Ibid.

10. AD LA, C 566.

11. AD LA, C 566.

12. Pétard, *Histoire,* pp. 123–30.

13. Ibid.

14. AC CBM, RP, 1783.

15. AD IV, C 2429; AD LA, G 202; APB.

16. AD LA, C 785.

17. AD LA, C 567.

18. Archbishop of Paris, *Traité de l'administration temporelle des paroisses* (Paris, 1845), intro., pp. 9–15.

19. Pétard, *Histoire,* pp. 80–94.

20. APB.

21. All Catholic Europe was subject to the same procedure; for example, there is a chest of this kind in the parish church of Pinner in northwest London.

22. Pétard, *Histoire,* pp. 80–94.

23. APB.

24. AD IV, C 2429.

25. APB.

26. A kind of porch open to the weather, sheltering the principal entrance to the church. Two stone benches were used as seats for the members.

27. Michèle Elder Ugland, *Une fabrique paroissiale au XVIIe siècle et XVIIIe siècle en Basse-Bretagne, Ploubezre,* master's thesis, Rennes, 1968, p. 22. Excerpt from the register of the Parlement copied in the record of deliberations no. 1 after the session of April 29, 1696.

28. Pétard, *Histoire,* p. 84.

29. APB.

30. Pétard, *Histoire,* p. 8.

31. APB.

32. AD IV, C 2296.

33. AD IV, C 2296.

34. AD LA, G 52.

35. AD IV, C2429.

TWO. *The First Revolutionary Accomplishments*

1. AM CBM, RP 1783.

2. AD LA, L 367.

3. AD ML, L 349.

4. AD LA, L 283.

5. The conditions established by the law were in flagrant contradiction to articles 1 and 6 of the Declaration of the Rights of Man and Citizen.

6. Alexis de Tocqueville, *De la démocratie en Amerique* (Paris: Garnier-Flammarion, 1981), vol. 2, part 2, chap. 3, p. 129: "These societies . . . are daily replenished with men who, having just achieved independence, are intoxicated with their new power: they assume a presumptuous confidence in their strength and, not imagining that they might need to call on their fellows for help, have no hesitation in showing that they think only of themselves."

THREE. *The End of the Honeymoon*

1. Secher, *Anatomie,* pp. 255–58.
2. APB.
3. APB, excerpt from the registers of the directory of the department of Loire-Inférieure. The document is a copy certified as identical to the original, September 1, 1790.
4. AN D, IV 40971. The document is signed René Bourdin, mayor, and by L. Lelore, Thomas, Mathurin Boussard, P. Corraud, and Fillion.
5. AC St J.-C.
6. AC PLB.
7. AC Saint-Etienne-de-Corcoué.
8. AD V, IL 998, January 2, 1792.
9. AD ML, L 321.
10. AD LA, L 46, commune of Saint-Lumine-de-Coutais, July 24, 1791.
11. AD LA, L 46.
12. AD V, L 44.
13. AD V, L 44.
14. AD V, L 44.
15. AD V, L 47.
16. AD ML, IL 12 bis.
17. AD ML, IL 12 bis.
18. AD LA, L 34, department council, folio 14.
19. AD LA, L 25.

FOUR. *The Mistakes of the Central Government and the Excesses of the Administration*

1. Alfred Lallié, *Le diocèse de Nantes pendant la Révolution* (Nantes, 1893), p. 30.

2. Fernand Mourret, *Histoire générale de l'Eglise* (Paris, 1915), vol. 7, p. 104; quoted by Canon A. Jarnoux, *La Loire leur servit de linceul* (Quimper, 1972), pp. 46–50.

3. Remark of General Adrien Carré.

4. Bonaparte's secret as a Mediterranean was to have much better understood the bases of French psychology than the members of the Constituent Assembly. Remark of Carré.

5. Jarnoux, *La Loire*, pp. 51 ff.

6. Emile Gabory, *Les grandes heures de la Vendée* (Paris: Perrin, 1963), p. 46.

7. AD LA, L 38.

8. François Chamard, *Les origines et les responsabilités de l'insurrection vendéenne* (Paris, 1898), pp. 48 ff.

9. Jarnoux, *La Loire*, pp. 51 ff. The address was printed by Gigougeux, Haute-Grande-Rue, in Nantes.

10. AD ML, IL 1911. The bishop of Angers was criticized for his mildness by the department council.

11. AD LA, L 123.

12. AD LA, L 123.

13. AD LA, L 123.

14. AD LA, L 123.

15. AD LA, L 123. As soon as he received this letter, the procurator of the commune sent the following letter to the directory, dated November 23: "I inform you of the escape without warning of our curé Robin. I enclose herewith a copy of my indictment, drawn up at the municipal offices, and a copy of the letter from the said Robin, a letter full of deception and calumny and worthy of contempt."

16. AD LA, L 1130 and L 658.

17. AD LA, L 34.

18. Jarnoux, *La Loire*, pp. 51 ff. By All Saints' Day, the bishop had not returned to his diocese, after his departing in late April 1790.

19. "We declare that any clergyman who has purely and simply sworn the oath required by the law must retract it within 40 days on pain of being suspended."

20. Carré, "Vendée, chouannerie et sociologie moderne," *SV* 92 (September 1970), pp. 5–26.

21. AD LA, L 658.

22. AD DS, L 172.

23. Lallié, *La diocèse de Nantes*, p. 82.

24. These statistics were established on the basis of files reconstituted within the dioceses and the departmental archives of Loire-Atlantique, Maine-et-Loire, and Vendée.

25. AD LA, L 1587.

26. Jarnoux, *La Loire*, pp. 55–56.

27. AD LA, L 34.

28. AD ML, 7 L 70.

29. AD V, VL 495–96. Letter from Abbé de Beauregard on the report made to the National Assembly.

30. AD V, L 495–96.

31. AD V, L 495–96.

32. AD LA, L 42. Situation in Saint-Etienne-de-Mer-Morte, September 23, 1790. Letter from the department council.

33. AD V, L 495–96.

34. AD V, L 496. Instruction given by the bishop of Luçon, March 29, 1791.

35. AD ML, IL 355.

36. AD ML, IL 357.

37. AD LA, L 112.

38. AD ML, IL 350.

39. AD ML, IL 356.

40. AD ML, IL 355.

41. AD LA, L 36, July 18–October 11, 1792.

42. AD LA, L 38, November 6–December 1, 1792.

43. AD ML, IL 357 bis.

44. AD ML, IL 357 bis. This was true in Saint-Georges.

45. AD LA, L 663.

46. Chamard, *Les origines*, pp. 180–83.

47. Verger, *Archives curieuses de Nantes et des departments de l'Ouest* (Nantes, 1837–41), pp. 159–60. In a long indictment, the department declared: "In the places in which another clergyman faithful to the law is called on to fill their offices [the refractories], even though they might show no open act of resistance or even of disapproval of their successor, their very presence and their silence would nevertheless have a nefarious influence. Their partisans would even dare to find, in their patience and their resignation, true or assumed, yet one more reason to favor their conduct and diminish the confidence due to the true ministers of the law."

48. Ludovic Sciout, *Histoire de la Constitution civile du clergé*, vol. 2; quoted by Lallié, *La diocèse de Nantes*, pp. 90–94.

49. Chamard, *Les origines*, pp. 183 ff.

50. AD LA, L 689.

51. On February 8, 1792, the department made obligatory the daily roll call of the priests held in forced residence in Nantes. They could thus be prevented from returning to their parishes.

52. AD LA, L 689.

53. AD ML, IL 745.

54. AD LA, L 663.

55. Jarnoux, *La Loire,* pp. 59–60.
56. AD LA, vol. 7, F 72.

FIVE. *The Role of the Refractory Clergy in the Resistance*

1. AD V, IL 998; AD ML, IL 357. The report notes that "things are going well."
2. AP Saint-Hilaire-de Mortagne, Abbé Fort, RP, 1830.
3. AC CBM, RP, 1792.
4. AD ML, L 357. Letter from Boussineau to de Daune.
5. AD V, L 46, September 28, 1792.
6. AD LA, L 35.
7. AD V, L 501, record of installation of the curé of Benêt, July 24, 1791.
8. AC CBM, RP, 1796.
9. AC CBM, RP, 1792.
10. AD V, IL 998, March 18, 1792.
11. René d'Anjou, "Le curé intrus de Saint-Lambert-du-Lattay," *SV* 119 (June 1977), p. 77.
12. AD ML, IL 357 bis and IL 364.
13. AD LA, L 404.
14. AC CBM, RP, 1796; AD ML, IL 364.
15. Pétard, *Histoire,* p. 217.
16. AD LA, L 720.
17. AD LA, L 692.
18. AD LA, L 47.
19. Pétard, *Histoire,* p. 218.
20. L.-P. Prunier, *Le martyre de la Vendée* (Fontenay-le Comte, 1902), p. 19.
21. R. P. Briand, *Les confesseurs de la foi au diocèse de Nantes* (Paris, 1903), vol. 2, pp. 679–81; AD ML, IL 364.
22. Prunier, *Le martyre,* p. 411.
23. AM CBM, RP, 1784.
24. AD LA, L 223.
25. These statistics were established on the basis of reconstituted files in the dioceses and the departmental archives of Loire-Atlantique, Maine-et-Loire, and Vendée.
26. AN, D XL 12; AD ML, IL 12 bis, August 30, 1792.
27. AD LA, L 123.
28. AN, F 19607 and D XIX 5, letter D.
29. Chamard, *Les origines,* pp. 210 ff. Historians have infrequently dealt with this subject, which seems to me to be essential.

30. AD LA, L 899.

31. Secher, *Anatomie*, p. 283.

32. AD LA, L 669. Letter from Abbot Derennes addressed to Abbé Robin, curé of La Chapelle-Bassemère, 1795; AD LA, L 733. Letter addressed to Abbé Jambu; AD V, L 497. Copy of a letter from the curé of Barbâtre to his parishioners, June 23, 1797, sent from Bilterbech in Westphalia.

33. AC CBM, RP, 1792–1801, etc.

34. AD LA, L 46.

35. AD LA, L 658.

36. AD ML, IL 350. We may mention La Chapelle-du-Genêt, May 18, 1792, and Beaupréau, May 5, 1792, among others.

37. AD ML, IL 350.

38. Charles Tilly, *The Vendée* (1964; reprint, Cambridge: Harvard University Press, 1976), and Paul Bois, *Paysans de l'Ouest* (1960; reprint, Paris: Flammarion, 1971), have developed these themes.

39. AD LA, L 740.

40. AD ML, IL 353, August 8, 1791.

41. AM CBM, RP, 1796.

42. AD LA, L 740.

43. Tradition preserved by Mme. Germaine Guillot, and confirmed by M. Lucien Jarry, present owner of the castle.

44. Peigné, *Histoire du Loroux Bottereau*, manuscript, AC Loroux Bottereau. Cited in future as *Histoire LB*.

45. AD ML, IL 745.

46. Prunier, *Le martyre*, pp. 37–38.

47. Claude Petitfrère, *Blancs et Bleus d'Anjou, 1789–1793* (Paris, 1979), suggests magical practices and the like, which is clearly inadequate.

SIX.   *The March Toward War*

1. AD ML, IL 350, October 6, 1791.

2. AD V, L 998.

3. AD ML, IL 12 ter.

4. AD ML, IL 350, October 1791.

5. AD LA, L 279.

6. AD LA, L 382.

7. AD LA, L 578.

8. AD ML, IL 350.

9. AD LA, L 48.

10. AD V, L 998.
11. AD ML, IL 351.
12. AD ML, IL 357.
13. AD ML, IL 366 and 387.
14. AD V, L 998.
15. AD LA, L 185.
16. AD ML, IL 357.
17. AD LA, L 401.
18. AD LA, L 188 and 477.
19. AD ML, IL 351 and 353. Report by Boissard, lieutenant of the national gendarmerie.
20. AD ML, IL 350 and 353.
21. AD LA, L 613.
22. AD ML, IL 350.
23. AD ML, IL 351.
24. AD ML, L 46, October 30, 1791.
25. AD ML, L 37, October 15, 1792.
26. AD ML, IL 357.
27. AD ML, IL 366.
28. AD LA, L 454.
29. AD ML, IL 366.
30. AD ML, IL 357 and 366.
31. AD LA, L 114.
32. AD LA, L 37, 49, and 348.
33. AD V, L 382.
34. AD LA, L 49, August 1792.
35. AD LA, L 48.
36. AD ML, IL 190.
37. AD ML, IL 368.
38. AD LA, L 1004.
39. AD V, L 45.
40. AD ML, IL 368.
41. AD ML, IL 368.
42. AD V, L 656.
43. AD ML, IL 353 bis.
44. AD ML, IL 12 bis.
45. AD ML, IL 12.
46. AD ML, IL 745. Remark of the mayor of Bouillé referring to his municipal officers "who violate the law or interpret it in a way to satisfy their passions."
47. AD V, L 45, June 26, 1791.

48. AD V, L 45.

49. AD LA, L 1130. Correspondence from the directory of Nantes sent to the municipal officers of Port-Saint-Père.

50. AD LA, L 46.

51. AD V, L 656.

52. AD ML, IL 351.

53. AD ML, IL 351. Example: May 3, 1792, denunciation of Desneux, surgeon and mayor of Chevigné.

54. AD ML, IL 357 ter. Denunciation of a member of the directory on September 15, 1791, for anticonstitutional statements and for having attempted to incite the population of the Cholet district to revolt and for having refused to bring his child to church for baptism.

55. AD LA, L 183.

56. AD V, L 45.

57. AD ML, IL 745.

58. AD ML, IL 745; AD V, L 45. The same thing in Pouancé and Bouillé; AD ML, IL 12 ter.

59. AD V, L 45.

60. AD V, L 998.

61. AD V, L 656.

62. AD V, L 45. "It [the national guard] shot for no reason," complained the directory of Challans.

63. AD ML, IL 357.

64. AD LA, L 1172.

65. AD ML, IL 366 and 745.

66. AD ML, IL 367; AD LA, L 1090 folio 60.

67. AD ML, IL 745.

68. AD LA, L 408.

69. AD LA, L 594.

70. AD LA, L 39.

71. Peigné, *Histoire LB.*

72. AD LA, L 39.

73. AD DS, L 8.

74. Peigné, *Histoire LB.*

75. Secher, *Anatomie*, vol. 2, pp. 200–300.

76. AD V, L 495 and 496. Commentary of Abbé de Beauregard on the report made to the National Assembly.

77. AD V, L 393.

78. This argument was advanced, among others, by Cavoleau, *Description du département de Vendée* (Paris, 1818); Petitfrère, *Blancs et Bleus;* Jean Meyer, *Histoire de Bretagne* (Paris: Flammarion, 1972), p. 134.

79. AD ML, IL 353. Deliberation of the municipal council of Clisson of April 3, 1792:

The nonjuring priests spread through the department of Loire-Inférieure have been presented to this administration as audacious men who, through their suggestions and their fanaticism are the cause of the disturbances troubling the department. It is said that they delay establishment of the tax rolls and the collection of taxes, that they pretend to misunderstand the voice of the established authorities, and that their disobedience is supported by the nobility and the connivance of a few subordinate administrations.

On the basis of these denunciations, produced by calumny and the spirit of intolerance and persecution, an administration driven by its zeal for the preservation of order and the execution of the law has been brought to act ruthlessly against six or seven hundred priests by a decree that would not be rigorous enough if they were guilty and that is extremely unjust if it strikes men who are innocent . . .

SEVEN. *The War Begins*

1. AN, F⁷ 3681 6. It seems, however, that the department was aware of the problem. In an excerpt from the registers of the directory dated June 12, 1792, we read: "There exists in the district of Guérande, of Clisson, etc., a hidden ferment. Public rumor declares that people are wearing the white cockade in the parishes of Saint-Joachim, Pont-Château, and Cressal; that there is recruiting for the émigrés, that cartridges are being made . . ."

2. AD V, L 382.

3. AHA, B⁵ 13. Report by Pierre Levieux, assistant to the adjutants-general.

4. AD LA, L 35, December 1791, folio 20.

5. AD LA, L 578.

6. AD ML, IL 350, May 18, 1792.

7. Léon Maître, "Le pillage des bureaux d'enregistrement en 1793 dans la Loire-Inférieure," *Les Annales de Bretagne*, 1913, pp. 17–37.

8. AD LA, L 137 and 668.

9. AD DS, L 137, October 29, 1789.

10. Maître, "Le pillage," report of citizen Monlien, tax collector in Le Loroux.

11. AD ML, IL 551 and 814.

12. Pétard, *Histoire*, pp. 220–23.

13. J. Senot de La Londe, "Les débuts de l'insurrection vendéenne sur la rive droite de la Loire, entre Ancenis et Nantes," *Bulletin de la Société archéologique de Nantes*, 1902, pp. 54–66.

14. AD LA, L 689. Declaration of the curé Caperon, dated August 31, 1793.

15. Pétard, *Histoire*, p. 223.

16. L. Guilbault, "Notes sur La Varenne," a manuscript completed on July 23, 1888, with the help of popular memory. In the possession of M. Chaisné, an inhabitant of La Varenne.

17. AD LA, L 760. Petitfrère, *Blancs et Bleus*, vol. 1, p. 204.

18. Guilbault, "Notes sur La Varenne."

19. Paul Mercier, *Un héros vendéen, Piron de La Varenne, le général au cheval blanc* (Nantes, 1938), p. 16; AD ML, IL 190.

20. Maître, "Le pillage."

21. AD LA, L 350.

22. La Londe, "Les débuts de l'insurrection."

23. AD ML, IL 551.

24. AD LA, L 349.

25. AHA, B^5 13, March 12, 1793; AD LA, L 278.

26. AD DS, L 8.

27. AD ML, IL 805 bis.

28. AD LA, L 40.

29. AD LA, L 349.

30. AD LA, L 183; Philippe Bossis, "Les réfugiés vendéens à Nantes lors du soulèvement de mars 1793," *Echange*, special issue 2 (2d quarter, 1980), pp. 7–12.

31. AD LA, L 350.

32. AD LA, L 350.

33. AHA, B^5 8.

34. AD LA, L 516 and 578; AD V, L 584.

35. Secher, *Anatomie*, pp. 305–6.

36. AD LA, L 237. It is difficult to provide exact figures for the number of deserters. In 1795, of the 1,100,000 men recruited in the "mass levy," there were 546,00 absent, deserters, or "rebels" for all of France.

37. AD LA, L 237. According to Carré, purchases of replacements were much more frequent in the West than in the South.

38. Some documents tried to explain that conscription was different from the militia: "No, citizens, there is no question of the militia; there will only be, as there were last year, registers open for the inscription of men who, eager for glory and devoted to the liberty of their country, wish to defend the nation, and in the unlikely case that not enough come forward, the assembled communes themselves will determine the most fitting means to make up the number of defenders that the nation asks of them. And who could refuse to take arms to preserve his property and his liberty!" AD LA, L 237.

39. Pétard, *Histoire*, pp. 167–70.

40. AD ML, IL 190.

41. Carré, "Vendée, chouannerie," pp. 4–24.

42. AC CBM, RP, 1794.

43. AC CBM, RP, 1796.

44. La Londe, "Les débuts de l'insurrection."

45. Peigné, *Histoire LB.*

46. Georges Bordonove, *La vie quotidienne en Vendée pendant la Révolution* (Paris: Hachette, 1974), pp. 172–73; AD LA, L 994: "Citizen Ferrand, commander of the Twenty-fourth Battalion, explained that it was particularly necessary to burn the mills."

47. AD LA, L 278; AD ML, L 1926. There were complaints about these tactics: "Trees are cut down to block the roads, bridges destroyed to intercept all communications, axles removed to starve troops and large towns . . ."

48. Jean Yole, *La Vendée,* pp. 17–18.

49. AC CBM, RP, 1796.

50. Emile Gabory, *Les Vendéennes* (Paris: Perrin, 1934), p. 56.

51. AD ML, IL 838, form concerning Chalonnes, and IL 834; AHA, B⁵ 6.

52. General Turreau, *Mémoire pour servir à l'histoire de la guerre de Vendée,* quoted by Bordonove, *La vie quotidienne,* pp. 166–72.

53. Secher, *Anatomie,* vol. 2, p. 314.

54. AD LA, L 278.

55. AD LA, L 126.

56. During the land consolidation around Vallet in about 1970, it was not uncommon to find in the hedges and bushes torn up by bulldozers a whole arsenal of tools and weapons eaten by rust which had been hidden by the Vendeans.

57. AD DS, L 137.

58. Dominique Jaudonnet de Laugrenière file, Dugast-Matifeux collection, vol. 7, 186; Carré, "Un document inédit: Le rapport de Jaudonnet de Laugrenière," *SV* 96 (September 1971), pp. 1–26.

59. AD ML, IL 834. Beaufort report; AHA, B⁵ 7. Report from Noméro, dated October 12, 1793, and B⁵ 16.

60. AHA, B⁵. Biron report, and B⁵ 9, called "Chouan papers." F.-L. Patu-Deshautschamps, *Dix années de guerre intestine* (Paris, 1840), pp. 49–63.

61. Jacques de Maupéou, "La cavalerie vendéenne," *SV* 57 (Christmas 1961), pp. 15–16.

62. AHA, B⁵ 14.

63. AHA, B⁵ 5.

64. AD ML, IL 834 and 839. There were other variants: "In the holy name of God and by order of the king———parish is asked to send as many men as possible to———at———. They will bring food for———days."

65. AD DS, L 186.

66. AD ML, IL 834 and 839.

67. Patu-Deshautschamps, *Dix années*, pp. 49–63.
68. AD ML, IL 834. Beaufort report.
69. AD ML, IL 834. Beaufort report.
70. Turreau, *Mémoire*, quoted in Bordonove, *La vie quotidienne*, p. 166.
71. Peigné, *Histoire LB.*
72. Kléber, *Mémoire sur la guerre de Vendée*, quoted by Bordonove, *La vie quotidienne*, p. 17.
73. J. Crétineau-Joly, *Histoire de la Vendée militaire* (Paris, 1896–97), vol. 1, p. 90.
74. Peigné, *Histoire LB.*
75. All these themes have been set forth by Carré, "L'Ouest catholique du XVIe siècle à l'insurrection de 1793," *SV* 122 (March–April 1978), pp. 19–41.

EIGHT.   *The Confrontation Between Legitimacy and Legality in the Same Territory*

1. AHA, B⁵ B, no. 3, document dated April 11, 1793, intended for the minister of war, Bourdonnaye.
2. AD LA, 2 R 124.
3. AHA, B⁵ 7; Chassin, *La Vendée patriote* (Paris, 1894), vol. 1, p. 79.
4. AD DS, L 8.
5. AD LA, L 91.
6. AD DS, L 34.
7. AD LA, L 87, March 13–26, 1793.
8. AD LA, L 99.
9. AD DS, L 8.
10. AD LA, L 88, and AD DS, L 8.
11. AD LA, L 88, and AD V, L 1279.
12. AD DS, L 8.
13. La Londe, "Les débuts de l'insurrection."
14. Ibid.
15. Peigné, *Histoire LB.*
16. AD DS, L 8–10, and AD V, L 302.
17. AD LA, L 41.
18. AD LA, L 41 and AHA, B⁵ 5.
19. AD LA, L 89 and AD ML, IL 12 bis.
20. AHA, B⁵ 13, April 23, 1793.
21. AD LA, L 236.
22. AHA, B⁵ 6. Letter of June 22, 1793.
23. AD LA, L 40.
24. AD LA, L 1131.

25. AD DS, L 8.
26. AD DS, L 67.
27. AD DS, L 69, September 27, 1793.
28. AHA, B⁵ 5. There was even a decree to punish deserters; AD DS, L 393.
29. AHA, B⁵ 5, June 18, 1793.
30. AD LA, L 1165.
31. AD DS, L 67 and 131.
32. AHA, B⁵ 5. Condition of the army: letter from Goupilleau, representative of the people to the army of the coast of La Rochelle, to his colleagues on the Committee of Public Safety, June 18, 1793.
33. AD ML, IL 12 bis.
34. AD ML, IL 12 bis.
35. AD LA, L 41.
36. AD LA, L 115 folio 166.
37. AD V, L 380.
38. AD ML, IL 12 bis.
39. AD DS, L 13.
40. AD V, L 393.
41. AD DS, L 8, May 7, 1793.
42. AHA, B⁵ 5.
43. AHA, B⁵ 143.
44. AHA, B⁵ 8.
45. AD LA, L 52 folio 195.
46. AC CBM, RP, 1796.
47. In fact, the crossing of the Loire took place on a very wide front. It had been prepared well before the battle of Cholet, "too well perhaps," notes Carré, "for it removed from the Vendeans the courage of despair. There were already Vendean troops on the right bank. The artillery that had crossed the river was already assembled at Liré. The mass of 'civilians' that accompanied the army had in fact already gathered in the region of Beaupréau. All this explains the speed with which the Vendean army was reconstituted on the right bank and the crushing victory over the Republican armies at Entrammes ten days after Cholet; it was the heaviest defeat of the Republican armies of the entire war. If the Vendeans had then returned to the other bank, the course of events might have changed. But the 'democratic' army, despite the desires of the leaders, wanted to continue toward the English Channel."
48. Archives of Joseph Berel, rector of Beauge, communicated by Father Georges Allain, superior of the community of Lazarist fathers of Rennes.
49. Archives and information communicated by M. Michel Houdusse, from Gahard.

50. AHA, B^5 16, third and fourth days of the second month of the year II.

51. Daniel Bonnin, "Les Vendéens au Mans en 1793," *SV* III (June–July 1975), pp. 11–15.

52. AD ML, IL 12 bis, decree of the general council of the department, March 23, 1795; AHA, B^5 8, 9. Two thousand people were thus enlisted in Orléans.

53. AHA, B^5 16 and 5; AD DS, L 37; AD ML, IL 12 bis.

54. AHA, B^5 13.

55. Elie Fournier, *La terreur bleue* (Paris: Albin Michel, 1984), p. 213.

56. Quoted by Prunier, *Le martyre*, pp. 76–77.

57. AHA, B^5 16.

58. AHA, B^5 16, December 16, 1793. Letter from Marceau, acting commander-in-chief of the army of the West, to the minister of war.

59. AHA, B^5 7.

60. Daniel Bonnin, "Les Vendéens au Mans en 1793," *SV* (March 1974), pp. 11–21.

61. AC CBM, RP, 1796.

62. G. du Plessis, "Les bateaux armés de la Loire et de l'Erdre pendant les guerres de Vendée," *Bulletin SAH de Nantes* 70 (1930), pp. 234–35.

63. AHA, B^5 16. *Le Moniteur*, December 28, 1793.

64. AC CBM, RP, 1796.

65. AHA, B5 16.

66. AD LA, L 2018.

67. AD DS, L 173.

68. AC CBM, RP, 1796.

69. Crétineau-Joly, *Histoire*, vol. 2, p. 57; *Le Moniteur*, December 28, 1793.

70. AD DS, L 173.

71. Expression of Carrier. AD LA, L 1493.

72. Lallié, *La justice révolutionnaire à Nantes.*

73. Dr. Charles Coubard, *Ceux qui ont été emmenés de force* (Cholet: Farré & Freulon, 1940), p. 27.

74. Henri Bourgeois, "Les noyades de Nantes," *SV* 119 (June 1977), pp. 26–28; *Le Moniteur*, January 2, 1794; Lallié, *La justice;* Lallié, *Les noyades de Nantes* (Nantes, 1898); Gabory, *Les grandes heures*, pp. 157–62; *Le Moniteur*, 10 frimaire year II, letter from Carrier of 17 brumaire; *Le Moniteur*, 26 frimaire, letter of 25 frimaire.

75. AC CBM, RP, 1793–96; AD LA, L 1005.

76. AD V, L 312.

77. AD LA, L 1005.

78. AD LA, L 1000.

79. AD LA, L 3 and 1005; AD ML, IL 810; AD V, L 382, 392, 394, and 656.

80. Crétineau-Joly, *Histoire*, vol. 2, pp. 37–102.

81. AC CBM, RP, 1796.

82. AD V, L 656.

83. AD ML, L 799. Proclamation of 12 frimaire year II.

84. AN, F¹⁰ 267.

85. Simone Loidreau, "Les colonnes infernales," *SV* 131 (June–July 1980), pp. 7–23; 132 (October 1980), pp. 7–45; 133 (December 1980–January 1981), pp. 15–30. These are remarkable articles that have provided the basis for this chapter.

86. Crétineau-Joly, *Histoire,* vol. 2, pp. 49 and 139. Letter from Francastel to the Committee of Public Safety.

87. AD DS, L 45.

88. Chassin, *La Vendée patriote,* vol. 3, p. 170. Complete text in *Le Moniteur,* October 7, 1795.

89. AHA, B⁵ 9.

90. AD ML, IL 380.

91. Loidreau, "Les colonnes infernales."

92. AD ML, IL 802; Carré, "Le général Turreau et les Bourbons," *SV* 130 (March–April 1980), pp. 9–35.

93. AHA, B⁵ 8; AN, A F II, 269, 2262, folio 25.

94. AN, A F II, 280, 2337, folio 33.

95. AHA, B⁵ 8.

96. AN, A F, II 280, 2337, folio 34.

97. Crétineau-Joly, *Histoire,* vol. 2, pp. 135–39.

98. Graslin-Doré, *Itinéraire,* pp. 105–6.

99. R. de Thivercay, "Les colonnes infernales en Vendée," *Revue du Bas-Poitou* (1896), pp. 424–32; Loidreau, "Les colonnes infernales"; AHA, B⁵ 8 and 9.

100. AHA, B⁵ 8.

101. AHA, B⁵ 8.

102. AD LA, L 1178.

103. Loidreau, "Les colonnes infernales."

104. R. de Thivercay, "Les colonnes infernales," pp. 424–32.

105. AHA, B⁵ 9, 23 messidor year II.

106. AHA, B⁵ 9, July 13, 1794. Instruction on defense, police, and composition of the camps.

107. Loidreau, "Les colonnes infernales."

108. This natural defense was seen as a kind of Maginot Line before the fact; it had the same disastrous consequences.

109. AHA, B⁵ 8. Letter of March 2, 1794, to the minister.

110. Peigné, *Histoire LB.*

111. AHA, B⁵ 9.

112. AC CBM, RP, 1796.

113. It has been possible to reconstruct the itinerary of the Republican troops over the territory of La Chapelle-Bassemère through the registers composed by Abbé Robin.

114. Many bone fragments can still be found there, because the dead were buried where they fell.

115. Peigné, *Histoire LB*, supplemented by the registers of Abbé Robin.

116. Tradition communicated by M. Lucien Jarry, present owner of the castle. The two daughters were shot a few days later. Legend has it that grass always has its springtime freshness on their graves. The father was condemned to the prison ships. Thanks to the tax collector of Le Loroux, whom she married, the youngest daughter was released by Carrier.

117. AC CBM, RP, 1796.

118. Interview with Mme. Irène Placier, née Tellier, resident of La Chapelle-Bassemère.

119. AD LA, L 889. Wound received at Granville.

120. Pétard, *Histoire*, pp. 242–43.

121. Comte Paul de Berthou, *Clisson et ses monuments* (Nantes: Imprimerie de la Loire, 1910), p. 391.

122. Abbé Joseph Le Clainche, "La noyade de la baie de Bourgneuf," *SV* 86 (March 1969), pp. 4–14.

123. AD ML, IL 1127/3.

124. Godart Faultrier, *Histoire du Champ des martyrs* (Angers, 1852). Incredulous, the author went to the site on May 31, 1852, to question personally the shepherd Robin. General Moulin was dressed in one of these skins, explaining his suicide.

125. Comtesse de La Bouère, *Mémoires* (Paris, 1890); G. Gautherot, *L'épopée vendéenne* (Paris, 1837), p. 427.

126. *Rapport à la Commission des Moyens extraordinaires*, IA, August 1793.

127. Comtesse de La Bouère, *Mémoires*, pp. 307–29.

128. Archives of the town of Angers; also quoted by Gautherot, *L'épopée*, p. 246, and by Raoul Mercier, *Le monde médical dans la guerre de Vendée* (Tours: Arrault, 1939).

129. AM Nantes, account 21, year II. A. Vélasque, "Les prisons de Nantes sous la Terreur (la prison de l'entrepôt des cafés)," *Revue du Bas-Poitou* (1913), pp. 51–54.

130. AHA, B⁵ 7.

131. Coubard, *Ceux qui ont été emmenés*, pp. 10–11.

132. AHA, B⁵ 5. Letter from Turreau of April 12, 1794. He concluded that the troops had to be changed "and that can be done without delaying military operations." Loidreau, "Les colonnes infernales"; AD V, L 380 and 914; AD ML, IL 812.

133. AHA, B⁵ 18. Letter of October 20, 1793, sent from Port-Brieux (Saint-Brieux) to Bernier.

134. AD LA, L 123. Letter sent to Doctor Martineau.

135. Loidreau, "Les colonnes infernales."

136. AD ML, L 812.

137. AHA, B⁵ 8. Letter of March 6, 1796.
138. AHA, B⁵ 9. Letter from Turreau, May 9, 1796. "We ought to accuse the moderation of some generals, the negligence of some, and the ignorance of others." AD V, L 907. Letter from Huchet.
139. AN, F¹⁰ 267. Letter from Guillemot.
140. AHA, B⁵ 7. Document dated December 25, 1793.
141. AHA, B⁵ 8, dated April 1, 1794.
142. AC CBM, RP, 1796.
143. G. du Plessis, *Les bateaux armés*, pp. 205–47.
144. Mantellier, "Histoire de la communauté des marchands fréquentant la Loire," *Mémoire de la Société archéologique de l'Orléanais*, vol. 7, p. 24.
145. AD LA, L 50.
146. AD LA, L 574.
147. The modifications were carried out in private workshops under the supervision of the competent authorities. They were almost all in the Chézine quarter of Nantes.
148. AD LA, L 575.
149. AD LA, L 574.
150. AD LA, L 574.
151. AC CBM, RP, 1794.
152. AC CBM, RP, 1794.
153. AC CBM, RP, 1796.
154. The disarmament of almost all the armed boats was decided on only in messidor, year IV (June 1794).
155. Crétineau-Joly, *Histoire*, vol. 2, p. 73.
156. AD LA, L 422.
157. AD LA, L 50.
158. AD LA, L 939. Trochu.
159. AHA, B⁵ 9; AN F¹⁰ 26.
160. AD LA, L 554.
161. AD LA, L 556.
162. AN, F¹⁰ 267; AHA, B⁵ 89. Further, in an order of July 27, 1793, General Kléber granted a reward of ten livres for each military or hunting rifle found "hidden in barns or attics, or in hedges and undergrowth; it is up to the citizen who finds them to declare them and account for them to the officer commanding the detachment."
163. AHA, B⁵ 80 and 8; AD LA, L 33; letter from Bluttel, 8 pluviôse, year II; AD ML, IL 802, 4 pluviôse, year II.
164. AHA, B⁵ 9.
165. AD LA, L 916, 18 brumaire, year III.
166. AHA, B⁵ 9.

NINE.   *Political Incoherence*

1. BM Nantes, Dugast-Matifeux collection, vol. 9, letter 73.
2. See AD LA, L 33 and 287.
3. AN, F^{10} 267.
4. AN AF II 269, 2267 folio 80, C 342 CII 1639, 1642; AHA, B^5 9. Letter from Vineux, June 26, 1794.
5. Crétineau-Joly, *Histoire*, vol. 2, pp. 300–310.
6. AD V, L 809; René de Dreuzy, "En 1794 la préparation des traités de pacification de la Vendée par les représentants du peuple," *SV* (June–July 1975), pp. 7–10.
7. AD ML, IL 809.
8. AD ML, IL 809.
9. Peigné, *Histoire LB.*
10. Crétineau-Joly, *Histoire*, vol. 2, pp. 370 ff.
11. AD ML, IL 812, 26 messidor, year III.
12. Abbé Blanchet, *Le district de Paimbœuf pendant la Révolution*, vol. 4, p. 166.
13. Doré-Graslin, *Itinéraire*, pp. 162–63.
14. Théodore de Quatrebarbes, *Une paroisse vendéenne pendant la terreur*, pp. 121–30.
15. AD ML, IL 995.
16. Blanchet, *Le district de Paimbœuf*, vol. 3, pp. 150 ff.
17. Crétineau-Joly, *Histoire*, vol. 2, pp. 389–90.
18. Blanchet, *Le district de Paimbœuf*, vol. 4, p. 166.
19. Crétineau-Joly, *Histoire*, pp. 411 ff.
20. This habit of announcing important events lasted until the Second World War.
21. Crétineau-Joly, *Histoire*, pp. 531–32.
22. AD LA, L 281.
23. AD LA, L 805.
24. AD LA, ML, DS, and V, series Q.
25. AD DS, L 73.
26. AD LA, L 39.
27. Peigné, *Histoire LB.*
28. AD DS, L 70.
29. AD LA, L 352, and AD DS, L 40.
30. AD DS, L 174.
31. AD DS, L 9.
32. AD LA, L 322.
33. AD LA, L 353 and 322.
34. AD DS, L 40.

35. AD LA, L 59. Central administration: 30 vendémiaire, year VI to 6 floréal, year IV.

36. AD LA, L 75.

37. AD LA, L 525. Imprimerie A.-J. Malassier, place du Pilori, 20 nivôse, year IV.

38. AD DS, L 47.

39. AD DS, L 47.

40. AD DS, L 47; AD V, L 394.

41. AD DS, L 47.

42. AD LA, L 341.

43. AD LA, L 345.

44. Blanchet, *Le district de Paimbœuf*, vol. 5, p. 206.

45. AD DS, L 13.

46. AD LA, L 488 and 60.

47. AD DS, L 13.

48. Blanchet, *Le district de Paimbœuf*, vol. 4, p. 191.

49. AD DS, L 72.

50. Blanchet, *Le district de Paimbœuf*, vol. 4, p. 189.

51. AD LA, L 524; AHA, B⁵ 8.

52. AD DS, L 68, 15 vendémiaire, year IV.

53. AD DS, L 129; AD ML, IL 2132.

54. AD LA, L 156 and 430; AD ML, IL 2132.

55. AD LA, 3160.

56. AD LA, L 313.

57. Blanchet, *Le district de Paimbœuf*, p. 113.

58. AD LA, L 133. Remark concerning the canton of Bouaye.

TEN.   *The Living Conditions of the Vendeans*

1. AD DS, L 61; AD ML, IL 801, 811, and 867; AHA, B5 4, etc.

2. Prefect Dupin, *Annuaire statistique de l'an XII*, pp. 249–50.

3. AHA, B⁵ 4. Letter from Bournou to the minister, March 12, 1793.

4. AHA, B⁵ 13. Letter from Minister Monge to Bouchotte, April 22, 1793.

5. Dupin, *Annuaire statistique de l'an XII*, pp. 259 ff.

6. AD DS, L 45; Carré, "La guerre des vivres en Vendée militaire, 1793–1795," *Presse-Océan*, March 24, 1971.

7. Peigné, *Histoire LB;* AD ML, IL 802.

8. AD LA, L 378.

9. AN, F¹⁰ 267.

10. AD V, L 907 and 908.

11. AD V, L 867. In Montaigu, there was not a single seed for sowing; Peigné, *Histoire LB;* AD LA, L 1298 folio 7.

12. AD DS, L 107.

13. Peigné, *Histoire LB.*

14. AD LA, L 485 and 1298; AD V, L 867.

15. AD DS, L 61.

16. AD LA, L 461.

17. AD LA, L 368.

18. AD LA, L 378.

19. AD ML, IL 12 bis.

20. Peigné, *Histoire LB.*

21. AD LA, L 312.

22. AD ML, IL 808.

23. AD LA, L 303; AD V, L 385.

24. AD DS, L 9.

25. AD DS, L 15.

26. AD LA, L 1168.

27. AD LA, L 306.

28. AN, F[10] 268.

29. AN, F[7] 3861[6].

30. AN, F[7] 3861[6]; AD V, L 380 and 392.

31. AD LA, L 370.

32. AD V, L 656.

33. Dupin, *ASDS an XII,* p. 512.

34. AD LA, L 309.

35. AD DS, L 72.

36. AD DS, L 38.

37. Excerpt from the *Journal des décrets pour les campagnes,* session of 8 vendémiaire, year III (September 29, 1794).

38. AD LA, L 360; AN, F[10] 267, 30 prairial, year II.

39. AD LA, L 360.

40. AD ML, IL 802; AD V, L 907.

41. AD V, L 907.

42. It was unquestionably a stimulant.

43. AN, F[10] 267.

44. AD LA, L 363 and 364.

45. AN, F[10] 267, 29 floréal, year IV. In this letter, Cavoleau observes that the farmers in the region "are rather enlightened about their interests and much less tied to routine than is commonly thought."

46. AN, F[10] 268.

47. AD ML, IL 802.

48. La Touche d'Avrigny, "Trois documents sur la pacification de la Vendée," *SV* (February 1950), pp. 1–8.

ELEVEN. *Local Authorities Confront Their Consciences*

1. Blanchet, *Le district de Paimbœuf,* vol. 4, p. 183.
2. AD LA, L 1168.
3. AD DS, L 154.
4. AD LA, L 55 folio 36.
5. Blanchet, *Le district de Paimbœuf,* vol. 4, pp. 184–85.
6. AD DS, L 9.
7. Blanchet, *Le district de Paimbœuf,* vol. 4, pp. 183–85.
8. AD LA, L 126.
9. AD LA, L 213.
10. Peigné, *Histoire LB;* AD LA, L 349.
11. AC CBM, RP, 1796, no. 740; AD LA, L 349.
12. AD DS, L 68; AD ML, IL 845 bis, etc.
13. AD LA, L 410.
14. Blanchet, *Le district de Paimbœuf,* vol. 4, p. 168.
15. AD LA, L 202.
16. AD ML, IL 992.
17. AD LA, L 124.
18. Secher, *Anatomie,* p. 369.
19. AD LA, L 1197.
20. AD V, L 217.
21. AD DS, L 147; AD ML, IL 192.
22. AN, F^7 3681^7.
23. AD ML, L 124, 6 floréal, year IV.
24. AD DS, L 120; AD LA, L 129.
25. AD DS, L 164.
26. AD LA, L 525.
27. AD DS, L 9.
28. AD DS, L 120.
29. AD ML, IL 808.
30. AD LA, L 525.
31. AD LA, L 1226. Instruction sent on 12 frimaire, year IV.
32. Baron de La Touche d'Avrigny, "Les conséquences de la loi sur les otages," *SV* (November 1950).
33. Article 26 of the law of 9 frimaire, year VI.

34. AD LA, L 127.

35. AD DS, L 68.

36. AD LA, L 587 (year IV).

37. AD DS, L 32, 11 brumaire, year II.

38. AD ML, IL 353.

39. AD DS, L 104.

40. AD LA, L 587.

41. AD LA, L 1121.

42. AD LA, L 1148 folio 95.

43. AD LA, L 1174.

44. AD LA, L 1262, 17 vendémiaire, year IV.

45. AD LA, L 222.

46. AD LA, L 292.

47. AD DS, L 68; AD LA, L 322. This law was the first establishing a true conscription in the modern sense of the word.

48. AD DS, L 47.

49. AD DS, L 9; AD ML, IL 192.

50. AD DS, L 47.

51. AN, F[7] 3681[7].

52. AD LA, L 303. "Which announces the presence of refractory priests . . ." AD DS, L 8.

TWELVE. *The Legitimacy of the Clergy and Its Activity*

1. Secher, *Anatomie*, vol. 2.

2. Doré-Graslin, *Itinéraire*, pp. 89–90.

3. Abbé Briand, *Les Confesseurs de foi dans le diocèse de Nantes* (Nantes, 1903), vol. 1, p. 753.

4. Ibid., p. 666.

5. Jacques Roulleau, "Des prêtres martyrisés à La Rochelle," *SV* 125 (December 1978), pp. 13–14.

6. Jean-Julien Savary, *Guerre des Vendéens et des chouans contre la République* (Paris: Baudouin, 1824–27), vol. 6.

7. These statistics were established on the basis of files contained in the departmental and diocesan archives in Maine-et-Loire, Loire-Atlantique, and Vendée.

8. Abbé Manson, *Les prêtres et les religieux déportés sur les côtes et dans les îles de la Charente*, vol. 1, p. 100.

9. AP Sainte-Marie, AD LA, L 767 and 1471.

10. Prunier, *Le martyre*, pp. 143–47.

11. Ibid., p. 149.

12. AE Angers, RP of the parish of Gené, 1797.

13. AP Saint-Lumine-de-Coutais.

14. AP Frossay. Père Mathurin Billot.

15. AP Frossay. Père Mathurin Billot.

16. AD DS, L 93.

17. AD LA, L 345.

18. AD LA, L 338, 687, 797, and 1047.

19. Célestin Port, *La Vendée angevine* (Paris, 1888), vol. 1, p. 615.

20. AD DS, L 93.

21. AE Angers, RP Issé. Abbé Charles Paizot was arrested by the gendarmes of Segré and taken to the castle of Angers.

22. AD LA, L 522.

23. The inhabitants of Auray did indeed make pilgrimages to the field of martyrs, the place where many prisoners taken at Quiberon had been shot. As for Vannes, according to Hoche himself (April 1796), every day priests were led to the scaffold: "Every day peasants come to dip their handkerchiefs in the blood of these unfortunates who will soon be transformed into religious martyrs." Beauchamp, *Histoire de la guerre de la Vendée* (Paris, 1820), vol. 3, p. 537.

24. Beauregard, *Mémoires*, pp. 375 and 494.

25. AC CBM, RP, 1793–99.

26. AD LA, L 338, 687, 797, and 1047.

27. AE Angers, RP Melay.

28. AE Angers, RP Coron; AD ML, IL 192.

29. AD LA, L 689.

30. AD DS, L 68.

31. AP Saint-Lumine-de-Coutais; AD LA, L 249, 539, and 938.

32. AC CBM, RP, 1796.

33. AD DS, L 68.

34. AD LA, L 724; AP Maumusson.

35. AP Boussay, RP, 1794.

36. AD LA, L 724; AP Maumusson.

37. AP Château-Thébaud; AD LA, L 414.

38. AP Ligné and Le Loroux-Bottereau; AD LA, L 808.

39. AD LA, L 724; AP Maumusson.

40. AP Frossay, RP, 1796.

41. AP Saint-Lumine-de-Coutais; AD LA, L 249, 539, 948, and 1163.

42. AC CBM, AP, 1796.

43. AP La Bruffière, RP, 1796.

44. AP Saint-Lumine-de-Coutais; AD LA, L 249, 539, and 1163.

45. AP Maisdon; AD LA, L 723.

46. AD LA, L 123.
47. AD LA, L 668. Letter from the minister Fouché, year VII.
48. AD LA, L 313.
49. AD LA, L 1345.
50. AN, F⁷ 3681⁶, report of Marnou, commissioner from the executive directory to the department of Loire-Inférieure.
51. AD V, 4 M 6/11.

THIRTEEN. *The Problem*

1. Fabienne Pichard du Page and Georges Gondinet, *Histoire des Vendéens* (Luçon: Fernand Nathan, 1982), pp. 326–27.
2. André Sarazin, "Le recensement des victims de la Révolution et de la guerre de Vendée dans l'Ouest," *Echange*, special issue 1 (1st quarter, 1980), pp. 60–62.
3. Lallié, *La justice révolutionnaire à Nantes;* A. Billaud, "Au pays de Galerne, combien?" *SV* 62 (March 1963).
4. AC CBM, RP, 1797.
5. AP Le Luc, RP, 1793–95.
6. AP Le Loroux-Bottereau, RP, 1794–96.
7. AC CBM, RP, 1796–97.
8. AP La Remaudière, 1793–99.
9. Dupin, *ASDS an XII*, pp. 188–89.
10. AD V, L 342.
11. Philippe Bossis, "Les réfugiés vendéens à Nantes lors du soulèvement de mars 1793," *Echange*, special issue 2 (2d quarter, 1980), pp. 7–12.
12. AD ML, IL 995.
13. AD V, IL 350 and 570.
14. AD V, L 520 and 340.
15. AD V, IL 343; AD ML, IL 994.
16. AD V, IL 350.
17. AD V, IL 343.
18. Charles Merle, "Bressuire et les guerres de Vendée (l'incendie de mars 1794)," *Bulletin de la Société historique et scientifique des Deux-Sèvres*, 2d series, vol. 15 (1982), pp. 253–72.
19. Secher, *Anatomie*, vol. 2.
20. Remark of M. Lagniau, president of the association *Souvenir Vendéen;* Sarazin, "A propos du recensement des victimes de la Révolution," pp. 60–62.
21. Dupin, *ASDS an XII*, pp. 188–89.
22. Merle, "Bressuire et les guerres de Vendée."
23. AD LA, 2 R 124; AD DS, 7 M 4/1; AD V, R 148.

24. B. Ledain, *Histoire de la ville de Bressuire* (Bressuire, 1880), p. 483. Quoted by Merle, "Bressuire et les guerres de Vendée."
25. AD LA, 2 R 124.
26. AN, F¹³ 1822.
27. AD LA, 2 R 124.
28. AD LA, L 1296, folio 32.

FOURTEEN. *The Human Aspect*

1. AD LA, L 1513, 14 ventôse, year II. Denunciation of Commander Martin-court by General Cordelier.
2. Dupin, *ASDS an XII*, pp. 12–13.
3. AP La Renaudière, RP, 1794–99.
4. Dupin, *ASDS an XII*, pp. 174–75.
5. Las Cases, *Le mémorial de Sainte-Hélène* (Paris: Gallimard, Bibliothèque de la Pléiade, 1948), vol. 1, p. 908.
6. AD LA, L 53.
7. Dupin, *ASDS an XII*, pp. 125 ff.
8. Las Cases, *Le mémorial*, p. 908.

FIFTEEN. *Assessment of Property Destruction*

1. These figures concern only the northern part of the department. AD V, IM 392.
2. Vallet is excluded from this study because no list exists.
3. AD V, IM 392.
4. Merle, "Bressuire et les guerres de Vendée."
5. AD LA, L 329.
6. AD V, R 148.
7. AD V, R 148. Remark of the mayor of Chiché (Vendée).
8. Dupin, *ASDS an XII*, pp. 25–26.
9. AD V, R 148. Remark of the mayor of Chiché (Vendée).
10. Merle, "Bressuire et les guerres de Vendée," p. 263.
11. Dupin, *ASDS an XII*, pp. 53 and 131.
12. AD LA, 2 R 124.
13. They were Aigrefeuille (+1.81 percent); Chauvé (+4.68 percent); Machecoul (+20.36 percent); Saint-Même (+31 percent); Pont-Saint-Martin (+23 percent); Port-Saint-Père (+18.5 percent); Cheix-en-Retz (+3.3 percent); La Chapelle-Heulin (+15 percent); Léger (+1.38 percent); Chavagne (+1.94 percent); Moncoutant

(+8.5 percent); Amailloux (+45 percent); Chapelle-Saint-Laurent (+19.7 percent); Nueil-les-Autiers (+7 percent); Montravers (+7 percent); La Forêt-sur-Sèvre (+19.45 percent); Terves (+5 percent); Le Breuil (+6.11 percent); and Moutier-Argenton (+8.4 percent).

14. AN, F¹³ 1822.

15. AD V, R 148. It received this sum in accordance with the edicts of March 1, 1810: 200,000 francs; August 2, 1810: 50,000; September 8, 1810: 100,000; March 11, 1811: 150,000; September 14, 1811: 68,214 francs, 15 centimes; January 11, 1812: 31,785 francs, 85 centimes; September 19, 1812: 17,785 francs, 85 centimes; and November 19, 1812: 82,214 francs, 15 centimes.

16. AD LA, 2 R 124. It received this sum in accordance with the edicts of August 17, 1811: 50,000 francs; September 14, 1811, 100,000; September 14, 1814: 20,000; January 10, 1815: 20,000; and February 14, 1815: 20,000.

17. AN, F¹³ 1822. It received this sum in accordance with the edicts of January 20, 1810: 20,000 francs; July 26, 1810: 50,000; August 30, 1810: 100,000; September 20, 1810: 13,044 francs, 25 centimes; December 4, 1810: 57,255 francs; January 17, 1811: 31,985; February 1, 1811: 27,175; February 19, 1811: 150,000; June 1, 1811: 55,410; October 1, 1811: 190,311 francs, 95 centimes; November 29, 1811: 10,237 francs, 25 centimes, plus 17,300 francs; November 13, 1812: 100,000; and 35,050 in 1815.

18. AD V, IM 393.

19. Emile Bonneau, "L'habitat rural d'autrefois," *Presse Océan*, August 1, 1975.

20. Now owned by Mme. Germaine Guillot.

21. Vivant and Glébeau, *Saint-Julien-de-Concelles et son passé* (Mayor's office, Saint-Julien-de-Concelles, 1975) pp. 101–3.

22. Yan Brékilien, *La vie quotidienne en Bretagne au XIXe siècle* (Paris: Hachette, 1960), p. 22.

23. This situation produced some jokes. For example, a vicar of La Chapelle-Bassemère accused the curé of Barbechat of using for light the last *rousine* candle in the diocese, implying that the parish of Barbechat was considered the most difficult and least lucrative.

24. Mme. Guillot, owner of La Petite-Charaudière, observed this in 1980, when her house was restored. A 5–centime coin from the year V was found between the stones of the charred wall.

25. AD LA, IM 1896.

CONCLUSION. *The Vendée-Vengé*

1. Comte Fleury, *Carrier à Nantes* (Paris: Plon, 1897), p. 439.

2. Ibid., p. 389. Expression of Commissioner Chaux, 6 frimaire, year II.

3. *Gazette nationale* (reprint, Paris: Plon, 1854), 24 pluviôse, year II (January 12, 1794), p. 447.

4. Ibid., 5 ventôse, year II (February 23, 1794), pp. 533 and 536.

5. Arthur Young, *Travels in France During the Years 1787, 1788 & 1789*, ed. Constantia Maxwell (1929; reprint, Cambridge: Cambridge University Press, 1950), p. 117.

6. Doré-Graslin, *Itinéraire*, pp. 207–16.

7. *GN*, August 7, 1793, p. 325.

8. Las Cases, *Le mémorial*, vol. 2, p. 777.

9. Robespierre, *Discours et rapports à la Convention* (Paris: Union Générale d'Editions, 1965), p. 240.

10. Ibid., pp. 221–22.

11. *GN*, vol. 18, p. 16, speech of October 1, 1793, printed October 2.

12. *GN*, vol. 19, p. 127, January 4, 1794.

13. *GN*, vol. 19, p. 336, January 30, 1794; AHA, B^5 8.

14. *GN*, vol. 19, p. 101, January 2, 1794.

15. *GN*, vol. 19, p. 537, February 23, 1794.

16. *GN*, id.

17. *GN*, id.

18. *GN*, id.

19. Le Bouvier des Mortiers, *Supplément à la vie de Charette* (Paris, 1814), p. 105.

20. *GN*, vol. 19, p. 21, speech of December 21, 1793, transcribed December 23.

21. Carré, "La Vendée, ses bourreaux et l'armée française."

22. *GN*, vol. 19, p. 81, December 30, 1793. Letter from Francastel: "We have taken no prisoners, something we no longer do . . ."

23. Carré, "La Vendée, ses bourreaux et l'armée française."

24. *GN*, vol 19, p. 620, session of March 4, transcribed March 5.

25. AHA, B 58.

26. AHA, B 58, February 25, 1794. For Hantz and Francastel, "the race of men who live in the Vendée is evil, it is made up of fanatics, who are the people, and federalists, who are the gentlemen."

27. *GN*, vol. 19, p. 503, session of February 17, 1794, transcribed February 19.

28. *GN*, vol. 19, p. 21, session of December 21, 1793, transcribed December 23.

29. All the revolutionaries adopted this term, including General Beaufort in a report of his operations on 3 pluviôse, year II. *GN*, vol. 19, p. 336, January 30, 1794.

30. AHA, B 58. Letter of February 19, 1794: "And it is still to be feared that the scoundrels of neighboring regions who are so hateful to the public spirit will withdraw into those woods, which are indestructible." For Turreau, "the repentance of the Vendeans could never be sincere"; *GN*, vol. 19, p. 537, February 23, 1794.

31. AHA, B 58. Letter of 25 pluviôse, year II.

32. *GN*, vol. 19, p. 127. Letter from Francastel of December 29, transcribed January 5, 1794, vol. 20, p. 93.

33. *GN*, vol. 18, pp. 376–77, session of November 9, 1793, printed November 10.

34. *GN*, vol. 19, p. 175, letter of Blavier, Bourbotte, Prein, and Turreau of 14 nivôse, year II, published January 11, 1794.

35. *GN*, vol. 18, pp. 376–77, session of November 9, 1793, printed November 10. Report of Barère, November 5, 1793, p. 355.

36. Chassin, *La Vendée patriote*, vol. 14, pp. 458–61.

37. AHA, B 58. Letter to the Convention, February 28, 1794.

38. Bouvier des Mortiers, *Charette*, tells us that "these death's heads were painted on their uniforms. On their red, white-bordered sabretaches, they had a skull and crossbones and the legend 'The Republic, one and indivisible or death.' They had the same emblems on their dolman sleeves and pelisses."

39. Loidreau, "Bilan des colonnes infernales," *SV* 133 (December 1980), pp. 15–29.

40. Père Marie-Auguste Huchet, *Le massacre des Lucs-sur-Boulogne et le martyrologue du curé Barbedette* (La Roche-sur-Yon, 1983). The plan of attack on Le Luc is known; it was set out in the letter of 14 ventôse, year II (March 4, 1794): "A part of the troops, under the command of Martin Court, will occupy the right bank of the Boulogne, toward Le Petit-Luc. The bulk of the division, commanded by General Crouzat, will follow the left bank, go around Le Grand-Luc, and attack the rebels, who cannot fail to be 'crushed or made to drink the Boulogne'" (AD LA, L I 513).

41. Cordelier boasted of having put "behind the hedges" six hundred people of both sexes. A list of 469 persons drawn up by Abbé Barbedette is known: 209 men (77 younger than fifteen, 100 between sixteen and sixty, and 32 older than sixty), and 260 women (82 younger than fifteen, 158 between sixteen and sixty, and 20 older than sixty).

42. Carré archives.

43. Remark of Carré.

44. This was notably the case in the canton of Le Loroux-Bottereau.

45. AD V, I M 390.

46. AP Le Loroux-Bottereau (Loire-Inférieure). Abbé Peccot was deported in 1792. The Sunday following his arrival on October 24, 1801, to celebrate his return, the parishioners presented him with a bell to bless.

47. Peigné, *Histoire LB.*

48. Archives of M. Lucien Jarry.

49. AD V, I M 391.

50. Peigné, *Histoire LB.*

51. AN, F I 9905.

52. Archives of the family of Renoul, doctor in Le Loroux-Bottereau, communicated by M. Henri Renoul.

53. Did de Gaulle not set himself in the plebiscitary tradition?

54. Las Cases, *Le mémorial,* p. 472: "Returning to the war of the Vendée, he [the emperor] recalled that he had been moved from the army of the Alps to the army of Vendée, and that he chose to hand in his resignation rather than continuing a service in which, given the impulses of the time, he could only have contributed to evil and be unable to claim personally to do any good. He said that one of the first concerns of his consulate had been to pacify that unfortunate region completely and to make it forget its disasters. He had done a good deal for it, the population had been grateful, and when he traveled through it, even the priests had seemed to be sincerely favorable to him. 'Thus,' he went on, 'the later insurrections did not have the same character as the first one; it was no longer pure fanaticism, but only passive obedience to a dominant aristocracy.'"

55. Fleury, *Carrier à Nantes,* pp. 481–83.

56. Carré, "La Vendée, ses bourreaux et l'armée française." On February 12, 1794, the representatives of the people to the army of the West asked for explanations of the orders and the behavior of Turreau.

57. Jules Michelet, *Histoire de la Révolution française,* p. 460.

58. Ibid., p. 484.

59. Ibid., p. 463.

60. Ibid., p. 460.

61. Sainte-Beuve, "Portraits de femmes : Mme. Roland," in *Œuvres* (Paris: Gallimard, Bibliothèque de la Pléiade, 1951), p. 1131.

REYNALD SECHER is a scholar, businessman, and author of several books and articles. He produces historical videos, and is a specialist in the field of identity and national memory.

www.ingramcontent.com/pod-product-compliance
Lightning Source LLC
Chambersburg PA
CBHW021543260326
41914CB00001B/144